Acclaim for
Reconstructing retii
Work and welfare in the l

"This book is to be highly recommended as making an important contribution to understanding the shifting nature of retirement. Policymakers and older people's advocacy organizations would be well advised to carefully weigh its implications, striking as it does a welcome and rare cautionary note."
Professor Philip Taylor in *Journal of Aging & Social Policy*

"Once they read this book, policy makers, thought-leaders in the fields of aging, and scholars should feel compelled to engage in difficult conversations about the extent to which employment pathways can and do lead to quality jobs that align well with older adults' preferences and priorities."
Professor Marcie Pitt-Catsouphes in *The Gerontologist*

"This is a very good book on an important and topical subject, which should form the basis of any critical assessment of the rights and wrongs of early retirement."
Professor John Macnicol in *Journal of Social Policy*

"The book is very well written and can also be of interest to anyone wishing to learn more about social determinants of work in later life."
Dr Katsiaryna Padvalkava in *Journal of Population Ageing*

"I recommend Lain's work to all occupational scientists interested in work and retirement, or more generally, in the ways government policy actively and passively influences people's occupational opportunities, choices, and experiences. These are indeed matters of occupational justice."
Professor Clare Hocking in *Journal of Occupational Science*

This book is dedicated to Véro, Jacob and Samuel, with love, and to my parents, Michael and Susan Lain.

RECONSTRUCTING RETIREMENT

Work and welfare in the UK and USA

David Lain

P

First published in Great Britain in 2018 by

Policy Press
University of Bristol
1-9 Old Park Hill
Bristol
BS2 8BB
UK
t: +44 (0)117 954 5940
pp-info@bristol.ac.uk
www.policypress.co.uk

North America office:
Policy Press
c/o The University of Chicago Press
1427 East 60th Street
Chicago, IL 60637, USA
t: +1 773 702 7700
f: +1 773-702-9756
sales@press.uchicago.edu
www.press.uchicago.edu

British Library Cataloguing in Publication Data
A catalogue record for this book is available from the British Library

Library of Congress Cataloging-in-Publication Data
A catalog record for this book has been requested

ISBN 978-1-4473-2619-9 paperback
ISBN 978 1 44732 617 5 hardcover
ISBN 978-1-4473-2624-3 ePub
ISBN 978-1-4473-2625-0 Mobi

Cover design by Andrew Corbett
Front cover image: istock
Printed and bound in Great Britain by CMP, Poole
Policy Press uses environmentally responsible print partners

Contents

List of figures and tables

Figures

Tables

Acknowledgements

My interest in older workers and retirement issues began over a decade ago, when I was a Researcher at the Institute for Employment Studies. Working on a project evaluating the 'New Deal 50+' programme, I was travelling around the country interviewing (formerly) unemployed older people who had joined the scheme. What struck me at the time was how diverse their circumstances were, and yet they had all faced challenges finding new work after becoming unemployed. I began to wonder how older people would fare in future, as state pension ages began to rise and pressures to work in older age intensified. This book therefore examines prospects for employment beyond age 65 in the UK and US in the context of state pension age rises. It was funded by a three-year Leverhulme Early Career Fellowship (2011–14); I thank the Trust for providing me with this opportunity. The University of Brighton Business School was an excellent environment in which to conduct this research, and I thank my colleagues, the Dean of the School, Aidan Berry, and my excellent PhD students – Dave Wright, Christine Lewis and Karen Hanley. Particular thanks go to my colleague, Jacqueline O'Reilly, who supervised my DPhil in Sociology when we were both at the University of Sussex. Jackie was an excellent DPhil supervisor, and is now a good friend and very supportive colleague.

Outside of my school, Sarah Vickerstaff, Wendy Loretto and Chris Phillipson deserve particular thanks for their support, guidance and friendship during the writing of this book. Sarah Vickerstaff was the external examiner for my DPhil, and made a particular effort to involve me in her research networks and projects afterwards. Sarah kindly read the manuscript of this book, and offered perceptive comments and suggestions about the concluding chapter. Wendy Loretto has also influenced the contents of this book, via work we have done together on the changing nature of employment at age 65-plus. Chris Phillipson has been supportive of my work in general, and kindly read an early draft of some of the analysis and gave me useful feedback. I worked with Sarah, Wendy and Chris on the ESRC 'Uncertain Futures' project, and I thank other researchers on this project that have influenced my work: Charlotte Clark, Mariska van der Horst, Ben Baumberg, Brian Beach and Sue Shepherd. I would also like to acknowledge the help of Tony Lynes, someone I admired greatly for advancing the cause of earnings-related pensions in the UK. We met on a number of occasions and he very kindly gave me publications from his collection that were extremely useful in writing Chapter Two. Tony Lynes sadly passed away in 2014.

The ideas and analysis in this book have also been enhanced by my involvement with the ESRC 'Rethinking Retirement' Seminar Series, which I co-organised with Sarah Vickerstaff and Wendy Loretto. Around 150 people attended the seminars between 2010 and 2012, and we were also able to collect together papers from the series on pension reforms (in *Social Policy in Society*) and employment in older age (in *Employee Relations*). This experience taught me a huge amount about work and retirement in older age, and I thank the participants, presenters and discussants. At the final seminar at the University of Kent I was able to present early findings from this book, and I thank my discussant, Lynne Robertson-Rose, and the audience for their extremely useful comments.

Given that this research concerns the UK and the US, I was grateful to the Leverhulme Foundation and University of Brighton for enabling me to travel to the US on research trips. I was a Visiting Scholar at the Aging Studies Institute, Syracuse University, in the summer of 2012. I discussed my research with a number of people at Syracuse, in particular Madonna Harrington Meyer, Chris Himes, Andrew London, Perry Singleton, Janet Wilmoth, and Douglas Wolf. I would particularly like to thank Madonna Harrington Meyer, who ensured that my trip was not only intellectually stimulating but also great fun. During this US trip in 2012, I also went to Boston, to present the early research findings at the Society for the Advancement of Socio-Economics Conference at the Massachusetts Institute of Technology. During this trip John B. Williamson kindly met up with me at Boston College, and was very generous with his time and ideas. I was also able to present my ongoing research at the Gerontological Society of America (GSA) conferences in New Orleans (2013), Washington (2014), and Florida (2015). I am a member of the Older Workers Interest Group of the GSA, and I would like to thank other group-members who have helped to enhance my understanding of the US situation.

In addition to US trips, I have been fortunate to gain a broader perspective by presenting my research to audiences in a number of European countries. Dominique Anxo kindly invited me to present at Linneaus University in Sweden in 2014; I would like to thank Dominique, Mirza Baig and Anna Herbert for making it an intellectually stimulating and enjoyable trip. I was also able to get policy-orientated perspectives by presenting my research to the European Economic and Social Committee of the European Parliament (in 2013); the European Foundation for the Improvement of Living and Working conditions (2012); and Age Northern Ireland (2014). I thank these organisations for the invitations to present at these stimulating events. I was also fortunate enough to present the ongoing research in this book at the conferences of the European Network for Social Policy Analysis (ESPAnet) (2013), the Social Policy Association (2013), and the British Society of Gerontology (2015).

I also thank Simone Scherger from the University of Bremen for inviting me to present my UK/US research at the symposium 'Paid Work Beyond Retirement Age in International Perspective'. Walter Heinz was the discussant for the paper I presented, and I thank him for excellent feedback on the theoretical side of the research. Alongside Simone, I would like to acknowledge the other researchers at Bremen working on the topic of employment beyond pension age: Anna Hokema, Thomas Lux and Steffen Hagemann. One of the major outcomes from the event was an excellent volume bringing together papers that were presented (Scherger, 2015). I thank Simone Scherger for her excellent work as editor on this volume; the supportive, constructive feedback given to my chapter proved to be really useful when I later came to write this book.

The staff at Policy Press deserve thanks for their enthusiastic and professional work on this book; thanks to: Isobel Bainton, Rebecca Tomlinson, Dave Worth, Jo Morton, Jessica Miles and Rebecca Megson. I also thank the four reviewers of the original book proposal and the reviewer of the full manuscript draft.

The main sources of data used in this book are The English Longitudinal Study of Ageing (ELSA) and the Health and Retirement Study (HRS). ELSA is produced by the National Centre for Social Research, the Institute for Fiscal Studies, University College of London Department of Epidemiology and Public Health, and The University of Manchester School of Social Sciences. It is sponsored by the National Institute of Aging (US) and the main UK departments of government. The HRS is administered by the Institute for Social Research at the University of Michigan. It is funded by the National Institute of Aging and the Social Security Administration. In this book I make use of harmonised data files; these were created by the RAND organisation (for the HRS data) and the Gateway to Global Aging Data (for ELSA) (see Phillips et al, 2014 and Chien et al, 2014). These harmonised ELSA/HRS data-files were funded by the National Institute of Aging. I am extremely grateful to all the researchers who worked on producing this data, and the interviewees who give up their time on a recurring basis to be interviewed.

Acknowledgements

I would like to thank my wife Véronique, and children Jacob and Samuel. They provided endless love, support and encouragement over the long period I was working on this book. I would also like to thank my father, Michael Lain, and remember with enormous appreciation and love my mother, Susan Lain.

David Lain
Brighton, March 2016

ONE

Introduction: reconstructing retirement

Introduction

Increasingly, it is being claimed that we need to 'rethink' retirement. Ros Altmann, recently appointed UK Pensions Minister, has stated that:

> As people are living longer, we need to re-think what 'retirement' looks like. This is not about forcing people to work on, but supporting those who want to maintain a fuller working life.... Our concept of retirement and ageing in the workforce must move with the times as people's lives and the population demographics change. (Altmann, 2015: 9)

In the UK, such arguments have led to the introduction of a 'Redefining Retirement Division' in the Department for Work and Pensions. The argument is clear and is found in other countries, such as the US. Retirement in your mid-60s, or earlier, may have made sense in the past, when life expectancy was much shorter and people worked in more physically arduous jobs. However, this is no longer feasible, it is argued, because of population ageing and the fact that these individuals will have to be supported financially for a longer period of retirement. In 2000, 16% of the population was aged 65+ in the UK; this has been projected to rise to 20% in 2020, and 25.6% in 2040. The US has a younger population but will also see a rise in the share of over 65s, from 12.7% in 2000, to 17% in 2020 and to 22.4% in 2040 (Bonoli and Shinkawa, 2005: 4).

Working longer is a positive development, it is argued, because it will keep individuals active and be beneficial for their health and mental well-being (Altmann, 2015: 18). In the US, this has been linked to generational debates about baby boomers, those individuals born after the Second World War. These individuals, who are now approaching or over age 65, are different from previous generations. They are more active and educated and they positively resist the notion of taking full retirement at a fixed age. Rix (2008: 77, emphasis in original) sums up the argument that is made:

Boomers, it has been maintained, are going to reinvent and/or revolutionise retirement. Not for them is an early labor force exit to full and permanent retirement. Rather, they will work longer, perhaps *much* longer, than their parents and combine work and leisure in new and more rewarding ways.

These arguments seem to suggest that we are entering a positive age in which older people are able to exercise greater degrees of choice and autonomy over their employment and retirement decisions. This book assesses whether this is the case. It explores employment beyond age 65 in two countries: the UK and the US. It argues that to a considerable degree, it is governments in both countries that have sought to 'reconstruct' retirement by using regulation and legislation to promote/necessitate employment beyond this age and dissolve the notion of a fixed retirement age. However, the degrees of choice that many individuals will have over whether to continue working are likely to be very constrained. The wealthiest, most highly educated individuals have probably never had better opportunities to decide whether to continue working if they want to. Many of the poorest individuals, on the other hand, have little prospect of being able to take opportunities to work beyond age 65. This is going to be highly problematic as state pension ages are to rise over time to 67 in the US and 68 in the UK, and the level and availability of financial support before this age will decline in both countries. In between these two financial extremes, an increasing number of individuals are likely to find themselves working past 65 for financial reasons, but many others on depleted incomes will find their expectations of working past 65 are not met. We therefore need policies that will support retirement and employment in older age. The book explores three questions:

1. How has policy in the UK and US attempted to 'reconstruct' retirement by increasing employment beyond age 65 and dissolving the notion of fixed retirement ages?
2. What are the consequences of policy attempts to reconstruct retirement in terms of the employment prospects and financial position of those over 65?
3. How can policies support retirement and employment beyond age 65?

This introductory chapter sets the context and provides an outline of the book. It gives a brief overview of research on retirement timing, explains policy changes since the early 2000s and reviews empirical evidence from the book that examines prospects for employment beyond age 65.

Explaining the rise of early retirement up to the early 2000s

Compared with early retirement, relatively little research has been conducted on people working 'late', for example, after state pension age or 65. This is perhaps not surprising. Across a range of Organisation for Economic Co-operation and Development (OECD) countries, 65 became institutionalised as the male state pension age in the post-war period (Ebbinghaus, 2006). However, up until the 1960s, it was nevertheless fairly common for men to work past 65 in countries such as the UK, the US and Denmark (Milhoj, 1968), and this was not seen as problematic (Phillipson, 1982). In the mid-1960s, across a range of countries, the employment of older men was also very high. For example, in 1965, the employment rates of men aged 60 to 64 were high in the UK (at 89%) and the US (79.2), with similar employment levels also found in Germany, Sweden, Denmark and Ireland (Ebbinghaus, 2006: 97). Since the 1970s, however, 'early' exit before state pension age became increasingly common. By the mid-1980s, only around half of men aged 60–64 were still working in the US, UK, Ireland and Denmark, with even lower employment found in countries such as Germany (Ebbinghaus, 2006). Women were also leaving work earlier, even if the absolute numbers of women in employment had increased (Ebbinghaus, 2006). Levels of early exit remained fairly stable across many countries from the mid-1980s to the early 2000s; it consequently became a phenomenon that researchers were eager to examine and explain. It is therefore important that we critically examine research on early retirement because this is likely to influence researchers' expectations about late retirement.

Explanations for this early retirement increase have tended to focus on 'push' or 'pull' factors (for discussion, see Jensen, 2005). Pull factors focus on financial incentives for retirement. For example, Costa (1998) highlights the importance of rising retirement incomes in the US for explaining the spread of retirement. Likewise, Gruber and Wise (1999: 35) conclude that 'there is a strong correspondence between the age at which benefits are available and departure from the labor force'. The authors note that in many countries, reduced 'early' state pensions or retirement incomes have been introduced. In the US from the 1960s onwards, individuals could take a reduced Social Security pension from age 62, and similar moves occurred in countries such as Germany and France. In this context, differences in early retirement between countries were explained by the extent to which pensions financially rewarded early exit. In the US, early exit was said to be lower than in Germany and France because the reductions for early receipt were smaller and more actuarially fair. While this explanation is no doubt part of the story, it is arguably incomplete. In the case of the UK, analysis in Gruber and Wise (1999) shows that early exit increased in the UK but the age at which pension benefits became available did not change. The explanation given was that invalidity benefits and income support benefits acted as quasi-early retirement benefits from age 60. However, there is no explanation for why changes to these benefits incentivised larger numbers to leave work. Instead, it is probable that individuals involuntarily exited from employment and *then* ended up on invalidity or income support benefits (Faggio and Nickell, 2003). If so, we need to consider broader changes in the labour market.

Push factors relate to changes in the labour market that push older workers out. The 1960s were marked by tight labour markets and a plentiful supply of work, including low-skilled work (Macnicol, 2006). It was therefore perhaps not surprising that early retirement rates were low. In the early 1960s, around half of men were still working at 65–66 in both the UK and the US (Milhoj, 1968: 292). After the mid-1960s, however, labour markets changed in ways that were unfavourable to older workers. Unemployment increased in many countries above the low levels found in the 1960s (Ebbinghaus, 2006: 226). Part of this development reflected a shift towards less labour-intensive forms of production and a decline in manufacturing. This, in turn, reflected a broader context of globalisation. Globalisation has resulted in low-skilled production shifting to low-wage economies, and has increased the exposure of countries and companies to global competition (Hofacker, 2010; Blossfeld et al, 2011). This is likely to have disproportionately affected older individuals. Older men were more likely to be in declining industries, and this increased their likelihood of being involuntarily displaced from work (Campbell, 1999: 39–40). Likewise, the decline in low-skilled work disproportionately affected older people as they had fewer qualifications than younger people, and the qualifications that they did hold were often deemed 'outdated' (Ebbinghaus, 2006: 30). Faggio and Nickell (2003) found that in the UK, the large rise in the number of men on disability benefits could be accounted for by a decline in low-skilled work; low-skilled older men with a health condition consequently found it harder to get and keep a job. More broadly, it is also probable that in the context of high unemployment in the 1980s and 1990s, employers became less inclined to employ older people (Taylor and Walker, 1997).

A number of authors have sought to bring together 'push' and 'pull' factors to explain early exit from employment. In this regard, Ebbinghaus (2006) makes a major contribution. He seeks to explain why early retirement was more common in 'conservative' welfare states (such as Germany) than in 'social democratic' countries (eg Sweden) and 'liberal' welfare states (eg the UK and US). He argues that across these countries, employers faced pressures to shed workers as a result of the industrial changes discussed earlier ('push factors'). However, the extent to which this resulted in mass early retirement depended, in part, upon the generosity of the welfare state and the extent to which social partners could collude in using social benefits to shed labour through early retirement. The welfare state typology of Esping-Andersen (1990) is an important part of this explanation. Esping-Anderson (1990) categorised welfare states on the basis of their degree of 'de-commodification', that is, the extent to which they reduced people's reliance on paid work for survival. 'Liberal' welfare states such as the US and the UK are classed as weakly de-commodified – cash benefits (including state pensions) are said to be very ungenerous, and the market is important in terms of securing individual welfare. Ebbinghaus's (2006) explanation for differences in early retirement rates is as follows:

- In 'conservative' countries, such as Germany, early retirement was higher because employers and unions colluded in offering generous social insurance benefits to older workers to leave employment. The ability of the social partners to cooperate in this way reflects the fact that these countries were 'Co-ordinated Market Economies' (Hall and Soskice, 2001).
- In Scandinavian social democratic countries, social benefits provided by the state were generous, but the social partners were not in a position to manipulate them to their own ends. At the same time, these countries had long traditions of active labour market policies, including retraining schemes, to promote full employment. As a result, early retirement in these countries remained relatively low, despite the generosity of the welfare state.
- In Liberal English-speaking countries, social transfers did not provide an accessible or attractive early pathway out of employment for older workers. The liberal welfare state (Esping-Andersen, 1990) was complemented by a liberal market economy (Hall and Soskice, 2001). Employers and unions were therefore not in a position to

easily collude in offering early retirement through generous social insurance benefits. Consequently, 'we would expect the push toward early exit to be largely market driven' (Ebbinghaus, 2006: 82). Exits were said to be more individualised and in response to market fluctuations, with private occupational pensions an important route to early exit for those wanting to leave.

These factors help explain why early retirement rates were lower in the UK and the US than in conservative countries such as Germany or France. However, it should be noted from the preceding discussion that early exit nevertheless became common in the UK and the US during this period.

From early to late exit since the 2000s

Since the early 2000s, there has been an increased interest in people working 'late', that is, after state pension age or after retirement. A key reason for this is that the state pension ages are set to rise across a range of countries, so there is an interest in those currently working beyond current pension ages (Dubois and Anderson, 2012). Actual empirical research examining how, and why, this differs across countries is limited (although see Scherger et al, 2012; Scherger, 2015). Early indications suggest that researchers will link employment beyond 'retirement' age to welfare state typologies, in the same way that Ebbinghaus (2006) used these to examine early retirement. Buchholz et al (2011: 22–3), for example, make the following prediction with regard to the UK and US:

> the institutional setting of these countries strongly follows the credo that individuals have to take care of their welfare on their own, and possible risks are hardly compensated through a welfare state, but directly shifted to the individual. Consequently, there is a strong need to be employed in these countries.... This implies that they may have to accept employment insecurities in their late life – such as unemployment, stop gap jobs and income losses – and may even be forced to work beyond retirement age in the case that they failed in accumulating enough pension savings, or in the case that stock market turbulence cause severe losses of private pension savings.

The logic of such accounts is that employment beyond age 65 is likely to be 'market-led' and at similarly high levels in liberal countries such as the UK and US. However, welfare state typologies, while useful, do not neatly account for past differences in employment levels beyond age 65. Figure 1.1 shows the proportions working at age 65–69 in 2002 and 2014 across a range of countries. We do see some clustering of countries that might be expected from the arguments of Ebbinghaus (2006) and Buchholz et al (2011). Employment at 65+ was low in most of the countries associated with high early retirement in Continental and Southern Europe. However, there were some striking anomalies in employment between countries within specific welfare state regime types. For example, employment was much higher in social democratic Norway than in Sweden or Denmark. Likewise, around a quarter of Americans were working at this age in 2002, around twice that of the UK, Canada and Australia. This was despite the fact that none of these English-speaking countries had a state pension age above 65 in 2002. These are large differences in employment that we might not expect in countries belonging to the same liberal welfare state typology. An examination of employment beyond age 65 in the UK and the US

Figure 1.1: Percentages working at ages 65–69 across OECD countries, 2002 and 2014

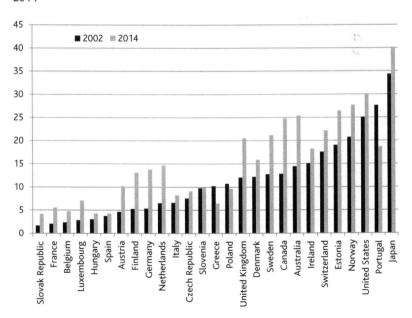

Source: Data downloaded from the OECD stats database: http:/stats.oecd.org/#

therefore requires a more finely grained approach, comparing policy in both countries in some depth.

For the remainder of the chapter, we explore the three questions raised earlier, each of which relate to a part of the book. First, we explore the attempt to 'reconstruct retirement policy' in the UK and the US by encouraging/necessitating employment beyond 65 (Part One of the book). Second, we review the possible consequences of such a policy shift in terms of employment at 65 (Part Two). Finally, we conclude by highlighting the need for policies to support retirement and employment (Part Three).

Reconstructing retirement policy (Part One of the book)

Reform context in the early 2000s: the legacy of different 'policy logics'

The US has historically done much more to encourage/necessitate employment beyond age 65 than the UK; this, in part, helps account for the higher US rate of employment past age 65 in the early 2000s. Since the early 2000s, however, UK policy has shifted towards promoting and necessitating employment beyond age 65. It is therefore important to look at the policy context of the early 2000s in this section, before examining changes that have occurred since this time.

Promoting self-reliance in the US

Lain (2009, 2011) has argued that different US and UK 'policy logics' underpinned social and employment policy for older people in the period up to the early 2000s. This notion of a policy logic is derived from O'Connor et al (1999), and is used to examine whether there is a broad consistency across policy areas about the expected role and behaviour of older people in relation to employment and retirement. Lain (2011) argues that the US policy logic of *self-reliance* was in operation, based on the expectation that it was the responsibility of the individual to ensure that they had adequate financial resources prior to retiring. The state's role was not therefore one of providing an adequate safety net, but instead to formally protect the employment of older people until they were in a financial position to leave work. The priority for state pensions policy was to reward individual endeavour through earned entitlements, rather than provide a safety net for the poorest. Lain (2009: 47) highlights the following key dimensions of the US self-reliance policy logic:

- age discrimination legislation preventing employers from setting mandatory retirement ages or getting rid of staff on the basis of their age;
- a state pension that rewarded 'individual endeavour' in the sense that it was based on previous earnings and closely linked to years in employment;
- a weak 'safety-net', with means-tested benefits that were difficult to access and set at very low levels;
- legislation to force employers to continue contributing to occupational pensions for as long as the person was employed, and legislation to prevent employers targeting early retirement incentives on individuals; and
- a shift towards 'defined contribution' (DC) occupational pensions, which operate similarly to savings accounts, and therefore place the onus on the individual to retire when pension wealth is sufficient.

US policy was not simply a case of leaving the market to operate, as a pure liberal model would imply, but of promoting employment even when this means strong market intervention. In this sense, this line of argument questions whether high rates of employment beyond age 65 can be explained simply by *pure* 'market outcomes', as implied by research drawing on typologies of welfare states (Esping-Andersen, 1990) and types of labour market (Hall and Soskice, 2001). It therefore questions the assumption that the US can be simply categorised as a weakly regulated, predominantly laissez-faire, country (see also Blyth, 2002; Prasad, 2012). Indeed, it is important to draw on the insight from Polanyi (2001 [1944]) that *all* markets are *built* upon the bedrock of legislation and regulation. Without legislation, markets would cease to operate. The market is undoubtedly important in the US, but market outcomes for older people are likely to be shaped by the rules that govern the market's operation. Most research on the employment of older people fails to mention the fact that US legislation constrains employers from getting rid of employees at 65, even when it includes people of this age.

It is important to note that the promotion of self-reliance is something that US policy has historically also attempted to do *before* people reach older age. In order to make sense of this, it is useful to draw on Leisering's (2004: 210) concept of 'lifecourse policies', which are 'intended by political actors to change the structure of the life course' in ways deemed normatively desirable. These cover three policy 'fields': education; risk management (benefits and services primarily during family/career years); and old-age pensions. Leisering (2004: 216) argues that:

> In the United States, public policy gives priority to education.... Risk management is stronger in the United Kingdom and in Germany than in the United States, where health insurance, unemployment benefit and social assistance are weakly developed. In short, the US model places a high emphasis on education, some emphasis on Social Security (old-age pensions) and least emphasis on risk management.

The US was a leader in the provision of education and a laggard in the development of social insurance (Lindert, 2004; Garfinkel et al, 2011). The US had a bias towards 'self-help' solutions such as education because of its racial, ethnic and religious diversity, its religiosity, and its history of being a frontier nation (Alesina and Glaeser, 2004; Garfinkel et al, 2011). Universal schooling developed early partly as a means of promoting self-reliance and integrating immigrants; it became an important aspect of nation-building. This legacy has had long-term consequences as older Americans are far more highly educated on average than their British counterparts. For example, 84% of Americans aged 55–64 in 2002 had completed secondary-level education, compared with only 56% in the UK and 50% for the OECD as a whole (OECD, 2004: 58). If we look at the cohort turning 65 over the next decade, in 2012, 55–64 year olds had a similar likelihood of being educated to post-secondary or tertiary level to those aged 25–34 (41.8% versus 44%). In the UK, like the vast majority of other OECD countries, older cohorts were much less likely to be educated to tertiary level: 32.6% of those aged 55–64 in 2012 had tertiary qualifications, compared with 47.9% of those aged 25–27.

In relation to 'risk maintenance', the US has been weak in the provision of social benefits and services covering family/career years; this includes medical insurance, family allowances and unemployment benefits. This has tied men *and women* to continuous full-time employment over the life course given the need for a full-time wage and the lack of fringe benefits commonly found in part-time work (Lyonette et al, 2011).

Paternalism and providing a minimum in the UK

In the UK, Lain (2009, 2011) identifies a policy logic of *paternalism* affecting older people in the early 2000s. This policy logic was not based on a strong set of social rights, as found in other European countries. Nevertheless, a key role of the state was to provide a financial safety net *aimed* at preventing poverty, rather than extending employment rights to the over 65s. Whereas the US has promoted self-reliance through individual effort, in the UK, an important role for the state in the past has been to protect the most vulnerable from the negative consequences of the market. The following aspects of the paternalistic policy logic were identified in the early 2000s (Lain, 2009: 48):

- a complete absence of age discrimination legislation, and very limited rights to claim unfair dismissal after the age of 65 (giving employers a virtual free hand in deciding whether, and who, to employ past 65);
- a 'basic' flat-rate state pension set below means-tested benefit levels (ensuring a key role for means-tested benefits in the system);
- a system of means-tested benefits from age 60 that were easier to access and more generous than in the US, covering a significant percentage of households with someone aged 65+; and
- a legislated 'second tier' of pension provision, primarily based on *one* of the following for those retiring in the early 2000s:
    - a 'State Earnings Related Pension', providing a modest supplement to the basic state pension, based on previous earnings above a threshold (therefore excluding very low earners); *or*
    - a defined benefit (DB) occupational pension, disproportionately received by higher earners (albeit of declining importance in the early 2000s).

Policy towards older people in the UK was therefore paternalistic in the sense that it recognised the potential vulnerability of older people. If individuals were unlucky enough to end up with low retirement incomes, there was little expectation that continued employment was the solution. Indeed, UK policy had tried to promote early retirement in the 1970s and 1980s, at the very point when the US was seeking to clamp down on it (see Chapter Two). Such a 'paternalistic' approach involved 'soft' social rights, rather than the provision of a generous state pension income. Figure 1.2 provides a visual representation of the different policy logics affecting older people in both countries.

Figure 1.2: Policy logics around retirement timing in the early 2000s, UK and US

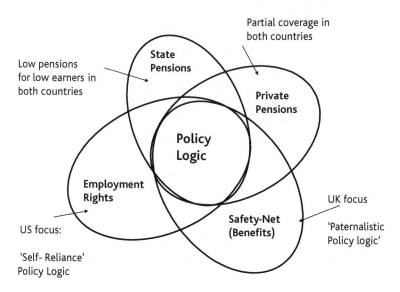

Source: Own compilation.

'Life-course policies' affecting people at earlier ages in the UK also focused on the provision of a 'safety net'; Sainsbury (1996) described the UK as 'The Guaranteed Uniform Minimum Welfare State'. In terms of social assistance provided for those with low incomes, Leisering (2004: 216) notes that the UK is closer to Germany than the US, a country that offers 'little security'. Benefits have been provided for a wide range of contingencies but lack the generosity of those found in other countries. These have recognised and supported (traditional) family roles to a greater degree than in the US (O'Connor et al, 1999: 195). This results in a UK 'male breadwinner–female housewife logic' (O'Connor et al, 1999), with part-time employment very common for women, which is in contrast to the US, where the lack of state provision more commonly ties women into full-time employment (Lyonette et al, 2011). This weak attachment to the labour market of UK women at earlier ages is likely to impact on their prospects for employment in later life.

Finally, as we saw earlier, education 'life-course policies' in the UK have resulted in older people having much lower qualifications than their US counterparts. In more recent cohorts, educational levels have risen in the UK but they remain stubbornly below those of the US (OECD, 2014). In 2012, 31% of the population aged 55–64 had below secondary-level qualifications in the UK, compared with 10% in the

US (OECD, 2014); this is the cohort that will potentially be working past 65 in the coming decade. This places older people in the UK at a particular disadvantage in terms of employment (see Chapter Five).

Reforms to encourage employment beyond age 65

Since the early 2000s, UK policy has shifted towards that of the US in terms of seeking to encourage/necessitate employment beyond age 65, particularly for those with inadequate retirement incomes. In the UK, a near consensus was reached that early retirement was problematic in the context of population ageing and persistently high rates of older male unemployment (Macnicol, 2006). At the same time, the New Labour government elected in 1997 wanted to increase individual responsibility for securing retirement incomes (Rowlingson, 2002). It is important to recognise that 'path dependency' is a factor shaping reform in both countries (Pierson, 1994, 2001). The choices open to policy reformers are strongly shaped by past policies. Most notably, attempts to encourage people to save more and work longer in the UK have to address the important (and growing) role of means-tested benefits; these benefits are withdrawn as a result of having earnings or other retirement income/wealth (Lain, 2011). Likewise, attempts to replace US Social Security with a privatised system have failed because Americans see the pension as an earned entitlement (Béland and Wadden, 2012). Nevertheless, there is an increasing recognition that incremental changes can lead to profound change over time (Streeck and Thelen, 2005), and this is true of policies to promote employment beyond age 65. A number of the policy changes covered in this book are summarised in Table 1.1. These reflect two policy dimensions: changes to retirement incomes (Chapter Two); and changes to the regulation of retirement (Chapter Three).

Starting with retirement incomes, the subject of Chapter Two, a key change has been a planned increase in the state pension age to 67 in the US and 68 in the UK, with further increases very possible. The strategy for introducing this while limiting opposition was a 'grandfather' clause (Pierson, 1994: 23), that is, at the time of enactment, it did not affect those immediately approaching retirement age. Increases in retirement age were also 'stepped', so that it rises in increments over time for different cohorts. Nevertheless, the changes are of current importance – the 'full' state pension age has already reached 66 in the US, and will reach 66 in the UK in 2020. In addition to these changes, the UK government has shifted the system of pensions further towards a 'single-tier' pension. This, it is hoped, will reduce the amount of

Table 1.1: Key changes impacting on need/ability to work past age 65

		Change	Method
Chapter Two: Retirement incomes	State pension	Increase in state pension age to 67 in the US and 68 in the UK	'Grandfather clause' and stepped change (delayed start and incremental rise)
	State pension – UK	Shift to 'single-tier' pension to reduce mean testing and promote saving/employment	Replacement of State Earnings Related Pension with State Second Pension, and erosion of earnings-related dimension over time. Then replaced with single-tier pension
	Private pensions	Shift from 'defined benefit' to less secure 'defined contribution' pensions in the UK and US	Occurred 'naturally' in the US In the UK, defined contribution pensions encouraged through 'auto-enrolment'
	Income assistance – UK	Age of entitlement for Pension Credit to rise from 60 to 68	'Grandfather clause' and stepped change
	Income assistance – US	Sharp decline in access to Supplemental Security Income for poor retirees	'Drift' – not increasing assets that recipients are allowed since 1989, restricting eligibility over time
Chapter Three: Regulation of retirement	Mandatory retirement abolished	UK follows US in abolishing mandatory retirement to encourage/support extended working lives, especially for the financially needy	'Conversion' – redeployment of earlier age discrimination legislation to promote employment at 65+
	Regulation of pensions	UK and US – reforms to pensions to make it easier to combine employment with pension receipt	

Source: Own compilation.

means-tested benefits that individuals would otherwise receive, and consequently encourage saving and employment among older people. There has also been a 'naturally occurring' decline in the number of people receiving salary-related DB pensions. In the US, these pensions have been replaced with DC plans, which do not offer the relatively secure paths to retirement found in DB schemes. In the UK, the government has encouraged the spread of DC saving through 'auto-enrolment', which is likely to end up in a similar outcome to the US.

The safety net of means-tested benefits available at, or below, 65 is also being undermined in both countries, increasing pressures to work past 65. In the UK, means-tested Pension Credit is rising in line with female state pension age, removing an important safety net previously available for men and women from age 60. In the US, access to means-tested Supplemental Security Income (SSI) is being eroded as a result of 'policy drift', whereby a policy is neglected and fails to adapt to changing circumstances (Streeck and Thelen, 2005). In the case of SSI, a small and declining number of people are entitled to this benefit because the assets that a recipient is allowed have not risen for over 25 years. Taken together, these changes significantly increase the financial need to work past age 65.

Chapter Three examines how the regulation of retirement has changed (see Table 1.1). A key change has been that the UK has followed the US in abolishing mandatory retirement in order to encourage employment beyond age 65. In both countries, the abolition of mandatory retirement was the result of 'policy conversion', the 'redeployment of old institutions [ie policies] to new purposes' (Streeck and Thelen, 2005: 31). In both countries, age discrimination legislation emerged separately to debates about extended working lives. However, conversion occurred later when discrimination legislation was extended, through the abolition of mandatory retirement, as a means of promoting continued employment in the context of concerns about retirement incomes. The rationales given at the time in both countries indicate that the move was aimed at helping those in financial need remain in employment. In addition to this, reforms to state pensions in both countries, and occupational pensions in the UK, have made it easier for individuals to work and receive a pension at the same time. Together, these changes alter the nature of retirement, making it less certain when 'full retirement' should or will occur.

Reconstructing employment and retirement behaviour (Part Two of the book)

Having established pressures to work past 65 in Part One, Part Two of the book assesses prospects for employment beyond age 65. It examines the factors influencing employment at 65 to 74 in the late 2000s through an analysis of the US Health and Retirement Study and the English Longitudinal Study of Ageing. Policy may seek to reconstruct retirement by increasing the pressures and opportunities to work past 65, but we cannot automatically assume that they will have the desired outcomes. We also cannot assume that UK employment outcomes will be identical to those in the US. Nevertheless, the US has a long track record of seeking to encourage employment at 65, with mandatory retirement being abolished in 1986; this compares with 2011 in the UK. The US analysis may therefore yield insights for the UK about what will happen to employment past 65 in the UK. The analysis of ELSA should be broadly reflective of the situation in the UK as a whole, because England represents 84% of the UK population (ONS, 2012).

Chapter Four examines the pathways to working at age 65–74 in 2012. It provides an overview of the employment transitions of people aged 65–74 in 2012 in both countries over the course of a decade. What this shows is that higher US employment was not simply the result of people remaining in career jobs a little longer. It is true that Americans aged 65–74 in 2012 were more likely than their English counterparts to still be employed in the job they were doing in 2002. However, Americans were also more likely to work at 65–74 as a result of changing jobs or returning to work following an absence. This typically involves being able to get a job as an employee as few people move from being an employee to self-employed in older age. Supplementary analysis shows that in England, there was an increase in the proportion of the over 65s staying on in long-term jobs during the 2000s but little evidence to suggest an increase in employment as a result of job movement.

In both countries, working past 65 typically involved shifting from full-time to part-time work. For some individuals, this may be the result of a simple preference. For others, it may be considered a necessity in order to reduce hours; in both countries, physically arduous work was not uncommon among workers age 65+, and evidence from the US suggested that work involving stress was also common. However, the wider literature suggests that only a fraction of those wanting to reduce their hours of work in retirement actually manage to do so. Overall, the analysis in Chapter Four shows that extending working lives beyond age 65 is likely to be more complicated than simply getting people to stay in their jobs a little longer.

Chapter Five examines the capacity of individuals to work past 65, including education, health and caring factors. This analysis suggests that qualifications increase the ability to remain in work, whether it be through staying in the same job long-term, moving jobs in old age or returning to work after having left. Health conditions were widely reported among this cohort in both countries, and they significantly reduced the likelihood of employment. However, among those with health problems, the highly educated were most likely to remain in work in the US. The effect of caring on employment is also examined, although the broader literature suggests that caring responsibilities have more impact on employment before age 65. Overall, the chapter suggests that health and education represent significant barriers to working beyond 65 for many individuals in both countries. However, for the historical reasons discussed earlier, older cohorts in England have low qualifications; this is likely to constrain their ability to move jobs in older age to a greater degree than in the US. In this sense, it is questionable whether reforms to retirement policies will result in the levels of employment found at 65+ in the US.

Chapter Six examines whether employment at age 65–74 is related to choice or financial constraint. This is of particular interest given the importance of the financial rationale for extended working lives. The analysis suggests that in both countries, the wealthiest were most likely to work at 65+, with the majority of this group in both countries attributing their employment to non-financial factors. These individuals have clearly benefited from the opportunity to work beyond age 65. At the other end of the spectrum, the poorest segments in both countries were least likely to work. Nevertheless, the poorest were more likely to work in the US than in England, and when the poorest did work in the US, they mostly said that they were working for financial reasons. In both countries, the lower likelihood of working among the poorest wealth segments disappeared once we controlled for education, health and a range of other factors that might explain their lower propensity to work. This suggests that these individuals faced significant barriers to working at 65+, something that policy has done little to recognise.

In the US, between the two extremes of rich and poor there were significant numbers of individuals who appeared to be in employment for financial reasons. Indeed, two thirds of US workers aged 65–74 in 2008 said that they would have left work if they could afford to. Workers in the 'middle' were not renters, but were often paying off a mortgage rather than owning their home outright. Likewise, they tended to have a private pension, but this was often in the form of a DC scheme, rather than a salary-related DB pension. Financially motivated employment was high for one group in England: those still paying off a mortgage. More generally, employment rates for those with apparent financial needs were low in England, and only around a third of individuals working at 65–74 said that they were working for financial reasons. This needs to be placed in the context of the time, however. The abolition of mandatory retirement only occurred in 2011, after the analysis in this chapter. Remaining in work therefore went against the 'norm', meaning that those with intrinsic work motivations were probably more likely to make the case to remain in work. Given that many people in the UK have very modest retirement incomes (see Chapter Two), we may expect a significant increase in people working beyond 65 for financial reasons. Indeed, among those *expecting* to work beyond 65, financial factors are a key reason (Smeaton et al, 2009). As we will see in Chapter Five, however, US experience suggests that fewer individuals may end up working than expect to; this suggests that policy should have an important role in ensuring that older individuals are in a financial position to support themselves without recourse to earnings.

The reconstruction of retirement? Current paths and policy alternatives

The concluding chapter summarises current paths towards a reconstruction of retirement and discusses policy alternatives to arrive at more equitable employment/retirement outcomes for older people. The reconstruction of retirement is not simply the result of a weak or inactive 'liberal' state. As the analysis in Part One shows, the state has played an active role in attempting to reconstruct retirement through the promotion of employment beyond age 65. The state will *necessarily* have an active role in seeking to reconstruct retirement; what is required, however, are 'life-course' policies that positively support opportunities for the employment *and* retirement of people when they reach older age. A range of policies are therefore proposed across the life course that would increase the financial security of older people and enhance individual autonomy over retirement and employment decisions. This would help bring about a new policy logic of 'self-determination', rather than self-reliance.

Part One
The reconstruction of retirement policy

TWO

Changing retirement incomes

Introduction

As we discussed in Chapter One, although both the UK and the US are commonly designated as having liberal welfare states, their pension systems have differed considerably. US state pensions are modest by international standards but are dominated by the notion of being an earned entitlement that reflects previous wages and work effort. The safety net of means-tested benefits for older people on low incomes is correspondingly weak. In the UK, a more paternalistic attitude to retirement incomes has been dominant. State pension provision has been very lacking in generosity but is geared more towards an analysis of social need, rather than an earned entitlement. Means-tested benefits have become an important source of income for many older people, particularly those without significant occupational pension income.

In this chapter, we examine how changes to retirement incomes in both countries have increased the need for individuals to work beyond age 65. In terms of making sense of these changes, it is first necessary to go back to the original guiding principles of state pension provision, namely, self-reliance in the US and paternalism in the UK. After this, the chapter then examines changes to retirement incomes in a number of areas that have increased the need to work past 65. In both countries, this includes increases in the state pension age, a withdrawal/reduction of social assistance benefits available at or before 65, and a decline in defined benefit (DB) occupational pensions. Throughout the chapter, it is clear that change needs to be understood as part of an incremental process, as per the arguments of Streeck and Thelen (2005). Policymakers have been crucial in constructing, and then reconstructing, the institutions that influence work in retirement transitions. In this light, policies to extend working lives in the 'liberal' UK and US cannot be viewed merely as market outcomes or the result of endogenous factors such as population ageing.

The roots of state pension provision

The roots of UK pensions

In order to understand changing state pension provision in the UK today, we need to recognise that the pensions that emerged were influenced by a concern for the social needs of older people (Rimlinger, 1971: 229; Thane, 2006: 79). In the early 1900s, laissez-faire capitalism existed in Britain and notions of the importance of self-reliance dominated, as they did in the US (Williamson and Pampel, 1993). Despite this context, a number of factors led to concerns at the political level about the conditions under which older people lived. Williamson and Pampel (1993: 45) argue that 'Great Britain is unique with respect to the role that social science played in the development of its old age pension policies'. A series of high-profile studies identified very high rates of poverty among older people; this made it harder to disregard poverty in old age as simply the result of fecklessness and irresponsibility. In 1887, Charles Booth's survey looking at the living conditions of the working class in London found that 30% were living in poverty. Booth subsequently reported that 38% of those over 65 were paupers, and that old age was the single biggest cause of poverty (Williamson and Pampel, 1993). Likewise, the Rowntree survey in York, published in 1901, found similarly high levels of poverty. Williamson and Pampel (1993: 45) argue that:

> this empirical evidence on the prevalence of poverty in the general population and among the aged served to undercut the assumption that poverty was due almost entirely to laziness and moral laxity; it became evident that destitution was often linked external economic circumstances and the hazards of everyday life (e.g. old age, widowhood, disability) over which the individual had little control.

Older people therefore came to be seen as the victims of life-cycle events, rather than the 'authors of their misfortune'. It is notable that the British state had examined pension proposals advocating compulsory saving among younger people as early as the 1870s (Thane, 2006: 79). After this, it became recognised that saving was difficult for most of the working classes (Thane, 2006) given the level of wages received. It was also identified that women were most likely to end up in poverty in old age and compulsory saving (eg through German-style social insurance) would be particularly ineffective given very low female wages.

The first state pensions in Britain were legislated in the State Pension Act of 1908. Pension proposals drawn up by Booth in 1891 had influenced the 1908 legislation in the sense that the pension provided would be flat-rate and not related to previous employment history (Williamson and Pampel, 1993). However, it would be provided at age 70 (rather than 65) and would be means-tested (rather than universal, as per Booth's scheme). The amount provided was set below a subsistence level in order to encourage family support and saving (Thane, 2006) and to make sure that it did not act as a disincentive to work (Williamson and Pampel, 1993). It would also only be provided to those of good 'moral character' so as to avoid paying it to the irresponsible, those who had squandered their resources or been in prison (Williamson and Pampel, 1993: 50; Thane, 2006: 80). According to analysis by Williamson and Pampel (1993), a number of political factors enabled the first state pension to emerge around this time. Industrialists believed that the workforce needed to be healthy and content for the country to be economically competitive; the surveys of Booth and Rowntree had suggested that this was not the case. Potential opposition to pensions from business was therefore reduced. Politically, the Liberal Party saw pensions as a way of gaining political support and preventing the growth of the Labour Party around this time. Finally, Friendly Societies came to be an important advocate for state pensions. These societies had previously provided pensions to their members and had opposed the development of state pensions. This changed in the early 1900s when their pension schemes were facing insolvency.

The first state pensions were therefore highly targeted and failed to reach large swathes of the population, in part, for reasons of political expediency. Nevertheless, the focus on flat-rate pensions as a means of addressing social need was now established and influenced the subsequent development of pensions in Britain. As Rimlinger (1971: 229) argued:

> in England, contributory old age pensions had evolved as an outgrowth of non-contributory old-age assistance, which in turn had been a modification of relief under the Poor laws. In this evolution the focus had remained on social needs, and they in turn governed the character of the protective measures.

State pension coverage was expanded in 1925 with the introduction of contributory pensions paid from age 65 (Thane, 2006: 80). Contributors were predominantly manual working-class men, although single women could also contribute. The 1925 legislation also introduced provision for widows for the first time.

Building on the logic of previous reforms, the 1942 Beveridge report, 'Social Insurance and Allied Services', represented the plans that would influence the mass expansion of state pensions in Britain. The idea behind the Beveridge proposal was to provide a flat-rate pension sufficient to lift individuals above absolute poverty (Bozio et al, 2010: 8). In this scheme, it was anticipated that people would earn an actuarially 'fair' pension – in other words, the contributions paid during a working life would pay for the pension received in retirement. The actual pension introduced in the National Insurance Act of 1946 deviated from these proposals in a number of ways. Notably, the notion that the pension was 'earned' through contributions paid was undermined from the start. As Bozio et al (2010) point out, a fully funded pension would not provide payments to older people at the time because they had not had time to accumulate one. As a result, the state pension was introduced on a 'pay-as-you-go' basis, and pensions were paid out from 1948 onwards to those that had not paid contributions. National insurance contributions were therefore paid by the working population in order to fund the pensions of older people, with only weak links between contributions paid and benefits received. The priority was understandably meeting the needs of a generation that suffered in two world wars and a depression, rather than being 'actuarially fair'.

The 'Basic State Pension', as it was to become known, also deviated from the Beveridge proposals by being less generous than anticipated. The intention to provide a subsistence-level pension was hard to achieve in the aftermath of the Second World War. As a result, from the very start, means-tested benefits were an important component of retirement incomes. According to Bozio et al (2010), the initial Basic State Pension for a single householder was £1.30 per week, compared with means-tested benefits from National Assistance of £1.20. As not everybody would build up a full pension entitlement, means-tested benefits would be received by many. Furthermore, the importance of means-tested benefits, relative to the Basic State Pension, would increase over time. In particular, the Conservative government in 1980 shifted the basis upon which the Basic State Pension increased over time from average earnings to average prices (Bozio et al, 2010: 13). As earnings typically rise faster than prices, this reduced the relative level of the Basic State Pension considerably, making it harder for people to achieve a pension above means-tested benefit levels. In 2009/10, the level of the 'full' Basic State Pension for a single pensioner was

£95, compared with £130 for means-tested Pension Credit (Bozio et al, 2010: 10).

The importance of means-tested benefits in the UK would have been higher were it not for so-called 'second-tier' pensions received by individuals. Occupational pensions provided by employers pre-dated the Basic State Pension, but their prevalence increased considerably after the 1950s. In 1953, just over a quarter of employees were covered by an occupational pension (28.3%); coverage was much higher in the public sector (54.9%) than in the private sector 19.1% (Clark, 2006: 149). Ten years later, in 1963, almost half of employees were members of an occupational pension through their job (48.5%). Coverage then fluctuated at around 50% until the year 2000, although this masked a decline in occupational pensions in the private sector and an increase in the public sector. In 2000, 88.2% in the public sector had an occupational pension, compared with 38% in the private sector. Clearly, throughout this period, public sector workers benefited from an expansion of occupational pension coverage (Bridgen and Meyer, 2013).

Uneven coverage of occupational pensions, and the low level of the Basic State Pension, led to calls for a supplementary earnings-related component within state pension provision. In 1961, the Graduated Retirement Benefit (GRB) sought to add an earnings-related addition to state pension income for those without an occupational pension. However, a lack of willingness to increase GRB levels 'earned' between 1961 in 1978 meant that inflation had rendered it insignificant (Bozio et al, 2010: 9).

The introduction of the State Earnings-Related Pension (SERPs) by the Labour government in 1978 represented the next attempt at an earnings-related supplement. This aimed to provide a pension worth 25% of 'covered earnings' (ie between certain upper and lower thresholds). Once again, social science had been influential in the development of SERPs. The prominent Professor of Social Policy Richard Titmuss was closely associated with the Labour Party's proposals (Lynes, 1997). It provided credits for periods out of the labour force for caring purposes, as was also the case for the Basic State Pension (Ginn, 2003). It was also to be redistributive, providing disproportionately larger pensions to low earners. However, as Myles and Pierson (2001) make clear, the Conservative government was in a position to undermine the pension because they took power in 1979 before a large constituency of recipients had developed to oppose the changes. The government cut future benefits so that they were to cover 20% of covered earnings, not 25%. The government furthermore halved 'survivors rights' within SERPs (previously the pension could be passed on to a partner upon death). The Conservative government also sought to promote private pensions in the place of SERPs in the Social Security Act 1986. The previous Labour government had enabled individuals to opt out of SERPs if they had a sufficiently good occupational pension; this was seen as a way of protecting occupational pensions already held by individuals. The Social Security Act 1986 enabled individuals to opt out of SERPs or their occupational pension and pay contributions into a personal pension bought by the individual. One of the outcomes of this was that many people were given poor advice and sold private pensions when it was in their advantage to stay in SERPs or their occupational scheme (Phillipson, 2013). A broader consequence was the development of a diverse range of supplementary pensions among the population. In 2000/01, around 44% of those covered by second-tier pensions had SERPs only; a further 17% had an approved personal pension, while the remainder had some form of employer-provided pension (Lain, 2009: 63). Pension changes since 2000 have further changed the pension landscape.

To summarise, the roots of pension provision in the UK were derived from a concern for the social needs of older people, rather than seeking to replicate market outcomes. The Conservative governments of the 1980s sought to promote the private pension market in the place of expanded earnings-related coverage. However, in the late 1990s, the low level of pension provision resulted in a dualised system: on the one hand, significant numbers were covered by occupational pensions; while, on the other, means-tested benefits were received by significant number of retirees. The safety net of means-tested benefits, which reflected paternalistic concerns with the welfare of older people, was more widely established than in the US.

The roots of US pensions

In contrast to the focus on social need in Britain, in the US, pensions have been framed around notions of an earned entitlement to a much greater degree. The first state pensions were provided in 1862 to Union soldiers injured in the Civil War or their dependants if they were killed in action (Skocpol, 1992; Williamson and Pampel, 1993). These were not provided on an assessment of need, although many would have been needy. Instead, the pensions were, in a sense, earned by the contribution made by the Union soldiers in the Civil War. Note, for example, that pensions were not provided to those injured/killed on the losing Confederate side despite the fact that they probably had comparable needs to Union soldiers. In 1890, the link between need and pensions was further weakened when all veterans of the Union Army were awarded a pension, even if they had never been injured or seen combat (Williamson and Pampel, 1993: 88). According to Williamson and Pampel (1993: 89), 'the benefits generally went to White native-born workers, who tended to be more affluent, and many of the lowest income workers were excluded'. While coverage of Civil War pensions expanded, when these individuals and their dependants died, this source of income inevitably diminished. An outcome of this expansion of pensions based on political patronage was also a concern about political corruption. This arguably made it politically harder to advocate for a more universal system of state pensions (Skocpol, 1992).

It was not until the Great Depression, following the 1929 Wall Street crash, that state pensions became a national political priority (Orloff, 1993: 283–7). The depression had highlighted the vulnerability that individuals faced, including in old age, and had led to mass movements pressing for pensions. The largest group was the Townsend movement; this had thousands of members and a presence in almost every congressional district in the US (Orloff, 1993: 286). The Townsend plan that they advocated was for a $200 pension for all Americans over 60, provided on the condition that they spend this money within 30 days. This therefore had the dual aims of creating a pension and stimulating the economy through the spending of older people. This was considered far too radical by President Roosevelt, who wanted a social insurance system that rewarded hard work and was aligned with notions of self-reliance. Fearing that 'unwise' legislation might be enacted, Roosevelt sidelined radical voices from the preparation of Social Security plans (Orloff, 1993: 286). No leaders from the labour or pensions movements were included in the drafting of the Old Age Benefits proposal that led to the introduction of Social Security Old Age Insurance. It was, however, supported by a number of business leaders, 'which was not surprising given that experts who shared the business values had a strong hand in shaping it' (Williamson and Pampel, 1993: 95). Large corporations had, by this time, realised that they would struggle to meet the pension needs of their employees single-handedly (Williamson and Pampel, 1993: 109). Gordon (1994: 280) argues that 'New Deal policies [including Social Security] were essentially business friendly measures in progressive clothing', although that did not stop business from having mixed, sometimes contradictory, attitudes to it.

Debates about what state pensions should look like were centred around two competing schools of thought (Williamson and Pampel, 1993). The Ohio School wanted substantial income redistribution between the classes in recognition of the social needs of those with low earnings. The Wisconsin School opposed the redistribution of income or non-contributory pensions; instead, the role of state pensions was to provide a system whereby individuals could set aside money for retirement. State pensions would therefore be consistent with market principles – those people paying in more to their pensions would receive more in retirement (Cates, 1983). When it was introduced in 1935, Old Age Insurance was closer to the scheme proposed by the Wisconsin School (Williamson and Pampel, 1993: 95). Roosevelt opposed non-contributory pensions such as those proposed by Townsend and pensions based on assessments of need; concerns about needs would be addressed through social assistance. Old Age Insurance would therefore be an earnings-related pension – better-paid individuals would pay higher contributions, which, in turn, meant higher pension levels. Roosevelt felt that an 'earned' pension such as this would be more in tune with American sentiments about individual responsibility and hard work. Resistance to social insurance within Congress could be overcome by framing Social Security on the basis of these sentiments. As Rimlinger (1971: 229) argues:

> Congress could be expected to have a natural affinity for forms of protection that were reasonably consistent with the dominant values of self-help and rewards related to individual effort. The proposals … met these requirements. A staff member of the committee … explained 'We wanted our government to provide a mechanism whereby the individual could prevent dependency through their own efforts'…. The central idea … was that the individual would earn his own benefits…. On a quasi contractual basis.

The Social Security pension was therefore influenced by private insurance (Williamson and Pampel, 1993: 97). Initially, no adjustments were to be made for family members. Employers and employees would pay equal contributions, and the original intention was for money to be paid into a large trust fund from which benefits would eventually be paid out. In the event, there were concerns that a large trust fund would distort the market, so Social Security was introduced on a pay-as-you-go basis – pensions were paid for by the contributions paid in. A reserve fund was created to collect contributions that were paid that were surplus to requirements at that time. Unlike in the UK, where social need considerations were stronger, pensions were not paid out immediately to older people. The first pensions were not to be paid out until 1940, and were paid at low levels given the short contribution period (the average was about $20 a month, one tenth of the amount requested by the Townsend movement (Williamson and Pampel, 1993: 96). Social security pensions remained low until the 1950s, which reflected the fact that they had to be 'earned' over a working life.

A number of concessions to social need were incorporated into Social Security. The pension had a 'tilt' in favour of lower earners, so it replaced lower earnings at higher levels than upper earnings. This meant that while the richest received the largest pensions, the poorest received larger pensions than they would in a strictly actuarial system (Lain et al, 2013). In addition, in 1939, the Social Security Old Age Pension introduced benefits for wives, equivalent to 50% of their husband's pension (if this was larger than their own entitlement). This, therefore, deviated from a pure market logic. However, the justification was based on an earned entitlement, rather than an assessment of need. As Rimlinger (1971: 233) points out:

> the Social Security planners seized on the concept of 'family protection'.... Stretching the original idea of individually earned benefits by extending it to members of the earner's family. In this manner, social needs could be met with a minimum of ideological conflict with individualistic principles.

The Social Security Act of 1935 also introduced Old Age Assistance, a non-contributory means-tested benefit. This proved to be a vital component of retirement incomes in the immediate post-war period given the slow rate at which Social Security Old Age Pensions accumulated. However, it is important to note that the levels at which this was provided varied across the US because states were allowed to set their own benefit levels and eligibility criteria. This was a compromise with Southern states, who did not want to pay high levels of Old Age Assistance due to fears that it would increase the wages of poor black farm workers (Williamson and Pampel, 1993: 96). Some of the poorest in the US therefore received extremely low levels of Old Age Assistance, or were deemed ineligible entirely.

In 1972, Old Age Assistance was replaced by the Supplemental Security Income (SSI) programme, which was provided to retirees with low incomes. The fact that such a policy would be enacted in the US is perhaps surprising. However, it must be seen in a wider context. SSI was originally a small part of a wider unsuccessful proposal called the Family Assistance Programme, which sought to protect a range of groups (Williamson and Pampel, 1993: 100). The fact that the SSI component provided to retirees was passed suggests that relative to younger age groups, older people were seen as a more deserving group. However, SSI was never to have the same level of support among the population as Social Security (Pampel, 1998). Public concerns about supporting the vulnerable came into conflict with concerns about the undeserving poor receiving help without having contributed. For example, one of the factors that undermined support for SSI was the inaccurate concern that lots of immigrants were arriving in the US in older age and claiming the means-tested benefit (Berkowitz and DeWitt, 2013).

The lack of political will to support SSI is illustrated by the way in which eligibility has declined dramatically since it was introduced; this has led Elder and the Powers (2006) to dub it the 'incredible shrinking programme'. The amount of assets (excluding housing) that the individual is allowed to have is only $2,000, the same amount as in 1989 and only 37% in real terms of the amount allowed in 1974 (Elder and the Powers, 2006: 343). In comparison, in the UK, individuals were allowed £12,000 of non-housing assets in 2004 in order to receive Minimum Income Guarantee (Lain, 2011: 496). SSI also only represented 20% of average earnings in the US in 2004, compared with 26% for the UK Minimum Income Guarantee (Lain, 2011). Out of the 52 states, 23 provided supplements to SSI, but typically only trivial amounts – the median being $31 a month (Lain, 2011). As a result of the strict eligibility criteria and low benefit levels, SSI has come to support only a small number of retirees with low incomes – around 3% of individuals aged over 65 (Lain, 2009: 146). This, therefore, represents an example of incremental change through 'policy drift' (Streeck and Thelen, 2005), whereby a policy is undermined because it fails to keep up with changing circumstances.

In summary, state pension provision in the US was designed around notions of earned entitlements and self-reliance. As a result, the safety net for those with low retirement incomes is weaker than in the UK, where policy has been more paternalistically oriented towards meeting the basic social needs of older people.

Reforms to state pensions

The state pension context in the early 2000s

In both the UK and the US, changes to retirement incomes since the early 2000s have increased the need for people to work beyond age

65. However, to fully understand the implications of these changes, we need to examine the situation of pensions in the late 1990s and early 2000s. In this regard, it is important to note that neither the UK nor the US faced the kind of pension crisis found in other countries in the early 2000s. To understand why this is the case, we need to examine the nature of pension provision in both countries in the early 2000s.

Figure 2.1 shows state pension levels in 1999 for those at different levels of earnings, ranging from half of average earnings through to twice average earnings (see the horizontal axis). Gross pension levels are shown on the vertical axis as a percentage of average economy-wide earnings. Pension levels are based on pension rules that had been enacted by 1999. In reality, people would have built up pension entitlements during different periods based on different rules. However, Figure 2.1 gives a good indication of the differences between pension regimes in different countries. It also shows the pension situation facing policymakers looking forward in the late 1990s as they sought to decide how to change the situation. It should be noted that the pension levels presented in Figure 2.1 assume that an individual has a full contribution record at state pension age. In some cases, this may be an unrealistic expectation in reality, particularly for women if they have had career breaks for family reasons (Ginn, 2003). Likewise, Figure 2.1 is based on the assumption that individuals have stable earnings throughout their careers – for example, they earn twice

Figure 2.1: Gross state pension levels across English-speaking countries, 1999

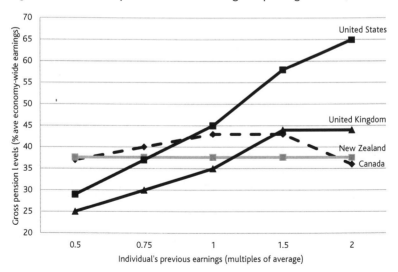

Note: **Figures** for England contain a full entitlement to the State Earnings Related Pension. State pension levels based on 1999 rules except for New Zealand, which is based on 2002 rules.
Sources: Whitehouse (2003) and OECD (2005b).

average earnings throughout their career. In some senses, Figure 2.1 presents an 'optimistic' indication of pension levels looking forward based on 1999 pension rules.

All of the countries in Figure 2.1 are English-speaking nations that would be classified as having 'Liberal' residual welfare states by Esping Andersen (1990). Despite this, however, different countries had clearly made different choices about how pension levels should vary across different income groups.

In the US, we see a visible increase in pension levels as you move up the earnings hierarchy, reflecting the earnings-related nature of these pensions. Somebody previously on half average earnings would receive a pension worth only 29% of economy-wide earnings. On the other hand, somebody on twice average earnings would receive a pension worth more than twice that (65% of economy-wide earnings). With such liabilities in the context of population ageing, cost containment is an issue for policymakers. However, US Social Security had less pension sustainability problems than other countries. It did not allow for the accumulation of very high pension liabilities for high earners. Americans on twice average earnings would receive a pension equivalent to 32.5% of *their* previous income, compared with 70% of previous earnings in the Netherlands (Whitehouse, 2003). The US also has a relatively young age structure, which considerably reduces pressure on the pension system going forward (Bonoli and Shinkawa, 2005). Finally, the US has the advantage of a reserve fund with surpluses in it, as we saw earlier; this helps offset the additional costs associated with an increasing number of pensioners. However, with little willingness to increase contributions, it was decided to increase the 'full' pension age (see 'Changing state pensions in the USA' later in the chapter).

In the UK, the very low level of UK state pension provision meant that, in 1999, the country faced no impending pensions crisis at all. Figure 2.1 shows state pension levels for those with a full entitlement to both the Basic State Pension and SERPs, based on 1999 policies. Somebody on half average wages would receive a pension worth only a quarter of economy-wide earnings, and somebody on average wages would receive a pension worth only around a third of economy-wide earnings. State pension levels stopped rising once individuals got to 1.5 times average earnings, at 44% of economy-wide earnings. This is because individuals stop paying National Insurance contributions above a certain threshold. The main outcome of this is that the state pension system fails to prevent individuals ending up with very low state pensions. To understand why this is the case, it is useful to look at the examples of New Zealand and Canada in Figure 2.1. New Zealand provided a flat-rate universal pension to all individuals above age 65 on the basis of residency, not contributions. As this was set at a relatively high level, it lifted individuals above means-tested levels, thereby preventing individuals from receiving the low levels of pensions found in the UK and US for those on low earnings. Canada, on the other hand, combines a universal flat-rate state pension with an earnings-related supplement (Canada Pension Plan). This combination helps limit the extent to which low earners end up with very small pensions, while including a modest earnings-related increase until individuals reach average earnings. In both the UK and US, there remained a problem of those with modest earnings receiving low pensions.

Means-tested pensions were an important component of retirement income for many older people in the UK in the early 2000s given relatively low state pension levels. Around one third of individuals aged over 65 lived in a household that received at least one means-tested benefit (DWP, 2007). Minimum Income Guarantee, later replaced by Pension Credit, was a social assistance benefit for older people with low incomes. In addition, Housing Benefit was received by those with low incomes in rented accommodation and Council Tax Benefit provided assistance with local taxes for those with low incomes. As Figure 2.2 shows, means-tested benefit receipt was particularly high for single men and women in the UK. Means-tested benefits were received by almost half of single women (47.1%) and two fifths of single men (38.6%). Approaching a fifth of married men and women received such benefits.

In the US, means-tested benefit receipt was much lower, at around 19% for single women, 15% for single men and 5% for married men and women. Included within this are SSI, housing benefits (provided in cash or kind) and food stamps.

One of the reasons for this was that the Social Security pension provided larger pensions for many individuals than in the UK, reflecting the extent to which it attempted to reward previous work and achievements. It should also be noted that any occupational pension income was in addition to a full Social Security pension, whereas in the UK, it was common for those with occupational pensions to opt out of their SERPs pension. As Figure 2.3 shows, people over 65 in the early 2000s in the US had higher median incomes than their UK counterparts before means-tested benefits and wages are included. Married men and women in the US had incomes (excluding benefits/earnings) equivalent to around 50% of full-time average earnings; this compares with around 42% of earnings in the UK. Single men had incomes equivalent to 38.5% of average full-time earnings in the US,

Figure 2.2: Percentages of those aged 65+ receiving means-tested benefits, UK and US, early 2000s

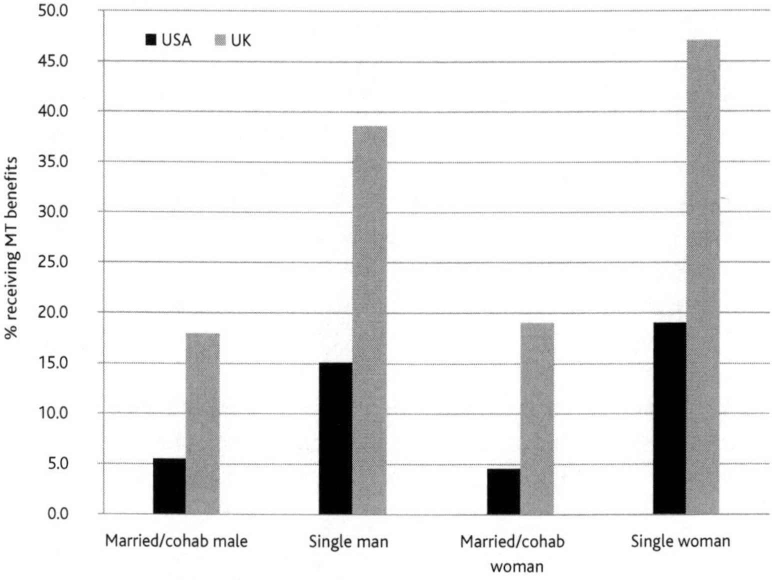

Note: **Means-tested** benefits include income assistance benefits, housing benefits/assistance and 'other' benefits such as Council Tax Benefit in the UK and Food Stamps in the US.
Source: Author's analysis of the UK Family Resources Survey 1999/2000, 2000/01 and 2001/02 and the US Current Population Survey March 2001.

compared with 31.9% in the UK. Likewise, single women had incomes of 31.4% in the US, compared with 27% in the UK.[1]

While we would expect fewer people to receive means-tested benefits in the US because they have higher average incomes, this cannot fully explain why such benefits are less common than in the UK. Another important factor is that means-tested benefits were easier to obtain in the UK, reflecting a greater legacy of trying to address social needs when they arise (Lain, 2011). In the early 2000s, around 12% of individuals aged 65+ living alone or in a couple in the UK received income assistance benefits (Minimum Income Guarantee/Pension Credit), compared with only 3% in the US receiving SSI (Lain, 2011: 496). As we discussed in the previous section, one cause of this was the strict eligibility requirements that restricted the benefit only to those with very low assets (only $2,000 excluding housing, compared with £12,000 in the UK) (Lain, 2011). In addition, the US benefit topped up incomes to lower levels than its UK equivalent (Lain, 2011), which further reduced coverage.

In relation to housing benefits, we see an even more extreme difference between the countries. In the UK, Housing Benefit was

Figure 2.3: Median incomes received by those aged 65+ as a percentage of average full-time earnings (excludes earnings and means-tested benefits), UK and US

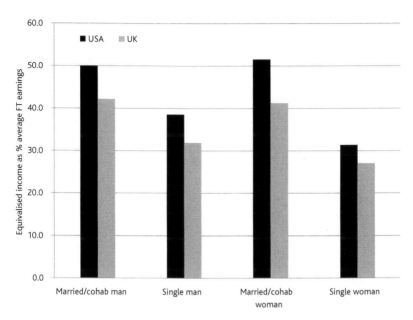

Note: Incomes are household incomes equivalised to the individual level using the OECD modified scale. This is based on the assumption that a couple needs 1.5 times the income of a single person to have an equivalent standard of living. Incomes exclude earnings and means-tested benefits.
Source: Author's analysis of the UK Family Resources Survey 1999/2000, 2000/01 and 2001/02 and the US Current Population Survey March 2001.

designed to ensure that no one in rented accommodation had an income of less than income assistance, once reasonable rental costs were deducted (Priemus et al, 2005: 587). This would mean that somebody on full income assistance would have their full reasonable rental costs met in UK. In the US, housing assistance was a more fragmented system, split between vouchers for private sector accommodation and low-rent housing programmes (Lain, 2011: 496). Nevertheless, the common principle was that recipients contributed 30% of their income, minus deductions, to the rent; this made it less generous than UK provision. Furthermore, in order to receive housing assistance, individuals had to join long queues and find suitable accommodation. In total, only 5% of individuals over age 65 in the US received housing assistance, compared with 20% in the UK. In 1999, only '29% of extremely low and very low income renter households were receiving housing subsidy' (Priemus et al, 2005: 582).

To summarise the situation in the early 2000s prior to reforms, means-tested benefits played a more significant role in the UK than in the US. This was because means-tested benefits were harder to access in the US, as well as the lower level of UK state pension provision. While UK state pensions based on 1999 rules were very ungenerous, it is important to note that they were to decline still further in the coming years. The decision to link pension increases to prices, rather than earnings, discussed earlier, would continue to erode the relative value of provision. Indeed, because of the declining value of state pension provision, the proportion of gross domestic product (GDP) spent on this was set to decline over the long term. In 2000, 5.5% of GDP was spent on state pensions, falling to 4.4% in 2050. In contrast, in the European Union (EU-15) countries as a whole, spending on state pensions was projected to rise from 10.4% in 2000 to 13.3% in 2050. While UK state pensions were declining, occupational pension coverage was also in sharp decline, as we will see in the next section.

Due to declining state and occupational incomes, the need for means-tested benefits in the future was projected to rise in the UK (Pensions Commission, 2004). This context presented a particular dilemma for politicians. Targeting income on the poorest pensioners helps those in most immediate need but, at the same time, the expectation that people might end up on means-tested benefits acts as a disincentive to save for the future. Means-tested benefits also act as a perceived disincentive to work in older age. In the UK in the early 2000s, people on low incomes could receive Minimum Income Guarantee/Pension Credit from age 60. With the exception of a small earnings disregard (of £5), these benefits would be quickly withdrawn when people worked (Lain, 2011: 497). In contrast, it is notable that the Organisation for Economic Co-operation and Development (OECD, 2005a) does not discuss means-tested benefits in its analysis of financial incentives to retire in the US. This was presumably because they offered such a week safety net for those on low incomes.

Changes to state pensions

Changing state pensions in the UK

When Labour looked likely to return to power in 1997, a number of commentators argued for a large increase in the Basic State Pension to address the decline that it had suffered under previous Conservative administrations, and for a revitalisation of SERPs (see, eg, Townsend and Walker, 1995; Lynes, 1996). These reforms, the National Pensioners Convention (1998) argued, would bring security to retirees. Instead, the New Labour government decided to encourage individuals to take greater responsibility for their own retirement incomes, while providing additional support for current retirees with low incomes (Rowlingson, 2002). The government's Green Paper *A new contract for welfare: Partnership in pensions* (DSS, 1998: 3) set out these principles as follows:

- Those who are able, should save what they can for their retirement.
- The government should support those who cannot save and regulate the pension system effectively.
- The private sector should provide affordable and secure second pensions.

The government therefore aimed to increase the share of pension income coming from private sources from 40% to 60% (DSS, 1998: 31–2). Recognising that administration fees could eat up pension assets, the government introduced a voluntary private 'stakeholder' pensions with caps on the annual management charges that could be made (see Waine, 2009). This, it was hoped, would increase the share of people actively saving for their own retirements. The government resisted big increases to the Basic State Pension and instead focused on increasing pension income for low earners from the 'second tier' of pension income. The principle of earnings-related pensions was criticised on the basis that SERPs 'gives least help to those on the lowest incomes' (DSS, 1998: 5). The State Second Pension therefore replaced SERPs in 2002; it was intended to provide larger pensions for those with low earnings and periods of caring and would become flat-rate over time.

Importantly, for those who had been 'unable' to save, the government increased the role of means testing in order to target those with low incomes. The Minimum Income Guarantee was introduced to replace Income Support, with the intention that it would rise in line with earnings and therefore be a significant safety net in future (DSS, 1998: 4). This reflected the focus on targeting increases in spending on the poorer pensioners. A problem with this targeting, however, was that people might not save if they thought that they would lose out on means-tested benefits as a result. The response to this was to introduce Pension Credit, which included a 'savings credit' element. This increased the scope for individuals with modest savings to receive some benefit income; it was hoped that this would encourage those on low incomes to save. With the introduction of Pension Credit, the numbers receiving income assistance benefits rose from 1.98 million people in 2003/04 to 3.15 million people in 2004/05 (ONS, 2013a: 16). In 2005, 40% of pensioner households were entitled to Pension

Credit (Pensions Commission, 2005: 11). Ironically, although Pension Credit increased savings incentives for some, because coverage was expanded, it introduced new savings disincentives for a larger number of individuals due to the tapering off of benefits (Bozio et al, 2010: 54). This problem was not going to reduce over time. Projections conducted in 2005 estimated that over 70% of pensioner households were likely to be entitled to Pension Credit by 2035 (Pensions Commission, 2005: 11).

It therefore became clear that the focus on means-tested benefits was incompatible with encouraging people to take individual responsibility for retirement finances. As Waine (2009: 759) points out, during this time, 'The introduction of the SHP [stakeholder pension] failed to increase the overall proportion of individuals saving for retirement through pension plans'. People were unlikely to save, or work in older age, if they anticipated that they would be little better off as a result. A consensus developed around the need for state pension income to lift more people above Pension Credit levels. The Conservative Party now argued for an increased flat-rate state pension, above which individuals would be responsible for their own savings (Willets and Yeo, 2004). This position was echoed by business (Bridgen and Meyer, 2007). Social activists, researchers and trade unions, on the other hand, had long argued that state pensions had to do more to protect individuals from very low retirement incomes. Means-tested benefits were complicated, stigmatising and a failure to claim them among a significant number resulted in poverty.

To address these issues, the Pensions Commission was set up in 2002 to review UK pensions and suggest reforms. The Pensions Commission was led by an industrialist, Adair Turner, but also included an academic and a trade unionist. It defined its remit as focusing 'constrained tax/NI [National Insurance] resources on ensuring as generous and non-means tested, flat-rate state pension provision as possible.... [And to] Improve the treatment of people with interrupted paid work records and caring responsibilities' (Pensions Commission, 2005: 21). The Pensions Commission envisaged arriving at a Basic State Pension from age 68 that would gradually become residency-based (Lain et al, 2013). This would expand coverage of people receiving a full pension. Increases in the Basic State Pension would also be pegged to average earnings rather than prices, halting its long-term decline. The State Second Pension was to become flat-rate over time, completing the two 'tiers' of flat-rate state pension provision. Individuals were now no longer able to opt out of the State Second Pension unless they had a DB occupational pension, further expanding coverage. The Pensions

Act 2007 introduced the main thrust of the Pensions Commission's recommendations. However, it was decided that the Basic State Pension would not become residency-based. Instead, the number of contributions years would be reduced to 30 (with allowances for caring responsibilities) (Price, 2007). This, it was hoped, would lead to 'near universality'.

This shift in focus to state pensions that lift people above means-tested benefit levels has continued under the Conservative governments elected since 2010. The 2011 Budget announced that both elements of state pension provision would be replaced with a new Single Tier Pension (STP) (Foster, 2014: 32). The new STP will be set just above the Pensions Credit Guarantee Level (£144 in 2012/13 prices) for those with 35 years of National Insurance contributions or credits (Foster, 2014). Pegged at means-tested benefit levels, UK state pension provision will therefore remain very modest by international standards (Ginn and MacIntyre, 2013: 97). The pension will be introduced from 2016, with many women eligible for a full pension making an immediate gain (Crawford et al, 2013). As Foster (2014: 36), points out, however, 'In the longer term, the STP will be less generous than the current system for most people'. This is because people will accrue lower STP pensions than was possible under the Basic State Pension and the State Second Pension combined. Women will also still be more likely than men to need to claim Pension Credit because years out of employment reduce pension entitlements.

In exchange for pension increases for (some) groups, state pension ages are to rise. To avoid strong resistance, immediate retirees were not affected by age increases (a 'grandfather clause'), and rises are to occur in increments. Nevertheless, the rise in state pension age will be very rapid; it will be 66 in 2020, six years earlier than planned by the Labour government in 2007 (Foster, 2014: 34). This is a particularly big increase for women, who had a state pension age of 60 in 2010. A significant number of older women (and men) will have to work much longer than they expected or planned to. The state pension age will rise to 67 by 2027, after which it will rise to 68 (DWP, 2013). The state pension age will also be reviewed every five years, as the Department for Work and Pensions (DWP, 2013: 4) explains:

> The Pensions Act 2014 provides for a regular review of the State Pension age, at least once every five years. The review will be based around the idea that people should be able to spend a certain proportion of their adult life drawing a State Pension. The first review must by completed by May

2017. As well as life expectancy, it will take into account a range of factors relevant to setting the pension age. After the review has reported, the Government may then choose to bring forward changes to the State Pension age.

This review process therefore reduces certainty in the minds of people about when retirement will come. It has been suggested that the pension age is likely to reach at least 70 if linked to life expectancy, as currently proposed (Clark, 2013). Unlike in other countries, including the US, there will be no entitlement to an early reduced pension. The age at which means-tested Pension Credit can be received will also rise to 68+, in line with the female state pension age. This means that this benefit will no longer provide a safety net for those exiting from work early. Reforms to state pensions therefore dramatically increase the need for individuals to work beyond age 65 in the coming years in the UK.

Changing state pensions in the US

In contrast to the UK, actual state pension reforms *enacted* in the US since the early 2000s have been minimal. President George Bush made a concerted, but unsuccessful, effort to allow individuals to 'opt out' of Social Security into private pensions (for a detailed account, see Béland and Waddan, 2012). Social Security was a mature pay-as-you-go pension programme, under which contributions from workers today paid the pensions of current retirees. In this context, it was difficult to explain how individuals could pay for their own pension while supporting the entitlements of current retirees. In addition, private pensions were thought of as more risky than Social Security, and the Republican administration was not trusted to introduce reforms in this area (Béland and Waddan, 2012).

While few reforms occurred in the 2000s, however, the impacts of earlier reforms have increased the need for individuals to work beyond age 65 in order to secure a 'full' Social Security pension. In the 1970s and 1980s, there had been increasing public and political concern about whether Social Security would be able to meet its commitments to retirees in the future. This public concern reflected the popularity of the programme, and the fact that the Trustees of Social Security report on the long-term financial solvency of the pension on an annual basis. In this political and economic context, President Reagan set up the National Commission on Social Security Reform in 1981 (Béland and Waddan, 2012: 130). Importantly, it was a bipartisan commission that included Republicans and Democrats. The Commission proposed that the 'normal' Social Security age be gradually raised from 65 to 67 between 2000 and 2027. Age increases were subsequently enacted in amendments to the Social Security Act 1983 (Béland and Waddan, 2012: 131). In 2004, the state pension age for a 'full' pension rose to 65 and two months and reached exactly 66 in 2009; it will remain at this age until 2020, after which it will increase gradually to 67 in 2027.[2] Once again, this change was therefore introduced through a 'grandfather clause', to borrow the terminology of Pierson (1994), and proceeded in incremental steps.

An early pension will continue to be available, from age 62, but the reductions for early receipt will rise in line with 'full' pension age. In 2003, when the 'full' Social Security age was 65, a pension taken at 62 was reduced by 20%; this reduction was 25% in 2009 and will be 30% in 2027. The viability of retiring early will therefore decline for many people. Reductions for receipt of Social Security at 65 between 2009 and 2020 will be less significant – 6.7%, rising to 13.3% in 2027. Social Security will therefore continue to offer early benefits to those involuntarily exiting from work, unlike the STP and Pension Credit in the UK. Early claiming at or before 65 is also likely to continue based on previous experience – currently, more than half of individuals claim Social Security before 'full' retirement age (Butrica and Karamcheva, 2013). Nevertheless, changes to the Social Security retirement age have increased the need to work past 65. At the same time, for those on low incomes, access to SSI will continue to diminish as the assets allowable decrease in real terms through a process of policy 'drift' (see 'The roots of US pensions' earlier in this chapter).

Looking forward, it is important to note that Social Security ages are not fixed in stone and may rise above 67 in the future. President Obama set up the bipartisan National Commission on Fiscal Responsibility and Reform in 2010, with the aim of suggesting policies to improve the financial sustainability of Social Security. The Commission has suggested indexing the 'full retirement age' and 'early retirement age' to increases in life expectancy (Béland and Waddan, 2012: 160). This would be expected to increase the full retirement age to 68 by 2050 and 69 by 2075, although it is impossible to fully anticipate how life expectancy projections will change over time (Béland and Waddan, 2012).

In sum, in both the UK and the US, changes to state pension incomes have increased the need to work beyond age 65 in the future. The US is currently ahead of the UK in terms of having a full retirement age of 66, but in the longer term, people in Britain will have to wait longer for a state pension. The UK STP retirement age will rise to 68, with no opportunities to obtain an early pension or Pension Credit. Working beyond 65 will therefore become particularly crucial in the UK. However, in both countries, we also need to look at changes to occupational pensions in order to obtain a more complete picture of how pressures to work beyond age 65 are increasing.

Changes to occupational and private pensions in the UK and the US

With comparatively modest or low state pensions by international standards, occupational and private pensions have been important in the UK and the US. Changes to these pensions in both countries have increased the need to work past 65. Historically, many employees have had DB occupational pensions in both countries. These pensions were paid to retirees on a regular basis for the rest of their lives, with the amount typically linked to an individual's final salary. DB pensions previously provided a significant route to early retirement (Laczko and Phillipson, 1991; Wise, 1993), but they have declined substantially in both countries. These pensions are being replaced with defined contribution (DC) schemes, which are unlikely to provide the same secure paths to retirement.

The shift from DB to DC pensions occurred earlier in the US than in the UK. So-called 401(k) DC schemes emerged in the US after a change to the tax code in 1978 that placed them on a legal footing. With DC schemes, employees themselves decide how much of their own money to contribute to these savings accounts, up to a fixed proportion of their earnings. *If they are lucky*, their employer will match a portion of their contribution. The employee also decides how they want the contributions to be invested, and upon retirement, they will be given a lump sum comprised of the value of the pension pot after investments have been made. In 1980, around 47% of private sector workers had an occupational pension, and only 8% had a DC pension instead of a DB scheme (Buessing and Soto, 2006: Table E). In 2003, the proportion of private sector workers with an occupational pension of either sort was similar to 1980, at 50%. However, the proportion of workers only covered by DC schemes had risen from 8% to 31% (Buessing and Soto, 2006). It is likely that the shift towards DC schemes has continued to increase since this period.

According to Hacker (2006: 119), there is a simple reason why US employers have been attracted to replace DB schemes with DB schemes: they are 'dirt cheap' and low-risk. Employers formally provided DB schemes to encourage employees to remain in the same company and because trade unions pressed for them. These factors no longer apply to the same degree because the commitment of employers to long-term employment relationships has diminished and trade unions have declined (Hacker, 2006). Shifting from DB to DC pensions has given employers the cover to dramatically reduce the contributions they make to employee pensions. In the late 1970s, employers devoted more than 4% of workers' payroll to pensions. By the late 1980s, on the other hand, they were only contributing 2.5% (Hacker, 2006: 119). Furthermore, if an employee makes no contributions to their 401(k) pension – as is the case for many workers – the employer does not have to contribute. Pension wealth in 401(k) plans is consequently strongly skewed towards the wealthy, who benefit greatly from the tax breaks available. The *median* amount held in 401(k) schemes was less than $20,000 in 2006 (Hacker, 2006). In addition to being cheap, 401(k) DC schemes are low-risk for employers because they do not guarantee a pension as a proportion of earnings for as long as the individual lives. It is the employee who takes the risk as to whether their pension pot increases, and pensions payable in retirement can vary dramatically depending upon when an individual retires. In some instances, individuals can make staggering losses to their pension wealth if they are unlucky with their investments. Furthermore, because employees take responsibility for deciding how the money will be invested, the employer avoids criticism if the pension outcomes are poor. Of course, some people will be lucky and see big increases in their pension wealth during periods of strong stock market performance. However, even for these individuals, we need to bear in mind the fact that employers are typically making smaller contributions in the first place. Furthermore, because 401(k) schemes to not provide an annuity, the individual – not the employer – bears the risk that they will outlive the assets that they have received (Hacker, 2006).

The shift from DB to DC pension schemes has therefore reduced the extent to which occupational pensions can provide a secure path into retirement and, on balance, it is likely to increase the need for individuals to work beyond age 65. Available US evidence consistently shows that, on average, people with DC schemes retire later than those with DB schemes (see, eg, Munnell et al, 2004; Friedberg and Webb, 2005). This may partly be due to individuals responding positively to financial incentives – another year of work contributes directly to the lump sum received upon retirement. On the other hand, DC schemes cannot provide the security of an annuitised DB pension, and employers contribute less to them.

In the UK, occupational pension membership in the private sector has been gradually falling overall since the 1970s. Occupational pension coverage has fallen particularly fast in recent years because closed DB pension schemes have not been replaced by DC schemes in sufficient numbers. Between 1983 and 2000, the number of private sector employees in DB schemes fell from around 34% to 22%, but the numbers in DC schemes only rose from around 1% to 4% (Pensions Commission, 2004: 118). Between 2000 and 2004, the numbers of private sector workers in active DB schemes fell by half, and is projected to fall even further (Pensions Commission, 2004: 114). Those that did have DC schemes also found that, as in the US, employers made smaller contributions than in the case of DB schemes (ONS, 2013b).

The decline in occupational pension provision for private sector workers created a problem for the future of retirement incomes. The solution suggested by the Pensions Commission (2005), and subsequently enacted, was 'auto-enrolment', which will increase membership of DC plans considerably. Starting with large employers in 2012, employees without an occupational pension will be 'automatically enrolled' into a workplace scheme. Individuals will therefore not have to decide to join a pension scheme, they will actively have to 'opt out' if they want to; this is an attempt to deal with the inertia and cynicism that prevents people from saving for retirement (Foster, 2014). The employer needs to select an approved pension scheme to enrol their staff into. This could be the default scheme, the National Employment Savings Trust (NEST). When auto-enrolment is fully established, the employee will pay 4% of their qualifying earnings into the pension, with the employer contributing 3% and the government contributing 1% through tax relief (Ginn and MacIntyre, 2013: 97).

The introduction of auto-enrolment signals the end of employer voluntarism with regard to workplace pensions (Bridgen and Meyer, 2011) − employers have to contribute if their employees do, which is not the case for 401(k) pensions in the US. On the other hand, as the STP pension will be lower than Social Security for most people, auto-enrolment arguably has to play an even more important role than 401(k)s in the US. The Pensions Commission estimates that somebody saving from age 30 until state pension age might receive an STP pension worth 30% of their previous wage, alongside an auto-enrolment pension of 15% after annuitisation. The amounts projected are therefore modest. Critics argue that it is difficult to project what outcomes might look like for auto-enrolment pensions given the unpredictability of private pensions (Ginn and Macintyre, 2013). The NEST scheme, which is likely to be the one disproportionately available to low earners, has been conscious of this concern and has developed a cautious investment strategy (NEST, 2014). It will remain to be seen whether NEST is able to generate the returns expected, or what will happen to the pensions of those enrolled in other schemes. Likewise, we do not yet know how many individuals will ultimately opt out of contributing via auto-enrolment, although early indications suggest that it may be around 10% of people (DWP, 2014a).

Auto-enrolment will therefore increase DC saving in the UK, benefiting some individuals, typically on low incomes, who would have otherwise had no workplace pension. On the other hand, when considered alongside the level of the STP, the projected total amounts are expected to be relatively modest by international standards. Individuals that would have had DB pensions in the past are unlikely to be better off under DC pensions. Furthermore, there has been a sharp decline in the regular income that an annuity will buy using a UK DC pension pot (Papworth, 2013). This has led the UK to join the US in not requiring 'DC pensioners' to buy an annuity, meaning that many individuals will now have to take responsibility for ensuring they do not run out of savings before they die.

The shift towards DC pensions, alongside increases in the state pension age, are likely to increase pressures to work beyond age 65 for many individuals in both the UK and the US. As noted earlier, people with DC pensions in the US retire later than those with DB pensions, and in the UK, DC pension-holders expect to retire later than those with DB pensions (Arkani and Gough, 2007).

Conclusions

In this chapter, we have examined how changes to retirement incomes have increased the need for individuals to work beyond age 65 in the UK and US. State pension ages are set to rise to 67 in the US and 68 in the UK, with further rises very possible. This will be a particularly big step for the UK because, unlike the US, there will be no early reduced pension available. Means-tested benefits for older people exiting from employment before state pension age are also being undermined in both countries. UK Pension Credit is to rise in line with the state pension age, removing an important benefit previously provided from age 60. SSI in the US will be rendered further irrelevant as policy drift results in even fewer people meeting the asset eligibility requirements. Finally, DB pensions have declined considerably in both countries. These are being replaced by DC pensions, but they are unlikely to provide the secure paths to retirement formally provided by many DB schemes.

In order to fully understand and appreciate the changes, it is important to place them in a broader context. As this chapter has shown, an emphasis on self-reliance and earned entitlements has historically shaped pension provision in the US. In the UK, on the other hand, retirement incomes have historically been guided to a greater degree by concerns about social need. It is certainly the case that recent UK policy reforms have also sought to improve the incomes of the poorest in a number of respects. The shift towards an STP should increase state pension levels for the poorest *once they reach state pension age*, even if most people will receive lower pensions in the longer term. Likewise, the introduction of auto-enrolment will spread coverage of workplace pensions to individuals that might have been unlikely to have had them in the past. Nevertheless, projected pension levels will remain low by international standards, and many people will have to wait a lot longer before they can access state pensions or benefits for older people. Likewise, DB pensions will play a smaller role in enabling early retirement. In this context, it is important to assess whether or not policies to promote employment beyond age 65 actually provide realistic opportunities to work. This is something that we address in Chapter Three in relation to the 'regulation' and rules governing employment past 65.

Notes

[1] In interpreting these figures, it is important to note that income levels reported have been equivalised to the individual level using the Organisation for Economic Co-operation and Development (OECD, no date) modified scale. Due to economies of scale of living in a couple, each individual in a couple is allocated 75% of the household income. For more on the data, see the statistical appendix to this book.

[2] These figures were taken from: https://www.socialsecurity.gov/planners/retire/ageincrease.html

THREE

The changing regulation of work and retirement

Introduction

In Chapter Two, we examined the increasing financial pressures to work past age 65 in both the UK and the US. As we saw, changes to retirement incomes began earlier in the US. However, it is also important to note that alongside these changes, the US was seeking to alter the regulation of work and retirement. A key moment in this regard was the abolition of mandatory retirement in 1986. As we shall see in this chapter, this move prohibited employers from getting rid of staff on the basis of their age, and sought to encourage individuals – particularly those with low incomes – to continue working. The UK followed the US by restricting the use of compulsory retirement ages in 2011. In both countries, the abolition of mandatory retirement arguably represented an example of what Streeck and Thelen (2005) call 'conversion' in policymaking. Legislation was initially introduced to protect individuals from age discrimination, but when it was amended, it became a policy to extend working lives. Alongside this, both countries altered the regulation of retirement incomes so that people could take their pensions while working. This chapter first reviews these changes. It starts by examining the period up to the late 1970s, when the US was seeking to address age discrimination and the UK was encouraging early retirement. We then examine changes since the late 1970s/1980s in both countries. Finally, the chapter examines the impact of age discrimination legislation, and considers the impact that this may have on employment beyond age 65.

Age discrimination and the position of older workers up to the 1970s

UK

It is important to note that before the expansion of pensions, the fear of poverty meant that few workers retired voluntarily. Two thirds of men over 65 in Britain were employed at the turn of the 19th century (Phillipson, 1982: 18). Employers often retained workers in older age, moving those engaged in physically arduous employment into 'light work' for the remaining years of their life. For those unable to work, the prospects were bleak – around one in 10 of the population aged over 65 lived in a workhouse, and by age 70, one in five would be a pauper (Phillipson, 1982). It was therefore seen by at least some employers as a moral duty to retain workers in employment over the age of 65.

Is important to note that during this time, there was nothing illegal about forcing someone to retire at a fixed age. However, it was not until the late 19th and early 20th centuries that we see the slow spread of mandatory retirement, the situation whereby individuals are required to leave work at a fixed age. Mandatory retirement started with bureaucratically organised professions such as the civil service and banking (Hannah, 1986). It became more common as organisations became more bureaucratic and rule-bound, and was used increasingly alongside pensions as a way of routinising the exit of older workers. Edward Lazear (1979) provides one of the most prominent explanations for why mandatory retirement came to exist. He argues that in modern organisations, mandatory retirement is used in conjunction with remuneration to instil employee loyalty and prevent shirking. Seniority wages mean that employees are underpaid relative to their productivity in the early years, but their wages increase over time if they remain in the same organisation. At some point, the employee becomes too expensive relative to their productivity (which will also inevitably decline). As a result, mandatory retirement is used (sometimes with a pension) to remove the older worker. Of course, the extent to which this explanation holds true depends upon the extent to which seniority wages have been paid (Lain and Vickerstaff, 2014). Nevertheless, it is evident that mandatory retirement did spread, and it represented a convenient way of managing the retirement process for employers.

Despite the gradual spread of mandatory retirement ages and pensions, employment beyond age 65 did not disappear overnight. In the aftermath of the Second World War, the government was keen to encourage people to continue working beyond age 65 due to labour shortages (Phillipson, 1982; Macnicol, 2006). Survey analysis from 1962 found that at age 65–66, half of men in Britain and the US were still in work; likewise, at age 67–69, around 40% were still working in both countries (Milhoj, 1968: 294). These workers were most likely to be in blue-collar employment in both countries, although this simply reflects the fact that this was the largest occupational group. In Britain, white-collar workers were just as likely as blue-collar workers to work past 65. In the US, white-collar workers were *more* likely to work past 65 than their blue-collar counterparts.

While workers over 65 were still a presence in the UK workforce in the mid-1960s, this was to sharply decline sharply later. Macnicol (2006: 81) argues that from the mid-1960s onwards, there was 'a 25 year period in which governments, employers and trade unionists shared the view that the modernisation of the British economy necessitated the exit of older workers via early retirement schemes'. A key turning point was the Redundancy Payments Act 1965; this attempted 'to facilitate industrial restructuring and technological modernisation by making it easier to dismiss workers' (Macnicol, 2006: 79). The Labour government of the time wanted employers to have the freedom to make people redundant in the context of industrial change, but restrictive workplace practices made this difficult. To help facilitate redundancies, the Act set out the minimum payments that individuals would receive upon being made redundant, based on length of service. While it was not overtly aimed at shedding older workers, older workers typically received larger payoffs than younger colleagues due to having longer job tenure. Consequently, employers were more likely to dismiss older workers that had most to gain financially, and older workers would sometimes take voluntary redundancy for this very reason (Macnicol, 2006: 81).

It has been argued that as a liberal market economy, levels of early exit in the UK were comparatively low relative to corporatist countries such as Germany, where the social partners conspired to encourage older people to leave work through early retirement schemes (Ebbinghaus, 2006). Nevertheless, declines in employment among UK men aged 60–64 were dramatic: from 89% in 1965 to around 50% between 1985 and 2003 (Ebbinghaus, 2006: 97). This decline was similar in magnitude to the one experienced in the US. The tight labour markets of the immediate post-war era began to give way to higher levels of unemployment, and were met with industrial restructuring that disproportionately affected older people. Many of these individuals ended up on unemployment or disability benefits. Individuals made redundant at aged 60 or over were also not expected to look for, or find, new work. As Banks et al (2008) points out, from 1981, men unemployed for a year were encouraged to sign on to higher-rate supplementary benefits rather than unemployment benefits that required the individual to look for a job. This was a way of getting the unemployment figures down, and arguably indicates a lack of support for older jobseekers.

At the same time, the government was signalling to employers and the general public that older people were a suitable group to leave the labour market when jobs were scarce. In this regard, the Job Release

Scheme (JRS) was introduced in 1977 and continued until 1988. Under the JRS, an employer could make older employees redundant if they filled the job with an unemployed jobseeker (Laczko and Phillipson, 1991). The older person was, in return, given a small flat-rate benefit called the Job Release Allowance until they reached state pension age. The scheme was only responsible for a relatively small fraction of early retirement, partly because the allowance provided was too low to be attractive to many workers (Laczko and Phillipson, 1991). Nevertheless, it reflected a culture of the time in which older people were being exited from employment. The sociologist Peter Townsend (1981) described this as the 'structured dependency' of older people, whereby they were pushed out of work early and often into a position of financial dependency on low state benefits.

Rather more significant than the JRS was the promotion of early retirement by employers through occupational pensions. By the 1980s, almost all occupational pensions allowed individuals to take early retirement and studies of manufacturing suggested that the use of occupational schemes to reduce the headcount was 'widespread' (Laczko and Phillipson, 1991). In addition, Laczko and Phillipson (1991: 236), writing in the early 1990s, argue that 'later studies have shown that early retirement continues to be used on a substantial scale by employers to affect reductions in headcount ... [and] managers are becoming more sophisticated in their use of early retirement packages'. It is notable that, unlike in the US, the government did not attempt to curb the targeted use of occupational pensions to promote early retirement.

In the context described earlier, it is perhaps unsurprising that employment beyond age 65 had reached very low levels by the 1980s, at around 7% for men and women combined. Assessing how much autonomy individuals actually had in practice in relation to working past 65 is difficult. However, survey analysis from 1994 suggests that around half of older employees faced a mandatory retirement age (Disney et al, 1997), which is similar to the proportions reporting a compulsory retirement age in the 2000s (Metcalf and Meadows, 2006). However, we should not assume that individuals *without* a mandatory retirement age could easily continue working beyond age 65. People beyond age 65 could not claim unfair dismissal or redundancy payments if they were retired off or dismissed, irrespective of whether or not they had a compulsory retirement age in the contract. Subsequent research from the 2000s suggests that line managers often decided whether somebody could work past 65 (Vickerstaff, 2006). When interviewed in organisational case-study research, most employees did not feel that they had a lot of choice about whether they continued in employment (Vickerstaff et al, 2004; Vickerstaff, 2006).

USA

It is perhaps surprising that legislation outlawing age discrimination occurred early in the US, a country that was slow to develop welfare policies. However, Macnicol (2007: 31) identifies three factors that seek to explain this. First, in the 1960s, the US had a strong civil rights movement, due to its history of racial discrimination and segregation. This strengthened the position of those campaigning against age discrimination because they could join with other social movements advocating change. In this regard, it is notable that age was originally included alongside race and sex in the 1964 Civil Rights Bill. However, it was decided that discrimination related to age was more complex, and this was dealt with separately in the later Age Discrimination in Employment Act 1967 (ADEA).

The second, and related, factor was the growth of 'grey power' pressure groups, most notably, the American Association of Retired Persons (AARP), which was founded in 1958. The AARP was particularly successful in highlighting the difficult financial position of many older Americans at this time, and the consequences of age discrimination in employment for individuals. These groups were effective in pushing for legislation at a state level. It is important to note that national legislation in the US is often preceded by earlier legislation at the state level. The emergence of legislation is therefore often a process of diffusion – a small number of states introduce legislation and its spreads (Boushey, 2010, 2012). This can be helpful for pressure groups because legislation can be introduced and effectively trialled in areas of the country that are sympathetic to it. Once it has been put into practice in one area, this provides a precedent (and evidence) that can be used by activists to promote it at a national level. There is little research on the process by which age discrimination legislation spread in the US. However, Neumark and Stock (1999) show that eight states had introduced some form of age discrimination legislation before 1960; the earliest was in 1903 (Colorado). In total, 22 US states had introduced age discrimination legislation before 1967, the year that the ADEA was passed. The ADEA should not therefore be viewed as a completely novel departure – it was a consolidation of developments that were occurring over time at a state level. These developments were influenced by the activities of pressure groups at the state level.

Debates about the modernisation of the economy in the US were a third factor influencing the development of age discrimination legislation (Macnicol, 2006, 2007). As in the UK, the US economy was shifting towards less-intensive forms of production in the 1960s. In the UK, this led to the expansion of early retirement/exit. In the US, on the other hand, debates about age discrimination were intertwined with debates about economic efficiency. There was a concern that the US economy was being damaged because, in the process of downsizing, employers were getting rid of some of the best older staff on the basis of outdated stereotypes. Legal protection for older workers therefore stemmed in part from a labour market policy that tried to encourage employers to 'retain the most efficient workers regardless of the age' (Macnicol, 2006: 82). In sum, the ADEA emerged in 1967 as a result of both social and economic concerns.

The original purpose of the ADEA was to 'Promote employment of older persons based on the ability rather than the age; to prohibit arbitrary age discrimination in employment; [and] help employers and workers find ways of meeting the problems arising from the impact of age on employment' (cited in Neumark, 2003: 298).

Under the ADEA, people were protected from 'arbitrary' age discrimination between the ages of 40 and 65. To quote the ADEA itself, an employer could no longer 'refuse to hire or to discharge any individual or otherwise discriminate against any individual with respect to his compensation, terms, conditions or privileges of employment, because of such individual's age' (cited in Macnicol, 2006: 236). The ADEA therefore protected individuals from being discriminated against in relation to recruitment and retention. Obviously, an individual between these ages could be made redundant, but this could not be due to their age (Mohrman-Gillis, 1978). It should be noted that protection provided was from *arbitrary* discrimination – an employer could argue that there was a 'bona fide occupational requirement' that meant a person of a particular age could not do a job. This would have to be a well-justified occupational requirement, however, for example, the need for an actor to play a character of a particular age (Macnicol, 2006).

It should also be noted that in some circumstances, the ADEA allowed practical considerations to override the legal principle of protection from age discrimination. In particular, due to the perceived burdens placed on small employers, employees in firms with less than 20 staff were not covered. It also only covered private sector workers – those working for federal, state and local governments were excluded until 1974 (Macnicol, 2006: 237). The ADEA was also ambiguous as to whether, or under what conditions, an occupational pension could have a mandatory retirement age below 65 (Mohrman-Gillis, 1978). Finally, the ADEA only covered people aged 40–65; it therefore viewed age discrimination above this age – and mandatory retirement – as being entirely legitimate. In this regard, it was originally about protecting the jobs of middle-aged workers, not about promoting extended working lives (Hansen, 1980).

Promoting extended working lives through age discrimination legislation

In both the US and the UK, age discrimination legislation came to be identified as a tool for promoting extended working lives beyond age 65. Age discrimination legislation was subject to 'conversion', to use the concept of Streeck and Thelen (2005) – it was redeployed to achieve ends other than those initially intended. We describe how this happened in the US, before returning to explain more recent developments in the UK.

The US: 1978 to today – extending protection to the over 65s

In 1978, the ADEA was amended such that it covered individuals up to the age of 70, rather than 65. This 1978 amendment arguably represented a key moment when age discrimination legislation was redeployed to promote extended working lives. Hansen (1980: 91) notes that, in 1967, the ADEA was initially 'viewed … as a mere expansion or extension…. Of the Civil Rights Act'. It was aimed at eliminating irrational and destructive age discrimination on the part of employers (Macnicol, 2006). In contrast, Hansen (1980: 94) notes that 'An impetus to the enactment of the [1978] ADEA amendment was the consideration given to … demographical factors…. [T]he average age of all American citizens is getting progressively older and there is a higher ratio of retirees to workers'. A key concern emerging around this time was that not enough people would contribute to Social Security in future to pay for retirees' benefits (Hansen, 1980). Extending age discrimination protection up to age 70 was therefore seen as a way of encouraging people to work longer, allowing people to continue contributing to Social Security. The amendment also tried to make the protection more consistent – a mandatory retirement age below age 70 could no longer be justified on the basis of occupational pension rules.

In 1986, the upper age limit for protection from age discrimination was lifted, thereby, in effect, outlawing employers from having a mandatory retirement age in most cases. The main exceptions were 'a small number of occupations where public safety was the issue – basically, airline pilots, firefighters and law enforcement officers' (Macnicol, 2006: 237). 'Bona fide' executives and those in higher policymaking positions were also exempt; these individuals could be compulsorily retired if they were aged 65 or over and entitled to annual retirement benefits of at least $44,000 a year (Macnicol, 2006). This was intended to only include a very small number of senior executives in large organisations. The exemption for employees in firms with less than 20 staff also remained.

Since 1978, the enforcement of the ADEA has been the responsibility of the Equal Employment Opportunity Commission (EEOC) (Macnicol, 2006: 238). If an individual wants to pursue a claim for age discrimination, they need to file it with the EEOC (Neumark, 2009: 45). The EEOC then decides whether to investigate it or to dismiss it if they see no law being broken. They can seek a settlement or mediation, or may launch legal proceedings. The individual retains the right to sue the employer regardless of the EEOC's determination (Neumark, 2009). Most charges brought relate to dismissal; in 2006, only 8.4% of cases brought related to hiring (Neumark, 2009: 46). It is generally felt that fewer cases are brought in relation to recruitment because it is harder for an individual to know, or to prove, if discrimination has occurred when they are outside the organisation (see, eg, Issacharoff and Harris, 1997). It is also pointed out by Neumark (2009: 48) that the potential payouts in cases involving discrimination in hiring are likely to be much lower than in cases of dismissal.

To give an indication of the enforcement of the ADEA, in 1999, 15,500 cases were resolved (Neumark, 2003: 301). Of these, 17.3% had a positive outcome for the claimant (a settlement, withdrawal of the case with benefits for the individual or successful legal action); 23.3% of cases were closed for 'administrative' reasons (eg a lack of communication on the part of the plaintiff). In 59.4% of cases, there was 'no reasonable cause' to conclude that age discrimination had taken place. The number of cases relative to the totality of employment was therefore small, and a minority of cases brought forward resulted in a positive outcome for the plaintiff. It should, however, be noted that the 'success rate' of ADEA cases appears to be similar to that of other cases resolved by the EEOC, covering race, sex, religion or national origin (Neumark, 2003). Furthermore, we cannot automatically assume that the ADEA had little impact given that it prevents employers from organising employment on the basis of fixed retirement ages and gives people the expectation that they will be able to work past 65 (Lain, 2011). We look at the consequences of the ADEA later in the chapter (see the section 'The impact of age discrimination legislation').

The abolition of mandatory retirement in 1986 was strongly opposed by business (Macnicol, 2006). This is reflected in a survey of 100 US companies belonging to the Equal Employment Advisory Council, an employer association representing business interests (United States Congress House Select Committee on Aging, 1982: 60–64). These companies were said to employ around 5.8 million people and cover a range of sectors. The survey found that:

> there is strong industry opposition to enactment of legislation that would prohibit mandatory retirement at any age. Those surveyed were sharply critical of the proposal as it would increase the exposure to liability and further encroach on an employers right to manage the enterprise productively. Nearly all companies were of the opinion that mandatory retirement at a reasonable age is the most effective means for both employees and employers to deal with the delicate issue of retirement.... Also, nearly all companies felt strongly that the removal of mandatory retirement would impact adversely on human resources planning as it would become increasingly difficult to determine when job vacancies would occur. Most companies felt that because planning for the replacement of key staff personnel is essential, a prohibition against mandatory retirement could result in inefficient management and declining productivity.

There was therefore strong feeling that mandatory retirement was necessary for planning, and for retiring off older workers with dignity as their productivity declined. Furthermore, it was argued that mandatory retirement ages removed blockages to promotion in the firm and assisted employees with their careers.

There are number of probable reasons why mandatory retirement was abolished under the Republican Reagan presidency even though there was so much opposition to this from business. First, the abolition of mandatory retirement built on previous legislation in 1967 and 1978, and was politically popular. Survey evidence from prior to 1986 suggested that the majority of US workers wanted to see mandatory retirement abolished (Hansen, 1980: 97). It is interesting to note that in the UK, people were much more accepting of mandatory retirement as part of the employment relationship (Hayes and Vandenheuvel, 1994).

Beyond political popularity, we can tease out the reasons for wanting to abolish mandatory retirement from the statements made to Congress by Malcolm R. Lovell Jr, Under Secretary, in the Department of Labour in 1982 (United States Congress House Select Committee on Aging, 1982: 20). The justifications can be divided into three categories. The first relates to productivity and health. Lovell Jr states that 'medical evidence clearly shows that productive work performance can easily continue long beyond age 70 and that forced retirement often has detrimental effects on health' (United States Congress House Select Committee on Aging, 1982: 20). In making this statement, it is striking how debates about older workers differed from those in the UK at the time. UK debates focused on the perceived collective benefits of early retirement for society. In the US, research was being drawn on to challenge the notion that productivity declines at around 65, and to highlight the perceived negative consequences of mandatory retirement on individuals.

A second justification relates to changes in the economy that make continued employment something that people no longer need to be protected from in a paternalistic fashion. Lovell Jr argues that 'our economy will continue to become more technologically orientated in the years ahead reducing the physical demands on employees' (United States Congress House Select Committee on Aging, 1982: 20).

The final justification given for abolishing mandatory retirement is arguably the most significant: enabling individuals to continue working if they need the money, and promoting continued working in order to help address pension problems. As Lovell Jr states:

> Forced retirement can result in financial difficulties for older workers with inadequate pensions who face lengthened periods of retirement. Also, mandatory retirement unnecessarily removes employees from the workforce who could otherwise contribute to the Social Security program and thus lessen the financial problems of that system. (United States Congress House Select Committee on Aging, 1982: 20)

In the context of low retirement incomes, abolishing mandatory retirement therefore represented a choice on the part of the government to focus on enabling people to stay on in employment. An alternative to abolishing mandatory retirement could have been increasing the safety net provided by Social Security. This, therefore, represents an additional stage in which age discrimination legislation undergoes 'conversion', towards a policy aimed at promoting self-reliance. It also needs to be understood in a broader context of changes discussed in Chapter Two, including a declining safety net of Supplementary Security Income and legislated increases in Social Security ages. Abolishing mandatory retirement therefore reflects a broader historical prioritisation of self-help solutions to social concerns, as identified by Garfinkel et al (2011).

Reforms to the ADEA in 1986 further sought to promote extended working lives by limiting the ability of employers to encourage early retirement through their occupational pension schemes. The 1978 amendment had outlawed the use of mandatory retirement clauses in occupational pension schemes, but 'workers beyond age 65 typically no longer accrued pension credits' (Quadagno and Hardy, 1991). In the case of individuals with defined benefit pensions, this meant that people might be encouraged to leave employment at 'normal' retirement age because of concerns that they will lose out on pension income. The Omnibus Budget Reconciliation Act 1986 amended the ADEA to address this; it required that employers continue to make 'contributions, credits and accruals under pension plans for service beyond normal retirement age' (Quadagno and Hardy, 1991: 473). It should be noted that the legislation did not state that the accrual of pension benefits beyond 65 should be actuarially fair, but it did 'increase the total compensation for work after age 65 and reduced the pension penalty for delayed retirement' (Quadagno and Hardy, 1991: 473). Age discrimination legislation was therefore used to increase the financial benefits of working beyond age 65.

Parallel reforms in 1986 to those discussed earlier also sought to prevent employers from using occupational pensions in a targeted way to promote early retirement. As in the UK, employers were increasingly using occupational pensions in a sophisticated targeted fashion to shed labour without incurring the expense of changing the scheme rules for everyone (Quadagno and Hardy, 1991). During recessions in the early 1970s and 1980s, US employers were offering incentives to retire to targeted groups or individuals, with individuals being given a short 'window' in which to decide. This might, for example, include the crediting of additional years of service to the pension scheme. In 1986, the US tax code was amended so that eligibility for special early retirement plans must be made categorically rather than individually. This meant that employers were no longer able to target early retirement incentives on individuals that they wanted to get rid of – they had to offer them more widely (Quadagno and Hardy, 1991:

473). This move made it much more cumbersome and expensive to use occupational pensions to shed labour. The rationale for the change was to 'prevent age discrimination by prohibiting companies from targeting individual workers' with regard to early retirement (Quadagno and Hardy, 1991: 473). The outcome, however, is arguably the adaptation of age discrimination legislation as a means of reducing early retirement. The context in which this occurred was one of 'concern[s] over the financial burden of supporting the growing population of retirees' (Quadagno and Hardy, 1991: 472).

Pension reforms also sought to alter the rules governing work in retirement. The Pension Protection Act 2006 enabled people to take an occupational pension from age 62 and continue working for the same employer (Johnson, 2011: 76). The US government also altered the regulatory framework for retirement in relation to Social Security. In the US, as in the UK, individuals needed to retire in order to receive Social Security when it was enacted (Rimlinger, 1971: 231). Rimlinger (1971) explains this with reference to 'the depression mentality', whereby they wanted to clear the labour market of older workers in the context of high unemployment levels. In 1999, Social Security was reduced by $0.33 for each dollar above a certain limit; this earnings test was abolished by the Senior Citizens Freedom to Work Act 2000. This meant that somebody could take their Social Security pension in full while continuing to work. In signing the Act, President Clinton made it clear that this was to encourage employment among those receiving Social Security:

> Increasingly, older Americans want to work. Many of them for various reasons need to work.... Yet, because of the Social Security retirement earnings test, the system withholds benefits from over 800,000 older working Americans and discourages countless more – no one knows how many – from actually seeking work.... It will mean more baby boomers working longer, contributing more to the tax base and to the Social Security Trust Fund.... When the percentage of younger workers paying into the system will be dropping. (Clinton, 2000)

To summarise US developments in full, age discrimination legislation emerged early in the US at the state level, and was consolidated in the context of the civil rights movement in the 1960s. At this point, age discrimination was viewed as another form of discrimination that needed to be addressed. From the late 1970s onwards, however, age discrimination legislation became a tool for encouraging people to continue working into older age, particularly those with low retirement incomes. Reforms to pensions also changed the regulatory nature of retirement, making it possible for people to take a pension and continue working. Taken together, these reforms attempted to blur the divide between work and retirement and encourage employment beyond age 65, particularly in the case of those with low retirement incomes.

The UK from the 1980s onwards: introducing age discrimination legislation and its expansion

In the late 1980s, we see evidence of a gradual shift away from the promotion of early retirement, towards a policy of promoting extended working lives. In the late 1970s and early 1980s, the JRS had been seen as a viable way of reducing unemployment by encouraging retirement. However, as Banks et al (2008: 9) point out, 'By 1988 the JRS had been phased out for new claimants, and in the 1990s the idea that reducing the labor supply of older workers could help mitigate unemployment was dropped altogether from the UK policy debate'. In addition, in 1989, the UK government abolished limits on the amount an individual could earn while receiving a state pension. When the UK state pension was introduced in 1948, it was a requirement that individuals had to leave work in order to receive it (Williamson and Pampel, 1993: 53). Not allowing workers over state pension age to take a pension while in employment was a cost-saving measure (Williamson and Pampel, 1993). In 1956, earnings below a certain threshold were allowed for those with a state pension, after which the pension was withdrawn by 50p for each pound earned. Margaret Thatcher, the then prime minister, showed no willingness to intervene in the market to outlaw mandatory retirement (Macnicol, 2006). However, her government saw it as an inequity that people should, in effect, be taxed heavily by working past state pension age. The 'earnings limit' was therefore abolished, allowing people to take their full pension while earning any amount. Econometric analysis suggests that this move resulted in a four-hour-per-week increase in work among employed men over age 65 (Disney and Smith, 2002).

As noted earlier, in the 1990s, it became less common in policy circles to argue that early retirement would help ease the unemployment levels of younger workers (Banks et al, 2008). Up until the late 1980s, it was often argued that the JRS had not succeeded in reducing unemployment because benefits provided to potential older 'retirees' were so low (Banks et al, 2008). In this context, the 1987 Labour

Party manifesto included a commitment to expand the JRS to address unemployment. After this period, it became increasingly common in policy debates about older workers to make reference to the 'lump of labour fallacy' (Banks et al, 2008): the 'fallacy' that there are a fixed number of jobs in the economy that can be redistributed from older to younger people. The types of jobs done by older and younger workers are likely to be different. Furthermore, older workers may themselves help create/facilitate jobs for younger people if, for example, they provide the labour required to manage younger staff. It is notable that a government report from 1999, *Winning the generation game*, even includes a box explaining what the 'lump of labour fallacy' is, and why such arguments should not be used to encourage the exit of older people (Cabinet Office, 2000: 39–40). Some academics have questioned the empirical evidence behind the 'lump of labour fallacy' arguments (Macnicol, 2006: 96–101). Nevertheless, in policy circles, these are useful arguments for promoting the employment of older people.

A key factor in terms of turning this debate around was the persistently high rate of early exit among older men. This raised concerns that older men were ending up on benefits for years with little expectation of returning to work (Macnicol, 2006: 92). Fears over public finances were raised as these individuals would build up lower pension entitlements in their own right. Added to this, the debate shifted onto concerns about the lost economic contribution of inactive older people. The *Winning the generation game* government report from 1999 estimated that early exit reduced gross domestic product (GDP) by £16 billion per year, and increased benefit expenditure by £3–5 billion (Macnicol, 2006). It therefore became a political priority to get older people back into work.

Following the election of a Labour government in 1997, the New Deal 50-plus was introduced in 2000; this aimed to address some of the perceived barriers to gaining employment for people aged 50 and over. Individuals joining the scheme were given a personal adviser to help them find a job. Those returning to work under the scheme were given a wage subsidy for the first year back in employment (£60.00 full-time, £40.00 part-time) and a grant of £750 that could be spent on training. The idea behind the programme design was that the wage subsidy would make it more financially viable for older people to take low-wage jobs. Having returned to work, the individual would then be in a position to advance in their job, drawing on the training grant if necessary. Research suggested that individuals tended to remain in their jobs, although advancement after one year was uncommon (Atkinson et al, 2003). The scheme nevertheless signalled a departure from policies in the 1980s that discouraged older individuals from seeking work.

In seeking to address age discrimination in employment, the government initially took a voluntarist approach. In 1999, for example, the government introduced a voluntary Code of Practice on Age Diversity in Employment. This sought to make a business case argument for having an age-diverse workforce and for adopting 'age neutrality' in decision-making. Assessments, however, suggested that this Code of Practice had limited impact, 'with low awareness found of its existence and content among employers, and with minimal changes having occurred or being contemplated in company policies as a result of the code' (Duncan, 2003: 111).

It was not until 2006 that age discrimination legislation was enacted for the first time in the UK. It is important to note that the roots of the Employment Equality (Age) Regulations 2006 stemmed from the EU, not the UK. In 2000, the EC General Framework for Equal Treatment in Employment and Occupation Directive (Council Directive, 2000/78/EC) was passed. The intention of this directive was not to promote extended working lives, but to protect individuals from discrimination on the basis of religion, disability, sexual orientation *and* age (Duncan, 2003: 112). This required countries to have age discrimination legislation in place by December 2006. Under the directive, compulsory retirement ages were not allowed unless a country made an 'objective justification' for them to remain. In practice, however, the definition of what could constitute an 'objective justification' was left fairly open. The UK government commissioned research to look at the possible impact of abolishing mandatory retirement, drawing on evidence from the US (see, eg, Meadows, 2003). In the event, the UK decided, like other EU countries, to continue allowing mandatory retirement. Protection from age discrimination in employment was introduced to cover people up until the age of 65. It became illegal for employers to use an employee's age to make decisions about their employment or vocational training. This, in effect, outlawed mandatory retirement ages below age 65 except where an employer could justify an Employer Justified Retirement Age (EJRA) (Sargeant, 2006). Relatively few employers had compulsory retirement ages below age 65; so the impact in this regard was relatively minor (Metcalf and Meadows, 2006: 4). The public sector and the financial services industry were most likely to be affected.

A significant innovation of the 2006 age discrimination legislation was the introduction of a 'right to request' continued employment beyond age 65. It was clear from government consultations that employers were not in favour of a complete abolition of mandatory retirement, and the government did not want to add to the 'bureaucracy' faced by firms (Sargeant, 2006). The 'right to request' was an attempt to straddle the middle ground and to encourage employers to *consider* allowing an individual to work past a Default Retirement Age (DRA) of 65. Under the law, there was a duty on the part of the employer to inform an employee in advance that they were approaching the expected retirement age for the organisation (typically 65). They were also informed that they had the right to request employment beyond this age. If an individual requested the right to continue working, the employer had to consider this, typically arranging a meeting unless this was 'not reasonably practicable'. The employer was completely free to decide whether or not they allowed the individual to stay. The only appeal that an individual could make against a decision was if the procedure had not been properly followed (Sargeant, 2006). It is hard to assess the impact of this legislation because we do not know what would have happened in the absence of such a measure. Employment of over 65s did grow between 2006 and 2011, although it is hard to know the extent to which this was influenced by the right to request continued employment. Flynn (2010) argued that 'a business case approach' was being used to allow people to continue working when it was in their perceived interests. At the same time, however, it is probable that the legislation encouraged employees to request continued employment and for employers to at least consider this (Lain and Vickerstaff, 2014).

In 2011, the DRA of 65 was removed and mandatory retirement ages were outlawed in most circumstances. This represented the completion of a policy 'conversion' (Streeck and Thelen, 2005): a directive to address multiple forms of discrimination led to the emergence of a policy to encourage people with inadequate retirement incomes to continue working. The 2006 legislation had committed the government to a review in 2011 over whether to scrap the DRA and abolish mandatory retirement. Following the financial crash in 2007/08, the political and economic situation changed dramatically. In the year leading up to October 2008, individuals with defined contribution pensions saw the value of their pensions fall by a third on average (*The Guardian*, 2008). At a time when individuals were being hit hard financially, it was considered politically difficult for people to be forced to retire at age 65. The government therefore reported the following in its paper *Building a society for all ages* (HM Government, 2009: 30):

> We announced that in 2011 we would review whether the
> Default Retirement Age was still appropriate and necessary.
> The very different economic circumstances today – for
> businesses, and for individuals coming up to retirement – in
> comparison to 2006 when the age regulations came into
> force, suggest that an earlier review is needed.

Elsewhere in the paper, it was hinted that people should be able
to remain in work beyond age 65 if they needed the money (HM
Government, 2009: 9): 'whether they want to boost their income
or keep enjoying the autonomy and sense of work that comes from
work, it will be important to allow those who want to keep working
for longer'. The review was brought forward to 2010 and the DRA
was abolished from 2011. As in the US, a key rationale for abolishing
mandatory retirement was that this move would enable people with
inadequate incomes to continue working. Mandatory retirement ages
are therefore now outlawed unless a legitimate EJRA can be established.
This justification has to be a 'proportionate means' of achieving 'a
legitimate end'; this 'legitimate end' must have a social policy objective
that is of public interest. It needs to be 'proportionate' in the sense
that: (1) mandatory retirement ages will achieve the desired end; (2)
the benefits outweigh the discriminatory effects; and (3) mandatory
retirement is the least discriminatory way of achieving the desired
end. A high-profile organisation with an EJRA is the University of
Oxford; they cite 'intergenerational fairness' and the promotion of
diversity among their justifications. This latter justification is based on
the argument that recruits are likely to have more diverse characteristics
than those retiring. The University of Oxford appears, however, to
be in a minority in creating an EJRA. In a survey conducted by
the Confederation of British Industry in 2013, only around 5% of
employers had retained a mandatory retirement age (CBI, 2013).
Around a third of employers said that they would ideally like to have
a mandatory retirement age, but saw this as too risky given uncertainty
about the legal basis for justifying these.

To compare the countries, the UK and US still allow mandatory
retirement ages in certain circumstances, but the basis upon which
they are allowed varies. In the US, mandatory retirement is allowed
in a narrow range of circumstances that are clearly specified, for
example, in relation to occupation and employer size. In the UK, any
employer can theoretically attempt to defend a mandatory retirement
age. However, the circumstances under which these can be justified
in legal terms are less clear, and employers at the current time seem

unwilling to test this. In both countries, mandatory retirement ages therefore appear to be a thing of the past for most employees. A key rationale for this change in both countries was to promote continued employment beyond age 65, particularly for those with low retirement incomes. Given this rationale, we now turn to examine what impact these changes had on employment in the US and other countries abolishing mandatory retirement.

The impact of age discrimination legislation

Changes to employment rates beyond 65 following legislation

Assessing the impact of US age discrimination legislation on employment beyond age 65 is not straightforward. During this period, there was a long-term decline in employment beyond age 65, in part, because of rising incomes (Costa, 1998). The question is not, therefore, whether age discrimination legislation increased absolute levels of employment after it was introduced – it did not. Instead, the question is whether or not employment beyond age 65 was higher than it would otherwise have been without legislative reform. We review US research on this in the following (see the next section, 'Research on the impact of age discrimination legislation in the US'). However, before this, it is helpful to examine changes in employment rates since the introduction of age discrimination legislation and abolition of mandatory retirement.

Figure 3.1 shows the employment rates of men in the UK and US between 1965 and 2007. We focus on men here because female employment more generally increased during this period, complicating the picture. Figure 3.1 shows that in 1965, prior to the ADEA, around a quarter of men aged 65+ were in employment in both countries. Other survey evidence from 1962 supports the fact that men aged 65+ had similar employment rates in both countries (Milhoj, 1968). After 1965, the decline in employment was smaller in the US, which is consistent with age discrimination legislation having an impact. Some of this divergence in employment between the countries occurred before 1978, when the ADEA was extended to cover individuals aged 70+. However, 15 US states introduced age discrimination legislation *without an upper age limit* before 1978, and these states contained 37% of the population aged 65 and over (Lain, 2011: 501). We might therefore conclude from this that state-based legislation helped stem the decline in employment past 65 prior to 1978. Labour market conditions from 1970 to 1981 cannot explain this divergence as male unemployment

Figure 3.1: Employment rates of men aged 65+, UK and US, 1965–2008

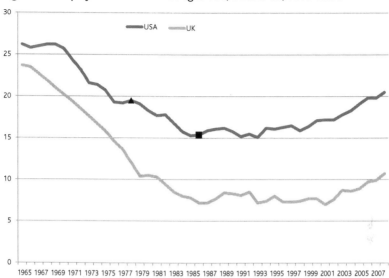

Note: The triangle indicates the ADEA extension to age 70 and the square indicates the abolition of mandatory retirement.
Source: Lain (2011).

levels were similar in both countries (Lain, 2011: 503). Changes in aggregate employment rates therefore suggest that age discrimination legislation had *some* impact on preventing the decline in employment beyond age 65 in the US. However, the UK context more broadly needs to be taken into account, including the fact that, as we saw earlier in the chapter, policy encouraged redundancy among older workers. We can gain further insights from examining employment in countries that have abolished mandatory retirement in recent years. A number of other countries abolished mandatory retirement prior to the UK in 2011: New Zealand (in 1999), Australia (2004) and Canada (2009) (Wood et al, 2010). Canada is a special case because it gradually eradicated mandatory retirement on a province-by-province basis, finishing in 2009. Figure 3.2 therefore presents employment rates at age 65–69 for all the countries just mentioned, excluding Canada. The 'European Union 15' (EU15) is also included as a comparison case because 14 out of the 15 countries continued to allow mandatory retirement.

Figure 3.2 shows that in 1986, employment was higher in the US than in the other countries, as you would expect given the legacy of earlier age discrimination legislation. Working at age 65–69 was around twice as common in the US compared with the UK, Australia and the EU15. The three non-US 'countries' and the EU15 had similar employment

Figure 3.2: Changing employment rates at age 65–69 in countries abolishing mandatory retirement

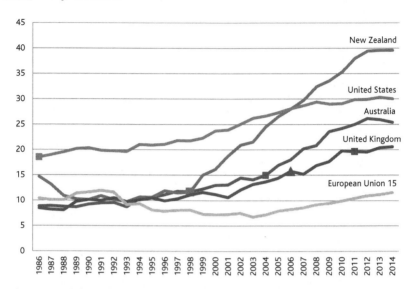

Note: A square indicates the year mandatory retirement was abolished and a triangle indicates the introduction of the right to request continued employment past age 65 in the UK.
Source: Data downloaded from the Organisation for Economic Co-operation and Development (OECD) stats database. Available at: http://stats.oecd.org/#

rates between the late 1980s in the late 1990s. However, after the abolition of mandatory retirement in New Zealand in the late 1990s, unemployment rates shot up, from around 10% in 1998 to 40% in 2014. Such is the rate of increase that employment at this age in New Zealand overtakes that of the US in the mid-2000s. Australia also sees a sharp increase in employment after the abolition of mandatory retirement in 2004. In the UK, the rate of employment growth increased after 2006, when the right to request continued employment beyond age 65 was introduced. After 2011, the year in which UK mandatory retirement was abolished, employment rates remained fairly flat. However, one does need to bear in mind the difficult economic climate during this period, which may have adversely affected older people below age 65 to a degree. In the US, employment at 65–69 grew from around 20% to 30% following the abolition of mandatory retirement in 1986. In the EU15, where mandatory retirement remained mostly legal, we see only modest increases in employment after 2003. Figure 3.2 therefore provides indicative evidence that the introduction of age discrimination legislation was associated with increases in employment beyond age 65. Increases in the state pension age above age 65 provide little explanation for the increases – only in the US did the 'full' state pension age creep above age 65 (from 2004).

While employment increased in all the English-speaking countries, Figure 3.2 suggests that the country context influenced the size of increases after mandatory retirement was abolished. The large employment increase in New Zealand is instructive in this regard. A range of factors were conducive to a big increase in employment beyond age 65 (Lain and Vickerstaff, 2014). There was a rapid increase in the state pension age from age 60 to 65 between 1993 in 1999 in New Zealand, which may have created a momentum for change. At the same time, this was a period of high labour market demand in New Zealand, and a government scheme was active in promoting older workers as a source of labour (Davey, 2007). In addition, opportunities to work part-time are common in New Zealand (Baxter, 1998), which may make employment for this group attractive (half of people working past 65 do so on a part-time basis; see Khawaja and Boddington, 2009). Finally, the New Zealand pension system is conducive to promoting employment. The state pension in New Zealand makes employment simple because it is provided to everyone on the basis of residency at age 65, irrespective of whether they work. Additionally, occupational pensions, which might encourage an individual to leave work, were also relatively uncommon (Lain et al, 2013). These factors may help explain why New Zealand overtook the US in terms of employment at age 65–69. In the UK, mandatory retirement was abolished during an economic downturn, which has probably suppressed the increase in employment beyond age 65 for the current time. Nevertheless, evidence from these countries suggests that abolishing mandatory retirement will have some effect in terms of increasing employment beyond age 65. The question, however, is how big this effect will be.

Research on the impact of age discrimination legislation in the US

In this section, we look beyond aggregate employment levels, towards a discussion of research on the impact of age discrimination legislation on employment in the US. The evidence from US studies suggests, quite strongly, that age discrimination legislation has resulted in older people remaining longer in jobs they already hold. There is *not* a body of evidence to suggest that this legislation improved the recruitment prospects of older people. However, it is important to examine how these conclusions were reached if we are to assess the impact of age discrimination legislation in the UK.

Research on the impact of discrimination legislation has tended to exploit the fact that some states introduced age discrimination legislation earlier than others. This provides a natural experiment whereby employment levels are compared between states with and without legislation. Neumark and Stock (1999), for example, examined the employment of white men between 1940 and 1980 using Census data. They found that in states where individuals aged 60 and older were protected from mandatory retirement, their employment rates were six percentage points higher. Adams (2004) also examined white men, this time using Current Population Survey data from the 1960s. He found that being protected from mandatory retirement increased the likelihood of working by 3.6 percentage points for those aged 60–65, and 4.1 percentage points for those aged 65 and over. Adams (2004: 240) drew the conclusion from this that 'age discrimination legislation has succeeded in boosting the employment of older individuals through allowing them to remain in the workforce longer'.

While age discrimination legislation may have boosted employment beyond age 65 overall, Adams (2004) finds no evidence that it helped with the recruitment of older people. He examined the employment rates of older men that had been inactive but looking for work the previous year. Rather worryingly, he found that jobseekers over 65 were significantly *less* likely to be in employment the following year if they were in a state that protected them from age discrimination. As Adams notes, this result needs to be viewed with some caution because the level of significance was relatively weak (at the 10% level). Nevertheless, some have argued that age discrimination legislation reduces the recruitment prospects of older workers because employers will fear recruiting older staff that they cannot retire off easily (see, eg, Heywood and Siebert, 2008). Research does, indeed, suggest that older people face discrimination when seeking work in the US. Lahey (2008), for example, conducted a field experiment in which employers were sent fictitious resumes for older and younger women. She found that older women were 40% less likely to be offered a job interview than younger women despite efforts to ensure that the resumes were equivalent between age groups. Whether or not this can be solely attached to age discrimination is debatable (see Neumark, 2003: 52–3), but it is likely that discrimination was a factor. The findings of a number of other studies can also be interpreted as being consistent with age discrimination. Hutchens (1988), for example, found that older workers were recruited to a smaller number of occupations and sectors than younger people; this would suggest that older workers have fewer employment opportunities. Perhaps most significantly, Johnson and Mommaerts (2011) found that older jobseekers that had been displaced from employment were less likely to return to employment than their younger counterparts. Men aged 50–61 who were displaced from employment were 39% less likely to be re-employed each month than people aged 25–34; older women were 18% less likely to be recruited. When older workers were recruited, they also tended to have a sharp decline in their hourly wage.

While the aforementioned research suggests that age discrimination in hiring has not disappeared, we should nevertheless be wary of concluding that age discrimination legislation harms recruitment. If this were the case, we might expect higher recruitment of older workers in countries where mandatory retirement was allowed. In reality, however, the US is known to have comparatively high recruitment of older people by international standards. For example, around 15% of those retiring from career jobs in the US returned to employment (Giandrea et al, 2010). In contrast, rates of re-entry after retirement were much lower in the UK (Kanabar, 2012) despite the fact that the UK made it easy for employers to retire off people after 65 (see Chapter Four). Those entering jobs in their 60s and working between 65 and 69 in the US have also been less confined to low-paid, typically part-time 'Lopaq' jobs than in the UK (Lain, 2012a). In the UK, it has been argued that employers have drawn on older workers to perform lower-level service jobs such as these because the 'queue' of 'core-age' workers was shorter (Lain, 2012a). It is therefore interesting that in the US, older workers were recruited to a broad range of occupations.

Survey evidence from 1997 also suggested that older people in the US were more likely to consider it 'very' or 'fairly' easy to find an acceptable job than their counterparts in Canada, Germany, Italy, Japan, the Netherlands, Sweden or the UK (Hicks, 2001: 15). A third of Americans aged 65+ or retired thought that it would be easy to get another job, compared with a tenth of individuals in these categories in the UK. Furthermore, 45% of Americans aged 50–64 viewed it as easy to get an acceptable job, compared with 16% in the UK (Hicks, 2001). Therefore, many older Americans realise that it would not be straightforward to get another job, and yet they are more optimistic about recruitment than comparable individuals elsewhere. This is not to say that their expectations were necessarily completely accurate. However, these findings as a whole do not suggest that the US is a country in which the recruitment of older people has been harmed by the abolition of mandatory retirement. Indeed, it is theoretically possible that the abolition of mandatory retirement actually *improved* recruitment prospects in the longer term (Lain and Vickerstaff, 2014).

US employers may be more likely to recruit older workers because they have positive experiences of employing people opting to continue working in older age (Lain, 2012a). There may also be a 'horizon affect' when mandatory retirement ages rise (Messe, 2011) or are abolished. Employers may look more favourably on hiring older workers because they can anticipate a longer period of potential employment. At the same time, we need to bear in mind the lower recruitment rates of older workers in Johnson and Mommaerts' (2011) study. Age discrimination legislation is clearly not a panacea for ensuring that everybody who needs to work can do so.

In considering the impact of mandatory retirement abolition on recruitment in other countries, we also have to consider the possible impact of broader employment legislation. The abolition of mandatory retirement might discourage employers from recruiting older workers in countries with strong employment protection legislation. However, the UK and the US both have weak employment protection legislation by international standards (OECD, 2013). Looking forward, evidence from the US suggests that in the UK, the abolition of mandatory retirement will increase the number of people remaining in their jobs. The evidence that it will increase recruitment is much weaker, although in the UK context, it is probably not going to damage the recruitment prospects of older people.

Conclusions: the conversion of age discrimination legislation to promote work at 65+

As we saw in the first part of the chapter, in the US and the UK, age discrimination legislation emerged out of concerns about discrimination and labour market inefficiencies. The roots of this legislation lay outside of the national political arena – state-level legislation pre-dated the 1967 ADEA, while the UK Employment Equality (Age) Act 2006 resulted from an EU directive. Following enactment, this legislation was extended in order to abolish mandatory retirement. This represented an example of 'conversion' (Streeck and Thelen, 2005), whereby discrimination legislation was enacted in order to promote employment beyond age 65, particularly in the case of those with low retirement incomes. For the UK, this represents a big change from the 1980s, when early retirement was actually encouraged by policy. In both countries, legislation has further regulated pensions so that people can take their pensions and work at the same time.

In the second part of the chapter, we examined the impact of age discrimination legislation in the US, and the possible impact of this in the UK. Evidence from the US suggests that protecting people from forced retirement above age 65 has increased the numbers of individuals *staying on* in their jobs. We might expect a similar outcome in the UK, which would appear to be positive in the context of pressures to work past 65 (see Chapter Two). However, we cannot assume that abolishing mandatory retirement in the UK will result in the same levels of employment at 65 found in US. The country context is clearly important in determining increases in employment beyond age 65 following mandatory retirement abolition, as the example of New Zealand shows. More importantly, evidence from the US suggests that recruitment rates of older people are relatively high by international standards, and yet there is little conclusive evidence that this is because of age discrimination legislation. Abolishing mandatory retirement *might* improve recruitment rates in the UK to a degree, but this is very far from certain. It is therefore important that we examine the pathways that people take into working at 65+ in both countries, something we do in Chapter Four.

Part Two
Reconstructing employment and retirement behaviour

FOUR

Pathways to working at age 65+

Introduction

In Part One of the book, we examined policy changes in the UK and the US that increase the financial need, and theoretical opportunities, for individuals to continue working in their jobs past age 65. However, we cannot automatically assume that working past age 65 will be as unproblematic as policy assumes. Part Two of the book therefore examines employment prospects at age 65+ through an original analysis of the English Longitudinal Study of Ageing (ELSA) and the US Health and Retirement Study (HRS). The focus of the analysis is on England, rather than the UK, because ELSA represents an excellent and comparable data source to the HRS (for more on the surveys see the statistical appendix). However, the results for England should broadly reflect those of the UK as a whole. This is because the legal/pension context in relation to retirement is identical across the countries of the UK, and 84% of the UK population live in England (ONS, 2012). We therefore draw inferences about the UK from our analysis of England.

In this chapter, we begin this analysis by exploring the pathways that people take to working at age 65+. We might expect high employment in the US to be the result of people in long-term jobs staying a bit longer. The US abolished mandatory retirement in 1986, and there is convincing evidence that it helped older individuals to *continue* in jobs past 65; it is not established that such legislation has helped with the recruitment of older people. The analysis here suggests that working beyond 65 is not simply a case of continuing a bit longer in a long-term career job. People in the US are more likely than their English counterparts to continue working in long-term jobs past 65. At the same time, however, Americans are also more likely to work past 65 as a result of moving into a new job in older age, or because they have returned to work following an absence. The wider literature suggests that movements into 'bridge jobs' and returns to work following retirement are not new in the US. However, they are clearly not a well-established route to working past 65 in the UK, which may create particular challenges if individuals need to move jobs in older age. At the same time, the literature indicates that fewer Americans work 'in retirement' than expect to, suggesting that it is not straightforward to acquire work in older age. A significant number of older individuals have stressful and/or physically arduous jobs, and most workers reduce their hours when they work beyond 65. However, opportunities to do this may be limited, leading to exit. Overall, the analysis in this chapter challenges the policy assumption that working beyond age 65 is straightforward.

Understanding employment at 65: job continuation or movement?

It has been established for many years that many Americans do not make simple transitions from full-time career employment to full retirement. They often move into so-called 'bridge employment', defined as 'the labour force participation patterns observed among older workers as they leave their career jobs and move toward complete labour force withdrawal (i.e. full retirement)' (Wang et al, 2014: 195). Our knowledge of these patterns stems from the long availability of US longitudinal panel surveys, which follow the same people over time. For example, Ruhm's (1990) analysis followed individuals aged 58–63 in 1969 until 1979. Of those with a career job lasting 15+ years, five out of nine individuals moved into bridge employment rather than fully retiring at that point. These bridge jobs were usually in different industries or occupations. With career employment terminating before retirement age, it is clear that for significant numbers of older workers, remaining in employment up to and beyond 65 involved moving into 'bridge employment'.

Subsequent research suggests that bridge employment continues to be of importance (Giandrea et al, 2009). However, the extent to which bridge employment occurs depends upon how 'career employment' is defined, and what constitutes a 'new' bridge job. In some research, bridge employment identifies employer changes (Jones and McIntosh, 2010); in other research, bridge employment involves working while being self-defined as retired or reducing working hours (which may, or may not, be with the same employer; Wang et al, 2008). Wang et al (2008), for example, define bridge employment as including people self-defining as partially retired who are still in employment. Using this measure, the authors find that a third of working individuals moved into bridge employment. However, the numbers of individuals moving employers is likely to be much lower than this. The authors make a distinction between 'career bridge employment' or 'bridge employment in a different field'; this was assessed based on whether the individual had the same occupational code at both time points. They find that 24.2% of individuals were in 'career bridge employment' – which probably includes lots of people reducing their hours in their current 'job' – and 10.2% were in 'bridge employment in a different field'.

Different studies take different approaches, and arrive at different rates of bridge employment; however, studies suggest that between a third and a half of individuals experience bridge employment (Wang et al, 2014: 197). Evidence also suggests that bridge employment is becoming more common. Giandrea et al (2009) compared cohorts aged 59–64 in 2000 and 2006, tracking each cohort in the 10 years leading up to 2000/06. They focused on people who had a full-time career job of at least 10 years, and then examined whether individuals moved into new 'bridge' jobs (which could be part-time or full-time). They found that 64% of those people moving out of career jobs moved into bridge employment in the more recent cohort, compared with 60% for the older cohort.

Another transition that some older Americans are known to make is 'unretirement', where an individual fully retires and then returns to employment. Once again, unretirement does not appear to be a new phenomenon. Ruhm (1990: 105) found that among individuals retiring between 1969 and 1979, around a quarter (23.4%) 'reversed' their retirement, with most re-entering within four years. A surprisingly similar percentage (23.8%) 'unretired' between 1992 and 2002 in Maestas's (2010: 722) study of older individuals between 1992 and 2002. This definition is based on individuals moving from work to full exit and back to work, without taking into account whether individuals define themselves as retired. When we define unretirement as being a return to work following an exit *defined as retirement* by the individual, the percentages going through this process are smaller (19.2%). A further 16% moved from full-time to part-time to full-time work over the period (which represents returning from 'partial retirement'). Likewise, 7.2% went from work to self-defined 'partial retirement' to full-time work. Clearly, the work transitions that people make are diverse.

While unretirement and bridge employment might signal some possibilities for the future of UK employment, current research does not establish that these types of transitions might be significant pathways to employment beyond age 65. Previous research suggests that levels of unretirement in the UK are currently lower than in the US. Kanabar (2012) estimated that only around 5.5% of retired men in the ELSA in 2002 had unretired by 2009. In comparison, Cahill et al (2011) found that 15% of men and women aged 51–61 in 1992 had returned to work at some point between 1992 and 2008 following full exit. However, neither study tells us how sustainable such jobs are for working past 65 because people could retire and return to work before this age.

A more general point is that it is important to separate out transitions involving moving employer, which may be particularly difficult, and those involving reductions in working time. Evidence from a range of countries suggests that employers are, on the whole, more likely to *continue* employing older workers than they are to recruit them (for the US, see Hirsch et al, 2000; for the UK, see Daniel and Heywood, 2007; Kidd et al, 2012; for Australia, see Adams and Heywood, 2007; for Hong Kong, see Heywood et al, 1999; for Germany, see Heywood et al, 2010, 2011). To some degree, this is likely to be a result of age discrimination. Although age discrimination is illegal in the US, it is easier for employers to discriminate unfairly in cases of recruitment rather than retention (Issacharoff and Harris, 1997; Adams, 2004). A recent US study by Johnson and Mommaerts (2011) found that older workers were less likely to be involuntarily displaced from a job, albeit only because they had spent more time with their employer. However, once older workers were displaced from employment, 'they appear to have more trouble finding work than their younger counterparts" (Johnson and Mommaerts, 2011: 19). The survey followed workers over an 18-month period after they had been displaced from employment. People that had dropped out of the Labour market after displacement – for example, through retirement – were excluded from the analysis. Johnson and Mommaerts (2011: 15) found that men aged 50–61 were 39% less likely to find new work each month than those aged 25–34, this was after controlling for demographic differences (including education), health, economic circumstances and previous job characteristics. People aged 62 or older were 51% less likely to find a new job. Women aged 50–61 were 18% less likely to find new work each month than those aged 25–34. Women aged 62 or older were 50% less likely to find new work.

Whether or not older people find it more difficult to find work in the UK, compared with the US, is not clear from previous research. However, there is ample evidence that older people perceive that age discrimination in recruitment, and employment more generally, is common (Porcellato et al, 2010). Likewise, UK employers have made it relatively clear that they like the *idea* of 'age-diverse workforces' but, in practice, prefer to recruit younger 'prime-age' workers over older workers (Loretto and White, 2006). According to this research, the recruitment of older workers tended to occur when employers had difficulty in employing core-age workers. This has led Lain (2012a) to argue that the recruitment of older workers is akin to a system of queueing (following the work of Reskin and Roos, 1990). In essence, older workers are towards the back of the queue for jobs, with recruitment opportunities in the UK disproportionately confined to so-called 'Lopaq' occupations that are less desired by much of the 'core-age' population. These are occupations typically organised on a part-time, low-paid basis with few formal qualification requirements. Lain (2012a) found that around half of recently recruited employees working at age 65–69 in the early 2000s were in Lopaq occupations. In the US, employers appeared to be more likely across a wide occupational spread, with a third of recent recruits of this age being in Lopaq occupations.

To summarise the preceding discussion, in order to understand prospects for employment past age 65, we have to understand the transitions that people make into employment at this age. Two transitions are potentially important for employment beyond age 65: (1) transitions involving the commencement of new work (moving jobs or returning from inactivity); and (2) transitions in working hours. We examine both in turn, starting with transitions between jobs and periods of inactivity.

Pathways to employment at 65–74

In order to examine the employment pathways that people make above age 65, we present analysis of the ELSA and the US HRS (see the statistical appendix). These are longitudinal studies that enable us to track individuals over time. We focus on people aged 65–74 in 2012, and track the employment transitions they report at each of the biannual waves from 2002 onwards. This means that all individuals were below age 65 in 2002. We first focus on those in employment at age 65–74 in 2012, breaking down the percentages working into three transition groups: 'Stayers', 'Movers' and 'Returners':

- 'Stayers' were employed at each wave and were in the 'same job' throughout, in the sense that they did not report having moved employers at any wave since 2002.
- 'Movers' were individuals who were working at each wave but who reported having changed employer at some point. This category overlaps with 'bridge employment'.
- 'Returners' were workers aged 65–74 in 2012 who reported being out of employment in a previous wave. It should be noted that employment returns might be to a new or former employer as it is

not possible to disentangle this. The category of 'Returners' overlaps with 'unretirement' transitions.

These breakdowns of employment at age 65–74 are presented as Figure 4.1. The first thing to note is the absolute levels of employment at this age. As we saw in Chapter One, US employment for this age group was twice that of England: 30.2% versus 14.8%. In both countries, women were less likely to work than men beyond age 65. This is likely to be, in part, because women in general are less likely to work at earlier ages, and because some couples coincide retirement timing (see Chapter Six). If men and women in a couple retire at around the same time, the man will naturally be more likely to work past age 65 because he is likely to be older. While this is the case in both countries, the disparity in employment between men and women was lower in the US than in England. In the US, men were 1.3 times more likely to be employed than women (35.3% versus 26.1%). In England, on the other hand, men were 1.7 times more likely to work

Figure 4.1: Percentages working at age 65–74, broken down by transition into employment, 2012

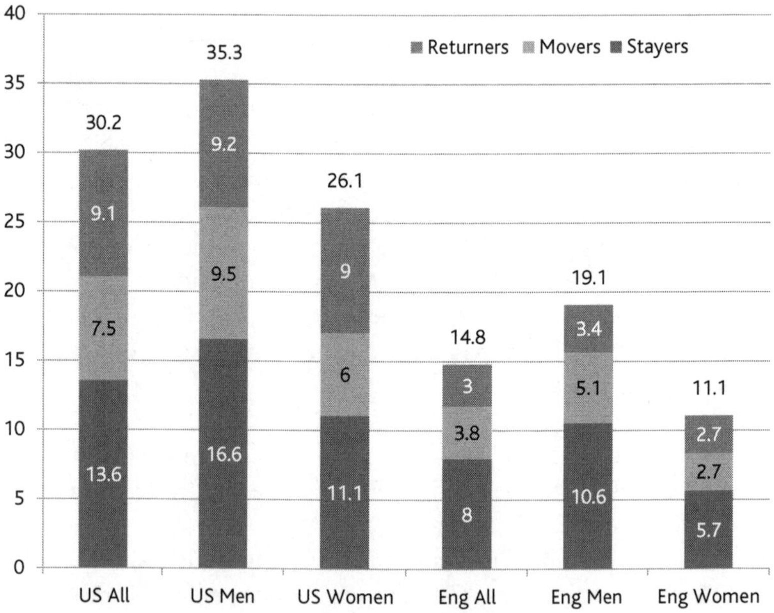

Notes: 'Stayers' remained in the same job between 2002 and 2012; 'Movers' were employed at each wave between 2002 and 2012 but moved job; 'Returners' were economically inactive at one (or more) wave(s) between 2002 and 2010 but were back at work by 2012. See text for more details.
Source: Author's analysis of ELSA waves 2002–12 and HRS waves 2002–12.

than women (19.1% compared with 11.1%). This may reflect the fact that US women have more substantial full-time careers prior to 65 than their English counterparts, which makes them less likely to follow their partners into retirement (see Chapter One). The influence of a partner on employment is examined in Chapter Six.

Moving onto the transitions that people make into employment, it is obvious from Figure 4.1 that US employment is not simply higher because people continue in long-held career jobs. Americans were more likely to be 'Stayers' than their English counterparts, working past age 65 in jobs that they had held for a least the decade leading up to 2012; 13.6% were in this category in the US, compared with 8% in England. However, Americans were also much more likely to be working past age 65 as 'Returners' who had previously been out of employment at some point in the previous decade; 9.1% were Returners in the US, compared with only 3.8% in England. Finally, Americans were also more likely to be working past 65 as 'Movers', working in jobs that started since 2002; 7.5% were in this category, compared with 3.8% in England. These trends were evident for both men and women. In the US, therefore, employment at 65+ often appears to involve the ability to navigate employment transitions that allow individuals to remain or return to work. We examine the factors influencing whether individuals make these transitions in Chapter Five.

While Americans were more likely to work past age 65, whether as a result of job continuation or change, it is likely that fewer Americans worked at this age than wanted to. Maestas' (2010) research found that working 'in retirement' was anticipated in advance by individuals: 82% of individuals that had unretired had previously said, in 1992, that they would like to do some paid work 'in retirement'. The explanation given is one of 'burnout and recovery' – people leave work because they need a rest, with the intention that they will return once they have had a break. However, only around half of those saying that they wanted to work in retirement actually went on to unretire (Maestas, 2010: 730). Gaining a job in older age may therefore be more difficult than is anticipated.

A slightly different perspective is gained if we examine changes in employment over time. Figure 4.2 breaks down employment for workers aged 65–69 by job tenure in 2002, in 2008 and in 2012; we focus on this slightly younger group because it will make changes over time more visible. We should note that job tenure information was not available for a significant number of workers in England, so we should treat the exact proportions with some caution. Nevertheless, the results for England are consistent with an increase in opportunities to *continue* working in jobs, rather than people increasingly working past 65 as a result of moving into new jobs. In 2002, 39.4% of workers aged 65–69 had started their job in the last five years; this fell to 31% in 2008 and 26.8% in 2012. The proportion of workers starting jobs more than 10 years earlier rose from around 40% to approaching 60%. A similar trend of increasing numbers continuing in long-held jobs past age 65 was found by Lain and Loretto (forthcoming), using the large-scale UK Labour Force Survey. Lain and Loretto (forthcoming) found that an increase in employees working at age 65–69 between 2002 and 2014 could largely be explained by an increase in people in long-term jobs working past 65. During this period, individuals were given the right to request continued employment (in 2006), with mandatory retirement abolished in 2011. The 2006 change may have encouraged more employers to allow people to work beyond age 65 (see Chapter Three). However, over this decade, there is little UK evidence of people working past 65 in greater numbers as a result of moving into new jobs (Lain and Loretto, forthcoming). In contrast, in the US, the proportion of people working at 65–69 who had started their job in the previous five years remained high at all time periods (see Figure 4.2). Greater recruitment of older people in the US cannot be explained by more favourable employment conditions than in England. Since the early 2000s, unemployment rates have been similar in both

Figure 4.2: Employment tenure of workers aged 65–69, various years

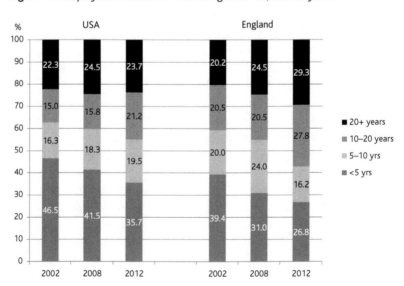

Source: Author's analysis of ELSA waves 2002–12 and HRS waves 2002–12.

countries, at 4–5% until 2009, and 8–9% thereafter. Early indications provide little evidence, therefore, that job movements in older age represent the kinds of pathways into work at 65+ found in the US. As chapter Five shows, one of the reasons for this appears to be the fact that job mobility in the UK is hampered by low qualification levels.

Pathways into inactivity at age 65–74

Figure 4.3 presents the transitions that individuals made to economic inactivity at age 65–74 in 2012. Those individuals are categorised into three groups:

- 'Leavers' were working in 2002 but left employment at some point after this time without returning to employment in any of the waves up to 2012.
- 'Out All' means that the individual was not employed at any of the waves between 2002 and 2012.
- 'Fleeting Workers' returned to work from an absence at one of the waves between 2002 and 2010 but were once again out of work in 2012. They are called 'Fleeting Workers' because they managed to return to work and leave within the decade and their employment was not a pathway into work at age 65–74 in 2012.

The main thing to note from Figure 4.3 is that individuals in England were more likely to be out of work for the entire decade leading up to 2012; 39.6% were 'Out All', compared with 26.8% in the US. This pattern of being out of work earlier in England, compared with the US, was true for men and women. The cohort of women aged 65–74 in 2012 in England was particularly likely not to work in any of the waves (45.5% were 'Out All'). This is likely to be, in part, due to the fact that these women were aged between 55 and 64 at the start of the decade in 2002, and the UK state pension age for women was 60. Nevertheless, a third of men in England were also 'Out All', which is higher than the fifth of American men in this position. The English were therefore less likely to be in work at age 65+ in 2012, in part, because they were less likely to have an attachment to the labour market in the previous decade. Analysis in Chapter Five shows that qualification levels among those 'Out All' in England were particularly low, which may help to explain why so many people were not working.

In summary, Americans were twice as likely to be working as their English counterparts due to a combination of staying in long-term jobs, moving jobs and returning to work after economic inactivity.

Figure 4.3: Percentages not working at age 65–74, broken down by transition into economic inactivity, 2012

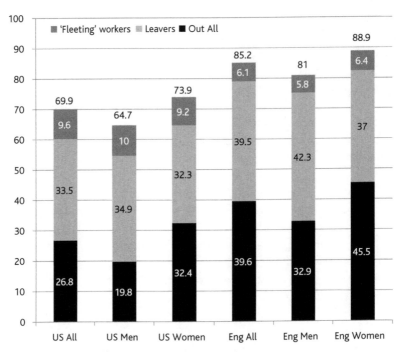

Note: 'Out All' indicates non-employment in all waves between 2002 and 2012; 'Leavers' were employed in 2002 but had left work by 2012 (with no subsequent returns); 'Fleeting Workers' had returned to work from an absence between 2002 and 2010 but were out by 2012. See text for more details.
Source: Author's analysis of ELSA waves 2002–12 and HRS waves 2002–12.

An increase in employment at age 65 in the UK may therefore require individuals to make job transitions in older age, and yet there is little evidence that this is increasing.

Transitions involving self-employment

In terms of understanding employment transitions, it is important to examine the contribution that self-employment makes. Research on employment transitions does not typically make a distinction between being an employee and being self-employed in older age, although we know that older workers are more likely to be self-employed than younger workers in the UK (Cahill and Quinn, 2014) and the US (Smeaton and McKay, 2003). In some countries, employment beyond age 65 is dominated by people in self-employment (Lain and Vickerstaff, 2014: 243). If this is not taken into account, we are in a weaker position to understand future prospects for employment beyond age 65 more generally, including among people working as employees. There are number of reasons why self-employed individuals may find it easier to remain in work past age 65. First, in some countries – including the UK until 2011 – employees could be forced out of work at age 65; self-employed individuals are naturally not confined by such organisational rules. Second, the self-employed may also have a greater ability to reduce their working hours and/or work flexibly. Reductions in working time, and the ability to work flexibly in a controlled fashion, are seen as important by many older people (Vickerstaff et al, 2008; AARP, 2014). Finally, the self-employed may have the advantage of being able to return to work, having left, without having to convince an employer to rehire them.

In addition to the self-employed, people working for small employers may find it easier to work past age 65 because they are less restricted by organisational policies. In the past, people working past pension age in the UK were disproportionately working for small employers (Smeaton and McKay, 2003). This may be because small employers are less rule-bound and better able to accommodate individual requests for reduced hours/flexible employment (Cebulla et al, 2007). In the past, they have also been less likely to have mandatory retirement ages for their employees (Metcalf and Meadows, 2006). This is not to imply that people had an automatic right to work past age 65 – employers still had the right to retire off workers at 65 even if they had an open-ended contract (Lain and Vickerstaff, 2014). However, the informality of smaller organisations and lack of rules forbidding employment beyond 65 may have made it easier for people to remain in work in the UK. In the US, as we saw in Chapter Three, small employers are exempt from age discrimination legislation. We might therefore expect people working for small employers to be *less* likely to remain in work in the US.

Figure 4.4 presents employment transitions for people who were self-employed or an employee in 2002; results for employees are broken down by employer size. Once again, transition categories include 'Leavers' and 'Stayers', the latter group being in employment throughout. 'Movers/Returners' have been combined into a single category because the self-employed are unlikely to be 'Movers'. People self-employed at all waves are defined as 'Stayers' given that it is unrealistic to identify whether the nature of an individual's self-employment has changed sufficiently to consider it as a new 'job'. It is also questionable whether we could make such a clear-cut distinction between 'new' and 'old' self-employment given that it is likely to adapt over time anyway. The only way a self-employed individual could

Figure 4.4: Employment transitions for those aged 65–74, 2012: self-employed in 2002 versus employees in 2002

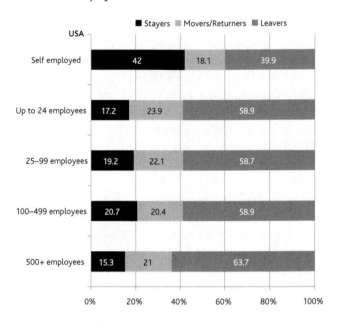

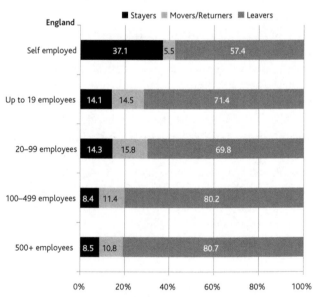

Notes: Employee results have been broken down by size of employer. Movers and Returners have been combined. For more category details, see the notes for Figure 4.1.
Source: Author's analysis of ELSA waves 2002–12 and HRS waves 2002–12.

become a 'Mover' was if they moved from self-employment to being an employee. As a result, it makes sense to combine 'Mover/Returners' for all groups as that they both involve new periods of employment.

As Figure 4.4 shows, in both countries, people who were self-employed in 2002 were more than twice as likely to be 'Stayers' than employees in any size of firm. The percentages of self-employed individuals still in employment in 2012 were 42% in the US and 37.1% in England. In the US, there was no statistically significant difference in the likelihood of being a 'Stayer' between employees in different sized organisations in 2002. This suggests that exemptions from age discrimination legislation for small firms have not resulted in people being more likely to be retired off on the basis of age alone. In England, people in small firms (with up to 19 employees) were more likely to be Stayers than those in large firms (500+ employees); the difference was statistically significant at the 5% level. This suggests that the formality of larger organisations resulted in fewer people remaining in work beyond age 65. An alternative argument is that large firms were more likely to provide occupational pensions, which encourage people to leave. We cannot entirely rule this out, but analysis of ELSA in Chapter Six does not suggest that those with an occupational pension were more likely to be out of work at 65-plus.

In addition to people staying on in self-employed jobs, people may move into self-employment as a means of working up to and beyond age 65. Self-employment might provide some of the advantages of flexibility discussed earlier, while also being a new and rewarding activity in itself (Cahill and Quinn, 2014). In the case of the US, it is not uncommon for people to see self-employment as a desirable component of retirement. In 2002, 10% of older people surveyed as part of the AARP Work and Career Study said that they planned to start their own business or work for themselves in retirement; in the 2012 survey, this had risen to 13%. The proportions working in self-employment rise sharply with age, which could imply significant movements into self-employment in older age. According to analysis of the HRS, just over 20% of men aged 51–61 were self-employed in 2002; when the men reached 61–71 in 2002, this had risen to 30% (Cahill and Quinn, 2014: 135). In 2006, when the cohort was aged 65–67, over 35% were self-employed (Cahill and Quinn, 2014: 135). However, the extent to which this represents transitions into self-employment in older age is not clear because the self-employed are more likely to *remain* in work.

Figure 4.5 shows the contribution that self-employment made to employment rates at age 65–74 in 2012. In order to assess the impact of transitions *into* self-employment, a separate category is included representing self-employed individuals in 2012 who were employees in 2002. Taking the self-employed as a whole, we can see that this form of employment made an important overall contribution to employment rates: 5.8% of people in this age category were self-employed in England, around a third of total employment; in the US, 7.4% were self-employed, a quarter of total employment. Self-employment was much higher among men than women. Just under half of male workers were self-employed in England (9.3% out of 20.1%), compared with a fifth in the case of women (2.5% out of 11.4%). In the US, a third of men in employment were self-employed (10% out of 35%), compared with a fifth of working women (5.2% out of 26.1%).

While self-employment was an important component of employment for men, relatively few people were working in 2012 as a result of having switched from being an employee in 2002. Only around 1% of people aged 65–74 were self-employed individuals that had switched from being an employee. This is consistent with previous UK research, which concludes that 'relatively few [older] employees and virtually no retirees switch into self-employment in later life' (Parker and Rougier, 2007: 697). The authors go on to state that:

> the switches [to self-employment] that do occur are motivated less by attempts to use self employment as a bridge job or 'stepping stone' to full retirement, than by self employment being the last resort for less affluent workers with job histories of weak attachment to the labour market. (Parker and Rougier, 2007: 697)

Consequently, such pathways *into* self-employment are unlikely to provide significant pathways into working beyond age 65 in either country. It is primarily individuals who were already self-employed that continued working, despite the fact that a significant minority in the US said that they planned to work for themselves in retirement. For those people who want to move into self-employment in older age, barriers may include the costs and risks of doing so (Cahill and Quinn, 2014). Likewise, people who have always been employees may find it harder than they expect to transition into self-employment in retirement.

Figure 4.5: Percentages working at age 65–74 in 2012 broken down by whether they are an employee or self employed

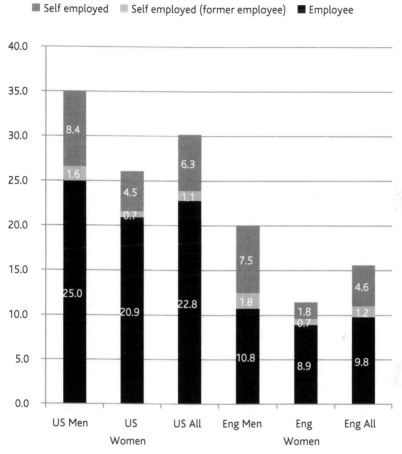

Note: The category 'Self employed (former employee)' represents people who moved into self employment having worked as an employee in 2002.
Source: Author's analysis of ELSA waves 2002 and 2012 and HRS waves 2002 and 2012.

Transitions in working time

As noted earlier, reductions in working time are considered by many in the US to be an important or desirable dimension for working 'in retirement'. Shorter hours help individuals to accommodate work with increased leisure activities in older age, or to deal with new responsibilities, such as caring (see Alden, 2012). It is also possible that some older people may feel that part-time work is more realistic as they age given changes to their health or the fact that they feel 'burnt out' by full-time employment. Evidence from the UK suggests that older people with health problems often consider the number of hours that they work as too many (Smeaton et al, 2009: 17); the ability to reduce working time may therefore help some people with health conditions to remain in work up to and beyond 65.

Reductions in working time may be a particularly important condition of working past age 65 in the US. By international standards, people in the US work long hours. Average working hours for men *and women* have been around 40 per week, with around a quarter of all US workers doing 48 or more hours per week (Kodz et al, 2003). It is noteworthy that Juliet Schor's (1992) book *The overworked American*, which identified a decline in holiday taken by workers, was a national best-seller. Reductions in working time are therefore arguably a necessity as people work up to and beyond age 65. A significant number of Americans also anticipate that they will be able to reduce their working hours. Abraham and Houseman (2005) found that in 1992, 18.3% said that they planned to reduce their working hours, with the proportion saying this peaking at 23% for those aged 61. In comparison, the proportions saying that they planned to change the kind of work they did was much lower (at 4.7%). Since 1992, there has been an increasing awareness of the need to work into older age, so it likely that more people expect to reduce their working hours as a way of extending their working lives. The AARP Work and Career Study 2013 found that 72% of older people surveyed planned to work in retirement (a similar proportion was found in 2002 and 2007) (AARP, 2014: 24). Of this 72%, 29% planned to work part-time for the sake of enjoyment, and a further 23% planned to work part-time for the income. These figures may overstate the extent to which people have actual plans to work part-time; nevertheless, they do suggest that it has become common in the US to view part-time work as part of extended working life transitions.

While a significant number may want to reduce their hours of work, research suggests that they may find it harder that they anticipate. Abraham and Houseman's (2005) study, discussed earlier, asked people when they planned to reduce their working hours; most (60%) planned to reduce their hours at or after the normal retirement age at their workplace. Only 35% of those planning to reduce their working hours actually followed through on these plans: 28% of individuals instead stopped work altogether, and 36% worked the same or more hours. It is not possible to say whether people failing to reduce their hours left work earlier than they would otherwise have done. However, this would seem plausible, particularly in the case of individuals struggling to work full-time hours.

The most obvious way to reduce working hours is to do so within the same company/job where currently employed. However, there are number of reasons why this may be difficult in the US. Few employers have formal policies that enable employees to reduce working hours in the lead-up to retirement (Johnson, 2011). Formal policies to reduce working time complicate the provision of benefits and run the risk of resulting in legal discrimination cases. For example, medical insurance and other benefits may be provided only to full-time employees; to make an exception for older people would be discriminatory (Johnson, 2011). Indeed, as mentioned earlier, the provision of medical benefits to full-time staff has been one of the reasons why part-time work in the US is generally less common than in the UK (Lyonette et al, 2011). As a result, opportunities to reduce hours are usually limited to informal arrangements made between employees and employers (Hutchens and Grace-Martin, 2006; Hutchens, 2010). Employers will be more likely to permit phased retirement if they employ part-time white-collar workers more generally, allow job sharing and have flexible starting times (Hutchens and Grace-Martin, 2006). In other words, employers that have integrated part-time and flexible working into their practices are more generally amenable to reduced hours of employment (Blau and Shvydko, 2011). Opportunities to reduce hours within firms are therefore likely to be limited due to rigidities within the workplace. The people most likely to reduce their hours in Abraham and Houseman's (2005) study were multiple job-holders (who could drop one job), those working very long hours (who could cut back on overtime) and the self-employed (who theoretically have full control over their working time).

For many US workers, reducing the number of hours that they work realistically requires that they move to another employer (Abraham and Houseman, 2005). Abraham and Houseman (2005) cite research by Altonji and Paxson (1990) which shows that married women are better able to reduce their working time if they change employer rather than remain with the same one. Research on older US jobseekers suggests that they are attracted to jobs/employers providing working time flexibility (including part-time work) (Gobeski, 2010). The ability of older people to find new work is, however, likely to be harder than people might expect. Abraham and Houseman (2005) suggest that older workers may lack recent experience in finding a new job, good connections to other employers and new skills required by available positions. Perhaps more importantly, however, older people face potential discrimination from employers when seeking work. As we noted earlier, evidence in relation to displaced older US workers suggests that they find it far more difficult to find new work than their younger counterparts (Johnson and Mommaerts, 2011).

As in the US, there is considerable evidence that the possibility of reducing hours in the lead-up to retirement is popular in the UK (Vickerstaff et al, 2008; Smeaton et al, 2009), as are flexible work arrangements enabling older people to combine work with greater leisure/external responsibilities (Alden, 2012). However, opportunities to reduce working hours for those in full-time employment do not appear to be widespread in the UK (Vickerstaff et al, 2004; Vickerstaff, 2007; Hedges and Sykes, 2009: 25). Analysis of ELSA, which tracked individuals from age 50 to state pension age between 2002 and 2008, showed that 9.3% of individuals moved from full-time to part-time work during the period (Crawford and Tetlow, 2010: 72). At the same time, a survey of older people showed that among people aged 50–59, a third thought that their working hours were not ideal (Smeaton et al, 2009). Most people wanted fewer hours or control over the hours that they did; very few wanted more hours. Among people with fair/poor health, 44% said that their hours were not ideal. This analysis suggests that there is unmet demand for reductions in working time, a demand that will inevitably be higher if we focus only on those in full-time jobs. Qualitative research suggests that in terms of getting people to work longer, part-time/flexible work is an important component for getting people to consider this (Vickerstaff et al, 2008). In this context, analysis of the UK Labour Force Survey suggests that only around 5% of employees working part-time at age 65–69 want a full-time job (Lain and Loretto, forthcoming).

It should be noted that part-time work is a stronger feature of the UK labour market than it is in the US. Part-time work is high among women of all ages, with around 40% of all females working part-time. This means that many women enter old age after a career of being in part-time jobs; for these women, reduced working hours may be a less attractive means of extending working lives (Loretto and Vickerstaff, 2015). More generally, however, because part-time work is integrated into UK workplaces in the UK, it may be a bit easier than in the US for older people to reduce their working hours within the same firm.

Figure 4.6 shows the extent to which employment at age 65–74 in both countries is associated with reductions in working time. In England, around 80% of all workers in 2012 worked shorter hours than they did in 2002, with no difference in this regard between men and women (note that people out of work in 2002 were excluded). Stayers, remaining in the same job throughout, were slightly less likely to reduce their hours than Movers/Returners starting new jobs in the period (74.9% versus 83.4%). Less than 1% of Movers/Returners were working the same number of hours in 2012 as they were in 2002; this suggests that an opportunity to change working hours *may* be important for a significant number of these job switchers. Nevertheless, the high percentage of UK Stayers reducing their hours (75.9%) suggests that relatively few individuals with inflexible working hours may have

Figure 4.6: Changes in working hours since 2002 for workers aged 65–74, 2012

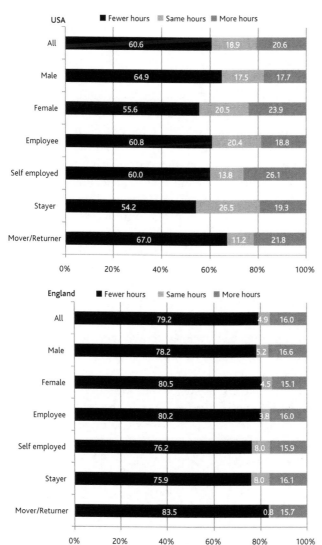

Note: Excludes those not working in 2002. Movers and Returners have been combined. For more category details, see the notes for Figure 4.1.
Source: Author's analysis of ELSA waves 2002–12 and HRS waves 2002–12.

remained in their jobs. Overall, only around 5% in England had the same number of hours in 2012 as they did in 2002, with around 15% working more hours.

Moving now on to the US, we see that around 60% of all workers age 65–74 in 2012 worked fewer hours than they did in 2002. The percentage of people working more hours was slightly higher than in England (around 20% versus 15%). A significant difference between the countries is therefore that around 20% of Americans worked the same number of hours as in 2002, compared with 5% in England. This is consistent with the preceding argument that there is a greater degree of inflexibility around working time in the US than in England. This is perhaps most evident when we note that 54.2% of Stayers in the US reduced their working time, compared with 75.9% of Stayers in England. On the other hand, the fact that over half of US Stayers reduced their working time suggests that people were probably more likely to remain with their employer beyond age 65 if they could reduce their working time.

These findings are interesting in suggesting that the feasibility of working past 65 for many individuals in both countries is likely to involve the ability to reduce working time. To get a better understanding of what these reductions mean in practice, Figure 4.7 shows mean working hours in 2002 and 2012 for workers aged 65–74. Once again, these figures only include people employed at both time points. If we take full-time work to be 35+ hours a week, we see that, overall, in both countries, people typically moved from full-time to part-time work. Mean working hours in 2002 were 41.3 per week in the US and 38.3 per week in England; when these individuals reached 65–74 in 2012, their hours had declined to 30.6 per week in the US and 24.8 per week in England. If we look at men, we see that those continuing to work past 65 in 2012 had worked relatively long hours in 2002 (45.9 per week in the US and 43.9 per week in England). This had fallen to relatively long part-time hours in the US in 2012 (33 per week), with shorter part-time work for men in England (24.8 per week). In the case of US women, working hours fell from relatively short full-time hours in 2002, 36.1 per week, to 27.9 per week in 2012. The situation of women in England was different because they were already in part-time jobs in 2002; this, in part, reflects the wider prevalence of part-time work among women in the UK more generally, as discussed earlier. Nevertheless, mean working hours fell considerably, from 30 per week in 2002 to 19.1 per week in 2012. In sum, the transition into employment for men and women past age 65 is not one of continuing in full-time work; instead, this transition typically involves reductions in working time for most individuals. This suggests that part-time work is a more plausible form of employment for many people beyond age 65, and yet constraints in the ability of older people to obtain part-time work are likely to reduce potential employment beyond this age.

Figure 4.7: Mean hours of workers aged 65–74, 2012, alongside their working hours in 2002

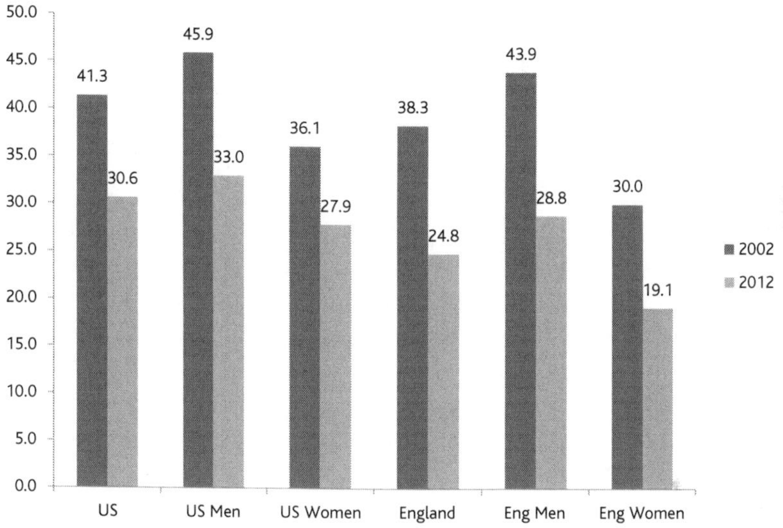

Note: Presents weekly hours in 2002 and 2012; excludes those not working in 2002.
Source: Author's analysis of ELSA waves 2002 and 2012 and HRS waves 2002 and 2012.

Work factors associated with making employment transitions

Work physicality

When examining prospects for employment beyond age 65, it is important to look at the nature of jobs done by, and available to, older people. As we saw in Chapter Three, one of the justifications for abolishing US mandatory retirement in 1986 was that jobs were no longer as physically arduous as they were in the past (United States Congress House Select Committee on Aging, 1982). According to Johnson et al (2011: 103), in the US, the 'shift from manufacturing to services and the professions has reduced the share of workers in physically demanding occupations and increased the share in cognitively complex jobs'. According to Johnson (2011), 7% of

American workers held highly physically demanding jobs in 2006, compared with 35% holding cognitively demanding jobs. This shift *might* be seen as advantageous to older workers as physical declines that occur with ageing become less of an issue, and work becomes more interesting given increased cognitive demands. However, as we shall see, work intensification and stress, and limited opportunities to move into less physically demanding work, are likely to remain barriers to employment beyond age 65.

Physical labour involving lifting heavy objects in the US has declined from about 20% of workers to 8% between 1950 and 1996 (Johnson et al, 2011: 107). With the decline of manufacturing in the UK in this period, we would also expect a similar decline. However, we need to look beyond these averages. Johnson et al (2011: 112) found that, overall, 7.3% of workers were in jobs with high physical demands, typically involving the need to lift/push/carry heavy objects and bend/twist/contort the body. This compares with 8.8% in 1971 using this measure. However, the percentages of workers performing this type of work varied considerably depending upon education level: 17% of workers with below high school qualifications were doing this very physically arduous work, compared with 1.6% of those with university degrees. The aforementioned definition of physical work is also extreme. When we look at jobs involving high degrees flexibility, dexterity and time spent handling objects, we see that around a quarter were in these jobs. The move from manufacturing to service industries has also not eradicated the need for work involving physical activity. Around 46% of the total US workforce were in occupations involving high or moderate general physical demands; for a third of jobs, spending time standing up was very or extremely important for job performance. Once again, there were stark differences between people depending upon their qualification levels: 77.8% of those with below secondary-level education were in jobs with high/moderate physical demands, compared with 23.5% of those with a degree. More than half of those educated to high school level were also in these types of jobs (58.4%). Clearly, lower-educated individuals depend upon their physical activity for employment, and yet these individuals are most likely to have poor health (see Chapter Five).

In order to examine this further, Table 4.1 presents the percentages of people working in physically demanding jobs for each country. The percentages are broken down by whether someone is a Stayer, Mover/Returner or a Leaver/Fleeting worker. Proportions are given for two time periods: 2012, when individuals would have been age 65–74; and 10 years earlier in 2002. For the US, the definition of a physically demanding job is one involving 'lots of physical effort' 'all' or 'most' of the time. As Table 4.1 shows, physically demanding work remained important in the US for this cohort. Overall, around 30% were in physically demanding jobs in 2002, when aged 55–64; this is consistent with previous research using this measure (Maestas, 2010). Previous research also shows that around 39% of people aged 55–64 were in jobs requiring high/moderate physical demands (Johnson, 2011). People who left work before 2012, however, were significantly more likely to be in physically demanding work than those who either stayed at the same job or move to another one. Just over a third of Leavers had been in physically demanding work in 2002, compared

Table 4.1: Physical job demands and job stress by type of employment transition: those aged 65–74, 2012

	Stayer (a)	Mover/ Returner (b)	Leaver/ Fleeting worker (c)
USA			
% in physically demanding job in 2002	27.1[c]	25.9[c]	34.6[a, b]
% in physically demanding job in 2012	26.1	26.7	N/A
England			
% in physically demanding job in 2002	29.5	29.0	29.8
% in physically demanding job in 2012	27.0	33.0	N/A
USA			
% in very stressful job in 2002 (strongly agree = stressful)	16.0	18.5	20.3
% in stressful job in 2002 (agree = stressful)	41.0	42.9	40.7
% in job that is NOT stressful	43.0	38.6	39.0
Total	100.0	100.0	100.0
USA			
% in very stressful job in 2012 (strongly agree = stressful)	13.2[b]	8.3[a]	N/A
% in stressful job in 2012 (agree = stressful)	38.7[b]	29.1[a]	N/A
% in job that is NOT stressful	48.1[b]	62.6[a]	N/A
Total	100.0	100.0	N/A
Base USA	543	534	1496
Base UK	156	118	812

Note: A physical job involves 'lots of physical effort' 'all' or 'most' of the time in the US; in England, it involved 'physical' or 'heavy manual' work. A stressful job is one where they agree that 'my job involves a lot of stress'. See Figure 4.1 for explanation of transition categories. A superscript of 'a', 'b' or 'c' indicates that the difference between columns is statistically significant at the 5% level.
Source: Author's analysis of ELSA waves 2002–12 and HRS waves 2002–12.

with just over a quarter of 'Stayers' and 'Movers/Returners'. Therefore, physically demanding work appears to have forced some people out of employment. At the same time, for 'Stayers' and 'Movers/Returners', a quarter were doing physical work in 2012, the same proportion as in 2002. This suggests that among those remaining with the same employer, few were moved into 'light work', as was common in the historical past (Phillipson, 1982). It also suggests that people moving jobs between 2002 and 2012 did not shift from physically demanding employment to more sedentary work (see also Maestas, 2010: 742). The importance of being able to do physically demanding work in order to remain employed does not therefore seem to decline as people age.

The results for England in Table 4.1 also suggest that physically demanding work remains important for the types of jobs done by many older people. The definition of physically demanding work differed slightly from that of the US, being 'physical' or 'heavy manual' work (versus 'sedentary' or 'standing' occupations). Despite the different measure used, the proportion of physically demanding work was similar to that of the US, at around 30%. It is important to note that the proportion of physically demanding work would be higher if we were to include standing occupations. In contrast to the US, 'Leavers' in England were no more likely to be in physically demanding work in 2002 than 'Stayers' or 'Movers/Returners'. We should bear in mind, however, that working past 65 was atypical in England at this time.

Job stress

In addition to recognising the physical demands of many jobs, is important to recognise that work intensification has occurred in the UK, US and other industrial countries (Green, F., 2006). Individuals are expected to perform more work per hour than they were in the past. One of the drivers of this has been the development of information and communications technology (ICT), which has enabled employers to monitor and manage performance much more closely (Burchell et al, 2005; Green, F., 2006). In addition to this, employers have arguably become much more competitive and market-oriented (Cappelli, 1999), increasing pressures on workers to perform. This has resulted in a decline in job satisfaction, particularly among older workers who have witnessed the change occurring (Smeaton and White, 2015). In the US, and no doubt in the UK, the shift towards more cognitively demanding jobs has occurred alongside a shift towards more stressful jobs (Johnson et al, 2011). From analysis of US survey data, Johnson et al (2011: 108) conclude that:

Stress is an important feature of many of today's jobs. Although just more than 9% of workers were in occupations involving high stress, with frequent conflict situations and much competition, about 39% of jobs involved time pressure, including strict deadlines. Overall, 44% of jobs involved stress under an expansive measure that included conflict situations, competition, and time pressures.

Johnson's (2011: 23) analysis showed that the proportions working in stressful occupations had increased considerably between 1971 and 2006. Being in a stressful job in 2006 was common across education levels, but highest among the highly educated (Johnson, 2011: 109).

In the context of increasingly pressurised workplaces, previous research suggests that stressful work is an influence on employment in older age. Wang et al (2008) found that work stress increased the likelihood of an individual taking full retirement rather than moving into a bridge job. When 'stressed' individuals did move into bridge jobs, they were more likely to be in a different occupation, presumably because they wanted to avoid the kinds of stresses previously experienced. These findings are consistent with those from the UK. Survey analysis by Smeaton et al (2009) found that at age 60–64, two fifths say that they have previously had a job involving high levels of skills, qualifications or responsibilities; this rises to 57% among those aged 65–74. Among all age groups, 17% of those working 'below capability' said that they preferred work that was not too demanding/ stressful, and a further 10% left their previous job because of stress or excessive demands.

The previous research suggests that remaining in employment for some individuals depends upon being able to work in jobs with manageable levels of stress. In order to investigate this further, Table 4.1 shows the percentages of US individuals in 'stressful' jobs broken down by type of transition made between 2002 and 2012. Table 4.1 defines people as being in 'stressful' jobs if they agree with the statement that their job involves lots of stress; 'very stressful' jobs required individuals to strongly agree with the statement. Unfortunately, no equivalent question is asked in ELSA, so the analysis is for the US only. Table 4.1 suggests that Leavers were slightly more likely to be in very stressful jobs in 2002 than Stayers (20.3% versus 16%), but the difference was not statistically significant. More broadly, it is notable that more than half of all groups were in jobs in 2002 that they considered either stressful or very stressful.

Alongside figures for 2002, Table 4.1 shows the perceived levels of stress for the jobs held in 2012 by 'Stayers' and 'Movers/Returners'. Once again, more than half of 'Stayers' defined their 2012 job as being stressful or very stressful. Remaining in a long-term job, up to and beyond age 65, therefore requires individuals to cope with work stress over a long period. For some individuals, it is likely that they will seek a less stressful job, perhaps in another occupation, as per the findings of Wang et al (2008) in relation to bridge jobs. Consistent with this, Table 4.1 shows that 'Movers/Returners' were significantly less likely than Stayers to be in stressful or very stressful jobs in 2012. Previous research has also shown that 'partial retirement' and 'unretirement' jobs are less stressful than 'pre-retirement jobs' (Maestas, 2010: 742). In total, 62.6% of 'Movers/Returners' were in non-stressful jobs in 2012. Some people therefore seem to be able to 'downsize' into less stressful jobs, a transition that probably occurs alongside a shift towards reduced hours or part-time employment.

Occupations

The final strand of analysis here relates to the occupations held by those working past 65. ELSA and the HRS do not have comparable occupational data. Instead, Table 4.2 draws on research examining the occupations held by *employees* aged 65–69 (note that this excludes the self-employed) (Lain, 2012a; Lain, forthcoming; Lain and Loretto, forthcoming). Table 4.2 shows that in 2000, employees aged 65–69 in the UK were disproportionately in so-called 'Lopaq occupations'. These low-paid, typically part-time, jobs required few formal qualifications and were less desired by much of the 'core-age' working population. These jobs included lower-level service and elementary positions, including shop and sales workers, waiters, bartenders, food preparers, cleaners, domestic helpers, personal health-care workers ('home help'), and caretakers, among others. Older workers could afford to take these jobs because they were subsidised by pensions and had often paid off mortgages. For employers, older workers represented a reliable/experienced source of labour relative to the main alternative – young people. Evidence in Lain (2012a) shows that UK employees aged 65–69 were disproportionately retained in, and recruited to, these Lopaq occupations. In 2000, 44% of employees age 65–69 were in Lopaq occupations, almost twice that of the 'core-age workforce' aged 25–49. In the US, in 2000, over 65s were over-represented in Lopaq jobs relative to those aged 25–49, but to a lesser degree than in the UK. By 2014, the proportion of 65–69 year olds in Lopaq jobs in the UK was lower, at 30.1%; this was much closer to the proportion at age 25–49 (25%). At the same time, the proportion in managerial professions at 65–69 was also closer to the core-age population: 34.8% versus 49.5%.

This shift away from a concentration in Lopaq jobs in the UK is likely to have occurred for two reasons. First, the cohort aged 65–69 in

Table 4.2: Occupational profile of employees by age, UK and US

USA 2000	16–24	25–49	50–54	58–59	60–64	65–69
Managers	5.5	15.2	16.9	15.2	13.5	11.0
Professionals	7.6	18.7	20.6	19.2	17.5	16.6
Technicians/Assoc. Professional	10.3	12.7	11.3	11.2	9.6	10.5
Crafts	8.9	12.0	10.2	10.3	8.8	6.1
Operatives	7.3	10.2	9.3	10.6	12.5	8.6
Clerks	21.3	13.3	14.5	13.5	16.3	19.1
Lopaq	39.1	18.0	17.2	19.9	21.8	28.1
Total %	100.0	100.0	100.0	100.0	100.0	100.0
UK 2000	16–24	25–49	50–59		60–64	65–69
Managers, Professionals & Assoc. Professionals	17.7*	44.0	37.5*		27.9*	24.0*
Crafts	10.6*	9.3	8.9		11.3*	7.5
Operatives	6.0*	8.6	10.0*		12.3*	8.3
Clerks	14.9	14.3	16.5*		14.1	16.2
Lopaq	50.7*	23.7	27.0*		34.4*	44.0*
Total %	100.0	100.0	100.0		100.0	100.0
UK 2014	16–24	25–49	50–59		60–64	65–69
Managers, Professionals & Assoc. Professionals	19.7*	49.5	44.2*		37.1*	34.8*
Crafts	9.3*	7.9	7.7		9.5	7.6
Operatives	3.5*	5.8	7.7*		9.2*	8.8*
Clerks	10.6*	11.1	14.0*		14.7*	18.6*
Lopaq	56.8*	25.8	26.4		29.6*	30.1*
Total %	100.0	100.0	100.0		100.0	100.0

Note: Data are from the UK Labour Force Survey and the US Current Population Survey. * = a significant difference from the 'core-age' workforce group aged 25–49 at the 5% level. Significance tests were not conducted for the US analysis.
Source: Lain (2012a) and Lain (forthcoming).

2014 was more likely to be in 'upper-level jobs' at earlier stages of the life course (Lain and Loretto, forthcoming). In addition, the increase in employment at 65–69 between 2000 and 2014 was primarily the result of people in long-term jobs staying on longer (Lain and Loretto, forthcoming); this is consistent with the preceding analysis. One might note the fact that individuals were given the right to request continued employment beyond age 65 in 2006. It is therefore to be expected that the occupational profile of people past 65 would become broader as people across a range of occupations work longer. It is, however, questionable whether older individuals would be able to attain 'non-Lopaq' jobs if they were seeking them in the labour market.

Conclusions

In the US and the UK, governments have abolished mandatory retirement in order to enable people to continue working in their jobs beyond age 65. The US was ahead of the UK in this regard, and we do see more Americans continuing in long-term jobs beyond age 65 ('Stayers'). However, for many individuals, working beyond this age is not simply a result of people working a bit longer in their career job. Even when people remained in their jobs beyond age 65, in both countries, most of them reduced their hours. For some, reducing hours would be a simple preference. For others, full-time hours of employment may have been seen as unsustainable. It is important to note that physically arduous work does not disappear in older age – around a third of people aged 65–74 in both countries were in physically demanding jobs. At the same time, stressful work was common among older workers in the US, and no doubt in England as well. In these instances, a reduction in working time may be seen as a necessity for continued employment to be sustainable, without suffering from 'burnout', to borrow the language used by Maestas (2010). However, the wider literature suggests that in both countries, opportunities to reduce working hours within companies, while popular, are often not available.

In this context, it becomes important that individuals be able to move jobs in older age. Movements into new work may also be necessary if an individual is to continue working given the possibility that individuals are made redundant or have to leave work temporarily for a range of factors, such as caring responsibilities. In the US, people were more likely than their English counterparts to work past 65 as a result of moving jobs in older age, or returning to work following an absence. Such movements appear not to be new, and we cannot assume that this is because of US age discrimination legislation. In the UK, job movements are clearly not as important a pathway to working past 65, and the evidence suggests that increases in employment at this age during the 2000s are primarily due to people staying on in long-term jobs, rather than moving employment (Lain and Loretto, forthcoming). The analysis in this chapter also suggests that men and women aged 65–74 in 2012 were more likely than Americans to have been out of work since 2002. If job movements are an important component of working past 65, it is debatable whether such a trend is occurring in the UK.

Although workers in the US were twice as likely to work past 65 as those in England, US evidence suggests that significantly fewer people work 'in retirement' than expect to (see, eg, Maestas, 2010). It is therefore important to examine the factors influencing working beyond age 65 in the US, alongside England. In Chapter Five, we examine how the capability to work, in terms of education and health, influences employment at this age.

FIVE

The capability to work at age 65+?

Introduction

As we saw in Chapter Four, US employment at age 65–74 was not simply the result of people in long-term career jobs staying on a bit longer. Americans were more likely to remain in long-term jobs beyond age 65 than their English counterparts. However, they were also more likely to work as a result of either moving jobs in older age or returning to work following an exit. Nevertheless, the wider literature suggests that fewer Americans work 'in retirement' than want to. In the next two chapters, we examine the factors influencing why some individuals end up working at 65–74, and why some individuals do not. In this chapter, we look at the influence of an individual's 'capability' to work. As we saw in Chapter One, the US has historically placed a greater degree of emphasis on educational attainment than the UK; we examine the influence of qualifications on employment first. Following this, we then examine the influence of an individual's health on employment, alongside the influence of a partner's health and other caring responsibilities.

Education and employment at age 65+

Previous research indicates that having qualifications increases the likelihood of working in older age in the US (Haider and Loughran, 2001), UK (Smeaton and McKay, 2003) and wider European Union (EU) (Komp et al, 2010). Haider and Loughran (2001), for example, found that only 16% of US 'high school dropouts' worked past age 65, compared with 42% of those with advanced qualifications. Likewise, Smeaton and McKay (2003: 20) found that men and women in the UK with no qualifications were significantly less likely to work past state pension age than those with degrees. Smeaton and McKay (2003) found that men were most likely to work with degrees, whereas for women, those with middle-level qualifications were most likely to be in employment. Qualifications are likely to increase the likelihood of employment because they help people retain the jobs they have, or find new jobs if they need or want new employment. Longitudinal research from Britain suggests that qualifications help facilitate more stable careers with fewer involuntary exits (Blekesaune et al, 2008). If individuals have managed to remain in work during earlier portions of their career, it therefore follows that they will be more likely to be able to remain in employment in older age. At the same time, however, evidence suggests that education facilitates job movement. US research suggests that the likelihood of older people entering new 'bridge' employment, rather than retiring fully, increases with the number of years of education a person has received (Wang et al, 2008). Likewise, Kanabar's (2012) analysis focusing on English men found that the likelihood of returning to work after retirement was higher for the highly educated. It should be noted that older workers in general have lower levels of qualifications than more recently educated cohorts, which is likely to place them at a general employment disadvantage.

Table 5.1 shows the educational levels of people making different transitions to work or inactivity at age 65–74 in 2012; this is based on an analysis of the English Longitudinal Study of Ageing (ELSA) and the US Health and Retirement Study (HRS). The analysis of ELSA focuses on England, but should broadly reflect the situation in the UK as a whole (see statistical appendix). As per Chapter Four, those working at 65+ are divided into three groups: 'Stayers', who remained in the same job between 2002 and 2012; 'Movers', who changed jobs between 2002 and 2012 but remained in employment at each wave; and 'Returners', who returned to work following an absence at a previous wave. Those not working at age 65–74 were also divided into three categories: 'Leavers' were individuals working in 2002 that had left by 2012 with no return to employment; 'Out All' indicates an individual who was not employed at any of the biannual waves between 2002 and 2012; finally, 'Fleeting Workers' were people who had re-entered employment between 2002 and 2010 but had left by 2012. Qualifications levels in Table 5.1 are the highest held by the individual; these have been harmonised with the measure used in the HRS Rand files (Phillips et al, 2014). The bottom two categories relate to whether an individual has received 'high school' secondary-level qualifications. This includes O-levels in the UK and a high school diploma in the US. 'Some college' refers to individuals with qualifications between high school and higher education; this includes, for example, English A-levels. Finally, 'College+' includes those with undergraduate or Master's degrees or a PhD.

Table 5.1: Breakdown of educational level by employment transition type

	Working at age 65–74 in 2012			Not working at age 65–74 in 2012		
	Stayers	**Movers**	**Returners**	**'Fleeting' Workers**	**Leavers (e)**	**Out All (f)**
USA – Education						
College+	39.3[ef]	40.8[ef]	32.9[f]	20.7	26.6[f]	15.2[e]
Some college	22.7	21.9	24.9	26.4	25.2	22.0
High school	30.2[f]	30.1	31.9	37.1	35.9	38.4
Below high school	7.9[f]	7.3[f]	10.3	15.8	12.4[f]	24.5[e]
Total %	100.0	100.0	100.0	100.0	100.0	100.0
England – Education						
College+	24.6[f]	24.0	30.3[f]	18.7	18.3[f]	12.6[e]
Some college	30.4	31.9	23.1	27.9	27.2[f]	20.5[e]
High school	19.3	16.2	15.9	18.8	19.8	16.7
Below high school	25.7[f]	28.0[f]	30.7	34.6[f]	34.7[f]	50.2[e]
Total %	100.0	100.0	100.0	100.0	100.0	100.0
Base USA	560	311	376	394	1381	1105
Base England	156	74	59	118	767	770

Notes: 'Stayers' remained in the same job between 2002 and 2012; 'Movers' were employed at each wave between 2002 and 2012 but moved job; 'Returners' were economically inactive at one (or more) wave(s) between 2002 and 2010 but were back at work by 2012. 'Out All' indicates non-employment at all waves between 2002 and 2012; 'Leavers' were employed in 2002 but had left work by 2012 (with no subsequent returns); 'Fleeting Workers' had returned to work from an absence between 2002 and 2010 but were out by 2012. A superscript of 'e' or 'f' indicates a significant difference at the 5% level from 'Leavers' or 'Out All', respectively.
Source: Author's analysis of ELSA waves 2002–12 and HRS waves 2002–12.

As Table 5.1 shows, in the US, higher education levels increased the likelihood of working at age 65–74, whether this was as a result of being a 'Stayer', 'Mover' or 'Returner'. In the US, College+ educations were held by around 40% of 'Stayers' and 'Movers' and 33% of 'Returners'; this compares with only 27% of 'Leavers' and 15% of those 'Out All'. The column percentages indicate statistically significant educational differences between groups. A superscript of 'e' indicates a statistically significant educational difference (at the 5% level) from 'Leavers'; a superscript of 'f' indicates a statistically significant difference from those 'Out All'. US 'Stayers' and 'Movers' had a statistically significant higher likelihood of having a degree than 'Leavers' or those 'Out All'. US 'Returners', on the other hand, were significantly more likely to hold a degree than those 'Out All'. At the other end of the educational spectrum, only around 7% to 10% of US 'Stayers', 'Movers' and 'Returners' had below high school qualifications, compared with 24.5% of those 'Out All'. Those with low qualifications in the US therefore seemed to be often out of work long before they reached age 65–74 in 2012. In this regard, it is noteworthy that those 'Out All' were twice as likely to have below secondary-level qualifications as 'Leavers'. Educational qualifications therefore appear to strengthen the attachment of individuals to the labour market, which, in turn, makes it easier for them to remain in work beyond age 65.

In England, education levels as a whole were lower than in the US (see Chapter One). However, the same pattern of higher education among those working was evident. Around a quarter of 'Stayers', 'Movers' and 'Returners' had college degrees, compared with only an eighth of those 'Out All'. At the other end of the spectrum, just over a quarter of 'Stayers', 'Movers' and 'Returners' had below high school qualifications; this compares with half of those 'Out All'. Once again, those with low levels of qualifications therefore had the strongest likelihood of being out of work long before reaching age 65–74 in 2012. Consistent with this, 'Leavers' were significantly less likely to have below secondary qualifications that those 'Out All'. It is also interesting to note that 'Fleeting Workers' in both countries did not have the same qualification levels as 'Stayers', 'Movers' and 'Returners'. These individuals would have had relatively short periods of employment at some point between 2004 and 2008; this suggests that more moderately educated individuals may sometimes have been able to re-enter employment but not remain in employment until age 65–74 in 2012.

While the preceding analysis indicates that highly educated people are most likely to work past 65, it is important to take into account factors that might influence their employment. For example, it may just be the case that highly educated individuals are more likely to work because they have better health. In order to examine this, Table 5.2 gives the *percentage probabilities* of individuals aged 65–74 working at different levels of qualifications in 2010. The results are presented as 'unadjusted' and 'adjusted' percentage probabilities of working. *Unadjusted* percentage probabilities represent the percentages working at each educational level. They are derived from logistic regression analyses on whether an individual is in employment or not using education as the sole independent variable. The coefficients from these analyses were converted into Average Adjusted Predictions (AAPs), as per the suggestion of Williams (2012), and then converted into percentage probabilities by multiplying them by 100. This enables us to see, for example, that 18.2% of those with below high school education worked compared with 41.3% of those with college qualifications (the reference category) – the asterisk indicates that this difference was statistically significant. Average Marginal Effects were calculated to ascertain whether these differences were statistically significant (see Williams, 2012).

Table 5.2: Percentage probabilities of working at age 65–74 by education, 2010

	All		Men		Women	
	% probability of working		% probability of working		% probability of working	
	Unadjusted	Adjusted (controls for other factors)	Unadjusted	Adjusted (controls for other factors)	Unadjusted	Adjusted (controls for other factors)
USA						
College+ (ref)	41.3	35.0	47.1	41.1	34.1	28.4
Some college	29.8***	28.8***	31.7***	30.8**	28.2°	26.3
High school graduate	26.9***	28.1***	31.9***	33.9*	22.9***	23.7*
Below high school	18.2***	24.0***	23.1***	29.0**	14.2***	19.7*
England						
College+ (ref)	21.4	16.0	25.2	21.0	15.2	11.0
Some college	17.7	15.8	21.4	19.7	13.4	12.3
High school graduate	15.4*	14.8	21.7	21.7	10.8	9.4
Below high school	9.7***	12.1°	12.2***	14.5*	7.9*	9.6
Base n USA	5339	5339	2329	2329	3070	2329
Base n England	2774	2774	1281	1281	1493	1493

Notes: Percentage probabilities are derived from Average Adjusted Probabilities (AAPs) from logistic regression analysis. 'Adjusted' probabilities control for the age, health, pension status, gender, partnership status, home ownership status and wealth (see the statistical Appendix). The difference from the reference category is statistically significant at the following levels: *** = $p < 0.001$; ** = $p < 0.01$; * = $p < 0.05$; ° = $p < 0.10$.
Source: Author's analysis of the ELSA 2010 wave and HRS 2010 wave.

Adjusted percentage probabilities are also presented because we are interested in whether the predicted likelihood of working varies between groups *after we take into account the potential impact of other influences*. As noted earlier, it might be the case that employment is high among the educated simply because they have excellent health, for example. Adjusted percentage probabilities take into account a range of other factors, included as independent variables in the regression, which might inflate or deflate employment levels among the group in question. These show the likelihood of working of an 'average' person within a category, such as 'some college', if they had average scores on other variables included in the regression. As educational groups are being compared *as if* they both had average levels of wealth, qualifications and so on, we can get closer to what might be described as the 'true' influence of education by 'controlling' for these other factors. 'Control variables' that are taken into account for the adjusted percentage probabilities in Table 5.2 are self-rated health, the number of health limitations, age, housing status, whether an individual has a private pension, partnership status, and household wealth 'equivalised' to the individual level (see the statistical appendix).

Table 5.2 confirms the extent to which the highly educated were more likely to work at 65–74. In both countries, someone with a college degree was twice as likely to be in employment as somebody with below high school qualifications (see unadjusted results). This is true for both men and women. In England, around a fifth of those with degrees worked, compared with a tenth of those with below high school qualifications (21.4% versus 9.7%). In the US, 41.3% of college graduates worked, compared with 18.2% of those with below high school degrees. The differences in the percentage probability of working between educational groups reduced in each country once other characteristics of these individuals were taken into account (see adjusted results). However, the overall adjusted results still show a significantly higher likelihood of employment for those with college degrees compared with those with below high school qualifications in both countries. This was true for men in both countries, and women in the US. In the case of UK women, there was no statistically significant higher likelihood of employment among the highly educated once we control for other factors.

The preceding analysis indicates that education as an important effect on the ability of people to remain in employment in both countries. However, the overall influence of education on employment will depend upon the educational profile of the population. As we saw in Chapter One, older cohorts in the US are far more highly educated than their counterparts in England as a result of life-course policies to promote self-reliance. Figure 5.1 presents the educational profiles of those aged 65–74 in 2010 in both countries. Overall, approaching half of the cohort had below high school qualifications in England (45.2%), compared with less than a fifth of Americans (17.1%). The English cohort was also less likely to have a college+ education (14.8%, compared with 23.6% in the US). As a result, the profile of American workers was skewed more to those with high qualifications. Around a third of American workers aged 65–74 had a college+ education (33.2%), compared with a fifth in England (21.2%). At the other end of the spectrum, only a tenth of US workers had below high school qualifications (10.6%), compared with a third in England (32.2%). In other words, although the low educated had a small likelihood of working, because of their sheer number, they represented the modal group among workers in England. Low levels of education among older cohorts in England are therefore likely to contribute to the low employment prospects at 65+, particularly when there is a wide educational disparity compared with recently educated cohorts (OECD, 2014). Those with low education have a weak attachment to the labour market prior to 65, which makes staying in employment difficult. They also appear to have difficulties in moving jobs or

Figure 5.1: Educational breakdown of workers and non-workers aged 65–74, 2010

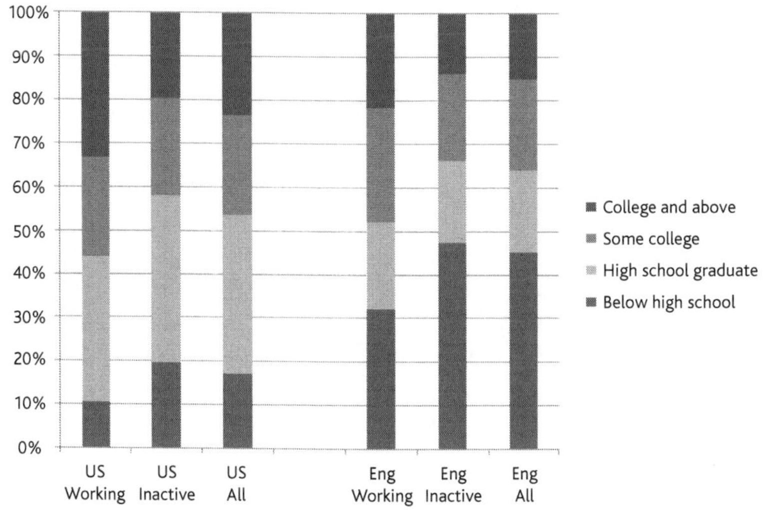

Source: Author's analysis of the ELSA 2010 wave and HRS 2010 wave.

returning to work following an absence. This presents potentially serious problems for the future as the state pension age rises.

Health

Health problems limiting employment

While it is true that life expectancy is rising, health remains a significant challenge in terms of promoting employment up to and beyond age 65 (Vickerstaff et al, 2012). According to the UK Marmot review, 'more than three-quarters of the population do not have disability-free life-expectancy as long as 68' (Marmot et al, 2010: 17). For people aged 50 to state pension age, almost one half have a long-term health condition (DWP, 2014b). Compared with the past, it has become easier for some people to manage a health condition while being in employment (Vickerstaff et al, 2012). However, in 2008–09, a quarter of people aged 50–69 had a work disability that limited the kind or amount of paid work that they could do (Crawford and Tetlow, 2010: 32). Of those with a work disability, only a quarter were in employment. Likewise, the influence of a health-limiting disability on being out of work was not identical across groups; being in the poorest wealth quintile reduced the likelihood of working with a work disability (Crawford and Tetlow, 2010: 37). This may be because the poorest wealth quintile have the least access to the kind of jobs that can be performed while having a health condition. This problem is exacerbated by a decline in low-skilled work; this means that low-skilled individuals with a work-limiting disability will find it harder to compete for work, and will disproportionately end up on disability benefits (Faggio and Nickel, 2003).

By the age of 65–74, health problems have become even more common. The top portion of Figure 5.2 shows that in 2010 in the US and England, around one in three individuals reported a health problem that limited the amount or type of work that the individual could do. Of those with such a health condition, only a small fraction were in employment: 13.2% in the US and 5% in England. This compares with 39.1% of those without a health condition working in the US, and 19.2% in England. Clearly, it is not uncommon for people in this age group to report that their employment prospects are limited by their health.

While 'work-limiting' health problems should be taken seriously, understanding the full implications of health on employment also requires us to look at a range of other health measures. The

Figure 5.2: Employment among those aged 65–74 with a work-limiting health problem, 2010

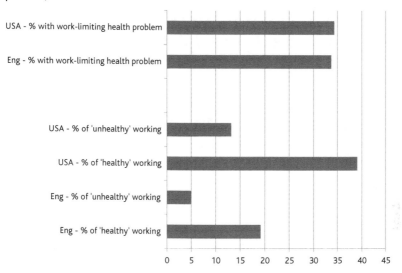

Note: 'Unhealthy' individuals have a 'work-limiting' health problem limiting the amount or kind of work that they can do.
Source: Author's analysis of the ELSA 2010 wave and HRS 2010 wave.

advantage of enquiring about work-limiting health is that it directly addresses individual perceptions about how their health influences their employment. The limitation of this measure, however, is that it may encourage individuals out of work to 'explain' their inactivity as being due to health problems. For example, a study by Faggio and Nickel (2003) found that men claiming to have an illness or disability limiting the kind of work that they could do rose from the early 1980s to 2000s. However, the proportions with a limiting long-standing illness (LLSI) that limits the kinds of 'things people normally do' remained fairly stable over the period. The explanation given was that low-skilled men with an LLSI lost their jobs due to a decline in low-skilled employment, were moved on to disability benefits and were more inclined to identify as having a work-limiting illness as a result. Consequently, this measure may theoretically be influenced by employment outcomes to a degree. Ill-health may also be seen as a socially acceptable reason for economic inactivity among older people (Lain, 2012b). This may be less of a concern beyond age 65, however, as people may be more inclined to define themselves as retired than in ill-health. Nevertheless, it is important to examine employment in relation to a range of different health measures in order to be confident about the influence of health on work.

Employment by self-rated health

An alternative to asking whether health limits work is to ask people to give a general health rating, for example, from excellent to poor. This is a useful supplementary measure because it provides a general perception of health without reference to employment. Given that individual behaviour is likely to be influenced by general perceptions, it is perhaps not surprising that previous research suggests that employment varies on the basis of these types of self-rated health measures. Using the British Household Panel Survey, Smeaton and McKay (2003), for example, found that 14–15% of those with 'excellent' health were in employment beyond the state pension age in 2001, compared with only 4–5% with 'poor' health. A subsequent logistic regression analysis using the Family Resources Survey found that those in 'good health' were twice as likely to work as those in 'poor health' after controlling for other factors. McNamara and Williamson (2004) also found that in the US, 'poor health' reduced the likelihood of men in their 60s to 80s from working.

Figure 5.3 presents employment rates for people aged 65–74 in 2010, broken down by self-rated health. In both countries, we see a clear pattern of increasing employment as people move up the health

Figure 5.3: Employment among those aged 65–74, broken down by levels of self-rated health, 2010

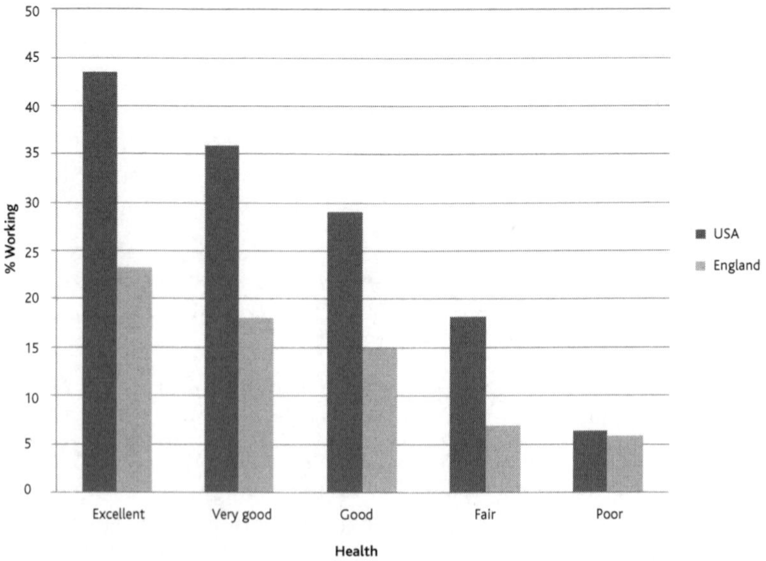

Source: Author's analysis of the ELSA 2010 wave and HRS 2010 wave.

rankings. At 'poor health', the proportions working were similarly small in both countries, at around 5%. It should be noted that only just over 5% of individuals in both countries rated their health in this way. At all other health points, we see much higher rates of employment in the US than in England, once again, suggesting that the national context influences the likelihood of working at different levels of health. Employment for those with 'excellent' health was particularly high, at 43.5% in the US and 23.3% in England. The positive influence of 'excellent' health on employment is sometimes overlooked in research; for some of these individuals, remaining in employment may be seen as a way of *maintaining* good health (Barnes et al, 2004: 38).

In addition to being a good general indicator, self-rated health is also shown to influence the likelihood of employment after controlling for a number of other factors. Logistic regression analysis (not shown) included self-rated health, broken down into two categories: those with fair/poor health; and those with good or above health. In both countries, having 'good+' health significantly increased the likelihood of working in 2010 at age 65–74, controlling for gender, education, household wealth, pension status, partnership status and the number of problems with 'activities of daily living' (ADLs). ADLs are another measure of health (see Lain, 2012b); the fact that self-rated health has an effect after controlling for ADL limitations suggests that general perceptions of health are an important influence on employment.

Figure 5.4: Self-rated health for those aged 65–74, 2010

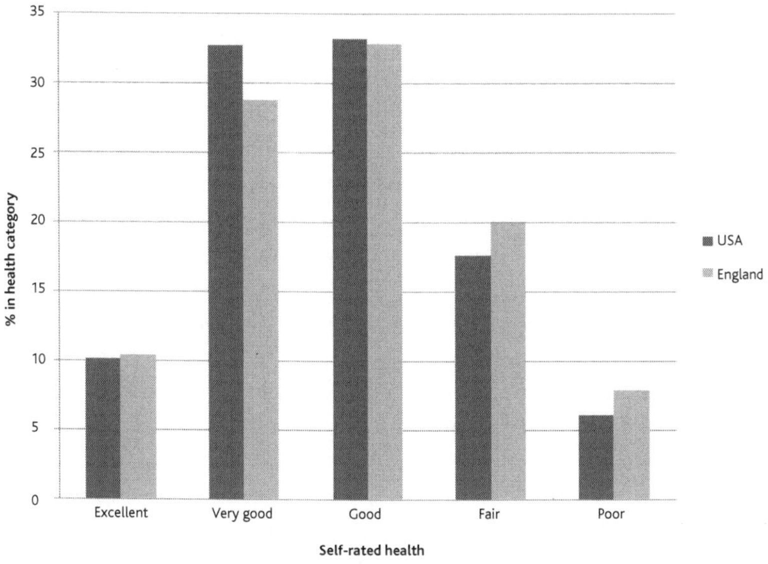

Source: Author's analysis of the ELSA 2010 wave and HRS 2010 wave.

In order to consider the broader influence of self-rated health on employment, it is useful to examine how people aged 65–74 rated their health (see Figure 5.4). As Figure 5.4 shows, self-ratings of health were similar in both countries, with around three quarters rating their health as 'good' or above. Only a small minority rated their health as being 'poor'. This perhaps seems a strange outcome given the fact that a third of individuals said that their health limited their work. In order to understand this, it is useful to consider how people arrive at the conclusion that their health is 'good'. McNamara and Williamson (2004) argue that individuals rate their health on the basis of what they think is appropriate for their age group. Analysis by the authors finds that the effect of self-rated 'poor health' on employment decreased for men between the ages 60–67 and 68–80 (McNamara and Williamson, 2004: 269–70). In this context, people in the older age group were probably rating their health as being good when their ability to work was limited because they were comparing themselves with other people of the same age with health limitations. As corroborating evidence, respondents with a functional limitation were less likely to report themselves as being in 'poor health' in the older 68–80 age group (McNamara and Williamson, 2004: 270).

Employment by health diagnoses

An alternative way of examining the impact of health on employment is to look at illnesses that individuals have been diagnosed with in the past. Previous research suggests that the major chronic illnesses in Britain are: musculoskeletal disorders (including arthritis); heart and circulatory problems; respiratory conditions; and 'mild to moderate' mental health disorders (Vickerstaff et al, 2012: 5). These health conditions are most common in the older population (Vickerstaff et al, 2012). More generally, musculoskeletal disorders and mental health issues were identified as the two most significant health problems compromising the ability of individuals to work across all age groups (Black, 2008).

Table 5.3 presents the percentages of people aged 65–74 in 2010 who have been diagnosed with a range of health conditions in the past; alongside this are the percentages working for those with a diagnosis. As Table 5.3 shows, Americans were more likely to be diagnosed with these conditions, in some cases, by a significant amount. Only 9.1% of Americans were diagnosed with none of the health conditions listed, compared with 20.9% in England. Consistent with this, previous research suggests that white Americans aged 55–64 are more likely to report diabetes, hypertension, strokes and cancer than their English counterparts (Banks et al, 2006). While Americans appear to be less healthy overall, those diagnosed with each condition were more likely to work than their English counterparts. The minority with no diagnoses did have a relatively high likelihood of working in both countries (45.9% in the US; 24.5% in England). However, between a fifth and a quarter of Americans with each health condition worked; the exceptions to this were strokes and psychiatric problems, which had lower employment rates. The relatively low rates of employment for those diagnosed with psychiatric problems in both countries reflect an underappreciated barrier to extended working lives.

Table 5.3: Percentages of those aged 65–74 reporting previous health diagnoses, and percentages with diagnoses in employment, 2010

	% diagnosed		% of diagnosed employed	
	USA	England	USA	England
High blood pressure	63.0	47.5	25.7	12.0
Diabetes	24.4	12.9	24.3	8.6
Cancer	17.0	12.2	26.0	9.7
Lung disease	11.5	8.3	20.7	7.9
Heart problems	26.1	20.3	24.2	10.0
A stroke	8.0	4.7	15.2	7.7
Psychiatric problems	17.9	9.6	18.3	10.8
Arthritis	65.4	41.7	26.0	9.8
No diagnoses	9.1	20.9	45.9	24.5
All 65–74 year olds	N/A	N/A	29.5	14.6

Source: Author's analysis of the ELSA 2010 wave and HRS 2010 wave.

While Table 5.3 provides some interesting insights, diagnoses are perhaps not the best measure for assessing the impact of health on employment (for discussion, see Lain, 2012b). We should not necessarily assume that health problems are being diagnosed on the same basis in each country. US clinicians are known to reach very different diagnostic conclusions to their British counterparts when presented with identical case histories (Fitzpatrick, 2008). A greater willingness to diagnose, and therefore treat, health conditions may, in part, be influenced by a US health system that financially rewards clinicians for performing health investigations and procedures (Fitzpatrick, 2008). In this context, the large difference between arthritis diagnoses between countries is questionable (see Lain, 2012b). Arthritis diagnoses were reported by

65.4% of Americans, compared with 41.7% of people in England. It is therefore possible that the label of arthritis is being applied to less severe joint problems in the US than in England. Musculoskeletal disorders such as arthritis are the biggest physical reason for receipt of incapacity benefits in the UK (Black, 2008: 43). It is therefore very important that measures of health adequately capture the extent to which physical constraints, caused by joint pain and other factors, limit employment prospects. In some cases, former diagnoses will be particularly inefficient in capturing levels of physical functioning. For example, some individuals may have limited long-term physical consequences from having cancer if it is successfully treated. In other cases, cancer may have greatly reduced the ability of individuals to work.

Employment for those with problems with activities of daily living

An alternative, or supplementary, measure is to try and ascertain levels of physical capability by asking individuals if they have any difficulties doing a range of ADLs. A selection ADLs are listed in Table 5.4 along with the percentages of people aged 65–74 in 2010 saying that they have difficulty with doing the activities. In addition, Table 5.4 shows the percentage likelihood of somebody with a particular difficulty being in employment. There is little obvious reason why Americans should be more likely to report difficulties with an ADL than their English counterparts, all else being equal. Americans, once again, appear to be less healthy than their English counterparts; it should be noted that

Table 5.4: Percentages of those aged 65–74 reporting difficulties with activities of daily living, and percentages with those difficulties in employment, 2010

	% with ADL difficulty		% with ADL difficulty employed	
	USA	England	USA	England
Sitting for two hours	19.8	13.8	20.4	6.8
Getting up from a chair	38.7	25.4	23.6	9.3
Climb several flights of stairs	47.4	38.2	22.5	6.7
Stooping/kneeling/crouching	48.0	39.0	23.1	8.8
Difficulty lift/carry 10 lbs	22.0	24.3	15.0	5.1
Reaching/extending arms up	16.7	11.0	17.7	5.4
Pushing/pulling objects	25.9	18.0	16.8	4.7
No difficulties	30.1	41.8	40.3	21.0
All 65–74 year olds	N/A	N/A	29.5	14.6

Source: Author's analysis of the ELSA 2010 wave and HRS 2010 wave.

obesity is more common in the US than in the UK (Wang et al, 2011), which may contribute to the lower reported physical capabilities of Americans. Overall, 30.1% of Americans reported no difficulties with the ADLs listed, compared with 41.8% in England. Employment rates were also higher for those with no reported difficulties: 40.3% in the US, compared with 21% in England.

One of the potential benefits of looking at ADLs is that they can be used as a cumulative health measure: summing the number of difficulties that people report gives us a measure of the degree to which their range of physical activity is constrained. Figure 5.5 presents the percentages employed for those with different numbers of ADL health limitations. In the US, employment drops from around 40% for those with no health limitations to around 30% for those with one to three ADL limitations. This plateauing at one to three limitations reiterates the fact that individuals in this age group do manage to work without having perfect health. After three ADL health limitations, however, the likelihood of working drops sharply, to 20% at four health limitations and 10% at six limitations. In England, we also see declining employment as the number of ADL limits increases, although employment rates were lower than in the US at all health levels. Most of the decline in employment in England had occurred by the time individuals report three health limitations. Between zero and two health limitations, the likelihood of employment halved from 20% to

Figure 5.5: Employment among those aged 65–74, by number of activities of daily living health limitations, 2010

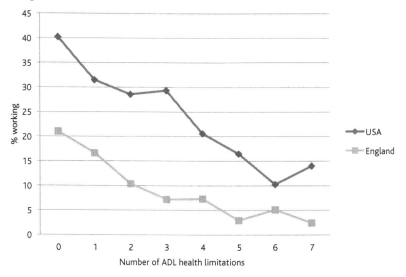

Number of ADL health limitations

Source: Author's analysis of the ELSA 2010 wave and HRS 2010 wave.

10%; by the time we reach three health limitations, only around 7% were working.

The interaction between health and education

The preceding analysis of ADLs suggests that physical capability has an important influence on whether somebody remains in work at age 65–74. However, Figure 5.5 shows that some people do remain in employment when they face physical health limitations. Previous research suggests that the influence of health on employment depends to some degree upon the level of education that an individual has. We saw earlier that past increases in male incapacity benefit receipt were related to a reduction in employment opportunities for *low-skilled* individuals with health limitations (Faggio and Nickel, 2003). We might therefore expect more highly skilled individuals with equivalent health problems to find it easy to remain in work. Lain's (2012b: 69) analysis of people aged 65+ in 2002 led him to conclude that 'having qualifications at secondary level or above reduces the impact of poor health on employment'. Qualifications may additionally reduce the extent to which individuals have to rely on precarious, physically demanding jobs that are hard to perform, and keep, if an individual has health limitations.

Figure 5.6 shows the probabilities of working in the US at different ADL health levels, with the results separately presented for people at different qualification levels. This is derived from logistic regression analysis examining the factors influencing employment at age 65–74. AAPs were calculated for the probability of working at different levels of ADL health limitations; these were calculated for people with different levels of qualifications (see Williams, 2012: 328–9). The health variable included was the number of ADL health limitations that the individual had (ranging from 0 to 7). In addition, a number of 'control' variables were included: education; gender; age; equivalised household wealth; pension ownership status; home ownership status; and partnership status (for more details on these variables, see the statistical appendix).

Figure 5.6 shows that, controlling for other factors, the probability of working with health limitations was highest for the most educated and lowest for the least educated in the US. In order to make the relationship visible on Figure 5.6, we have not included confidence intervals for the probabilities of being in employment. However, a comparison of those in the highest- and lowest-educated groups revealed no overlapping confidence intervals; this indicates that differences in the probability of working were statistically significant between the two educational

Figure 5.6: Probabilities of working for those with activities of daily living health limitations, broken down by educational level, US, 2010

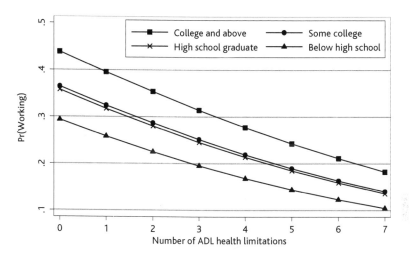

Note: Includes those aged 65–74 in 2010. Reports AAPs from logistic regression analysis; controls for education, gender, age, wealth, pension ownership status, home ownership status and partnership status. Source: Author's analysis of the HRS 2010 wave.

groups at all health points. Figure 5.6 therefore presents evidence that the influence of health on employment is mediated by an individual's education level. It is not just *whether* somebody has health limitations, as most individuals in this age group do; it is also whether or not their education enables them to do the kinds of jobs that are compatible with having a health condition. The important, statistically significant, difference is between those at the top and bottom of the educational hierarchy.

In relation to England, the main difference in the probability of working is between those with the lowest education, who were least likely to work, and the rest (see Figure 5.7). Those with high school qualifications and above appear to have relatively similar likelihoods of working when they have comparable levels of health, controlling for other factors in the regression. It should be noted that the confidence intervals for the estimates overlap between groups, so we cannot make any inferences about statistical significance. However, the sample was smaller than in the case of the US and had a stronger concentration towards one group (those with below high school education). Due to these factors, the estimates have large confidence intervals, which make it harder for the results to arrive at a position of statistical significance. Nevertheless, these results are consistent with US evidence that individuals with low education find it particularly hard to remain in work if they have health conditions. If we do not take into account the compounding influence of education, we are therefore likely to underestimate the extent to which people with health conditions are going to be able to continue working. In England, as we saw earlier, almost half of individuals had below secondary education. Prospects for extended working lives in England are therefore likely to be even more constrained than in the US.

Figure 5.7: Probabilities of working for those with activities of daily living health limitations, broken down by educational level, England, 2010

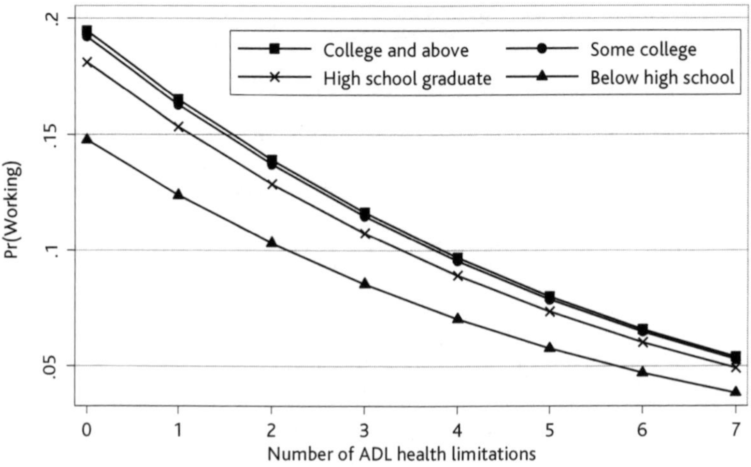

Notes: Includes those aged 65–74 in 2010. Reports AAPs from logistic regression analysis; controls for education, gender, age, wealth, pension ownership status, home ownership status and partnership status. Source: Author's analysis of the ELSA 2010 wave.

Partner's health and other caring responsibilities

Partner's health

In addition to individual health, it is important to recognise that the majority of people live in couples, and the health of their partner might influence their employment (Vickerstaff, 2015). These effects are, however, likely to be complex and not straightforward to measure (Siegel, 2006). If a partner has a 'health shock', for example, in the form of an illness, the employment of the other person in the couple could be affected in a number of ways. If the illness causes the partner to leave work or reduce their hours, this could result in the person delaying retirement in order to compensate financially (McGeary,

2009). In the US, a person with an ill partner may remain in work because they have medical insurance that covers their partner (see Chapter Six). This should affect people aged over 65 less because Medicare health insurance covers this age group. Nevertheless, there may be instances where employer-provided health insurance is more comprehensive in terms of covering costs, thus encouraging continued employment. As an alternative to remaining in work, an individual may leave work because a health shock increases their partner's 'need for attention' (McGeary, 2009). As a result, it is potentially difficult to identify whether a partner's health has an important influence on employment overall. It can pull people in the directions of exit or delayed retirement, with positive and negative consequences potentially cancelling each other out to some degree.

Previous research suggests that in the US, a partner's poor health does influence employment, but the effects differ to some degree by gender and the particular health condition or limitation (Siegel, 2006; McGeary, 2009). McGeary (2009) uses the US HRS to examine the influence of a partner's 'health shock' on employment for those aged 50–75; health shocks include new diagnoses of diseases and changes in levels of physical functioning (measured using ADLs). Individuals included in the study were those working full-time prior to the health shock. The analysis reveals that women had an increased likelihood of retiring if their partner was diagnosed with heart disease or arthritis; men, on the other hand, did not respond to any diagnoses with an increased likelihood of retiring. Instead, men had an increased likelihood of retiring if their partner suffered a decline in their ability to perform ADLs. This suggests that men may be more likely to wait until a partner has reduced physical functioning, and be in need of nursing, before they retire. Interestingly, for women, a decline in the ADL physical functioning of their husband *reduced* the likelihood of them leaving work; this is attributed to women working to replace the lost income of their partner. Siegel (2006) also found that women were more likely to continue working if their partner's physical functioning was reduced. At the same time, however, Siegel (2006) finds that different diseases have different impacts on employment. For example, for women, the likelihood of employment increased if their partner had heart disease but decreased if they had a stroke.

Clearly, the influence of a partner's health on employment is complex, and while it is likely to have an effect, it is hard to quantify in simple terms. In this light, analysis of the British Household Panel Survey by Jones et al (2010) found no statistically significant effect of a partner's health on employment. However, rather than suggest that health is unimportant, they note that this 'may reflect the fact that there are offsetting effects of pressure to provide personal care and to maintain household income when a partner becomes ill' (Jones et al, 2010: 874).

While the studies just reviewed provide useful context, it should be noted that they all include people below 65 or state pension age. The situation may be different for those over age 65 because they typically have access to pensions that may make it easier to leave work to care for somebody. Table 5.5 presents the percentage probabilities of working among married/cohabiting people aged 65–74, broken down by whether their partner has defined themselves as having a work-limiting health problem or 'poor health'. Percentage probabilities are included in the table; these attempt to take into account other influences on

Table 5.5: Percentage probabilities of working at age 65–74 by partner's health

		USA		England	
		Unadjusted	Adjusted (controls for other factors)	Unadjusted	Adjusted (controls for other factors)
All	Partner with work-limiting health (ref)	26.4	29.3	11.0	13.2
	Partner without work-limiting health	33.2***	31.8	15.9**	14.9
Men	Partner with work-limiting health (ref)	30.9	33.6	16.5	19.7
	Partner without work-limiting health	39.8***	38.6*	20.1	18.9
Women	Partner with work-limiting health (ref)	21.4	24.3	5.5	6.7
	Partner without work-limiting health	24.9	23.6	11.3**	10.5
All	Partner with 'poor' health (ref)	28.3	35.4	4.8	6.3
	Partner without 'poor' health	30.8	30.4	15.1***	14.9**
Base	All	3471		1769	
	Men	1778		918	
	Women	1693		851	

Note: The analysis in this Table only includes people in couples. Percentage probabilities are derived from Logistic Regression analysis. Please see the text for the control variables included for the adjusted results. The difference from reference category is statistically significant at the following levels: *** = p<0.001, ** = p<0.01, * = p<0.05, ° = p<0.10
Source: Author's analysis of the ELSA 2010 wave and HRS 2010 wave.

employment. For example, people with ill partners may be less likely to work because they are themselves more likely to have health problems. The factors 'controlled for' are: the individual's health (self-rated and in the form of ADL limitations); age; gender; housing status; pension status; and household wealth quartile (for more on these variables, see the statistical appendix).

Table 5.5 shows that in both countries, people were significantly less likely to work if their partner had a work-limiting health problem. A quarter of individuals with an 'ill' partner worked in the US (26.4%), compared with a third of those with a partner without such health problems (33.2%). The equivalent figures for England were 11% versus 15.9% for those with and without an 'ill' partner, respectively. Once we adjust for other factors, there are no longer any statistically significant employment differences between those with and without a partner with work-limiting health. For the US, this masks an interesting difference on the basis of gender, however. In the case of men, those with a partner with work-limiting health were significantly less likely to work; this remained true for the adjusted results. This is consistent with previous research suggesting that men leave work when their partner has functional limitations (Siegel, 2006; McGeary, 2009). In the case of US women, on the other hand, there were no significant employment differences related to whether the partner had work-limiting health. In England, a partner's health status appears to have more influence on employment for women than men, with an 'ill' partner significantly reducing the likelihood of working (see adjusted results). There remained a difference in employment for women in the adjusted results, although this is no longer statistically significant (perhaps reflecting the smaller sample of female workers).

The final section of Table 5.5 gives percentage probabilities for working, broken down by whether an individual's partner defines their health as being 'poor'. This is a narrower definition of health, with only around 5% of people aged 65–74 categorising themselves in this way (see Figure 5.4). As Table 5.8 shows, in England, only 4.8% of individuals with a partner in 'poor' health worked, compared with 15.1% of those with a partner in 'fair' or above health. Furthermore, those with partners in poor health remained significantly less likely to work once we control for other factors in the adjusted results. In the UK context, where working past age 65 was against the 'norm', it would appear that working while a partner was in poor health was particularly uncommon. In the US, on the other hand, there were no significant employment differences between those with and without 'poor health', either before or after adjusting the results for other factors.

This may, perhaps, reflect some Americans working for undetected financial reasons when their partner's health was poor. It is unlikely that health insurance had much influence in this regard, however, as only 19.4% of those working when their partner was in 'poor health' were covered by employer insurance (supplementary analysis not shown). Overall, therefore, this analysis suggests that a partner's health does have an impact on employment, although this is likely to be complex. Some may have to do leave work to care for a partner, while others may need to stay on to replace the lost income.

Caring responsibilities

While a partner's health may influence employment, older age is more generally a period when informal caring responsibilities are significant. In England, at age 50–64, 17% of men and 24% of women provided at least one hour per week of informal care for somebody (DWP, 2014b: 35). At age 65+, around 15% of men and 13% of women provided this care on a weekly basis. The hours of care provided tended to be fairly polarised, with individuals typically providing 1–19 or 50+ hours a week. This care might be provided to parents, partners, children, friends or neighbours, or parents-in-law/other relatives. In some instances, individuals provide care to multiple generations of family members, including parents and parents-in-law, children, and grandchildren. There is limited research on the impact of caring on employment beyond age 65, and a lack of comparable caring variables in ELSA or the HRS. However, caring responsibilities are known to reduce the likelihood of working before people reach age 65. In the UK in 2010, around 12% of economically inactive individuals aged between 50 and state pension age were caring for a sick/disabled or elderly person for 20+ hours a week; this compares with only 3% of workers of this age (DWP, 2014b: 36). The amount of care provided seems to be an influence on early exit from employment – it is men and women providing 20+ hours of care a week who are most likely to be inactive. Research covering people aged over 50 in other EU countries also finds that 'informal-care provision was associated with significant lower employment probability for both men and women' (Bolin et al, 2008: 728).

Research from the US also provides evidence that the provision of care in the period leading up to 65 is common, and that this care influences employment exit. Lee and Tang (2015: 471) find that 30.4% of respondents to the 2004 HRS aged 50–61 took part in at least one type of caring role: 4.2% of respondents were spousal carers;

20% cared for parents (100+ hours a year); and 15% looked after their grandchildren (100+ hours a year) – 4% of individuals were involved in two or more caring roles. Lee and Tang's (2015) logistic regression analysis found that, after controlling for a range of other factors, caring significantly reduced the likelihood of working for women but not men. Note that personal care (which excludes errands) was provided by 5.6% of the total male and female sample. Likewise, women looking after a grandchild had a statistically significant reduction in the likelihood of working. Finally, women performing multiple roles had a reduced likelihood of working. It is suggested that men typically have greater financial pressures to remain in employment, hence the fact that male carers are not more likely to leave work than their caring counterparts. It may also be possible that men can accommodate caring and working because they do less caring. Overall, the preceding research suggests that in the case of women in particular, caring is likely to be an important reason why people leave work in their 50s and early 60s in both countries. Once out of work, we can hypothesise, it will be less likely that they will be in work beyond age 65.

Research also suggests that caring for grandchildren influences employment (Minkler and Fuller-Thomson, 2000; Wheelock and Jones, 2002; Hughes et al, 2007; Koslowski, 2009; Wellard, 2011). Grandparent relationships are common in this age group. Over 60% of people aged 65–74 in the UK had a grandchild aged under 16 in 2009 (Wellard, 2011: 6). We saw earlier that according to Lee and Tang (2015), 15% of US grandparents aged 50–61 in 2004 looked after their grandchildren for at least 100 hours that year. However, broader estimates of grandparent care provision vary according to the measure of grandparent care used, the survey and the age group under investigation. Examination of the HRS by the current author showed that 30% of people aged 65–74 cared for a grandchild for at least 100 hours in the previous year; there was no difference in this regard between men and women. The proportion caring would also be higher if the number of hours of care was not specified. According to analysis of the British Social Attitudes Survey, 63% of grandparents say that they provide at least some care for their grandchildren. When we look at the number of hours they say that they provide, we can see that a significant minority provide at least 10 hours a week: 19% of grandmothers and 14% of grandfathers (Wellard, 2011: 12). In both countries, high childcare costs for working parents have helped create a need for grandparent care (Glaser et al, 2010; Harrington Meyer, 2014).

While there is an appreciation of the amount of care provided, there is much less UK research on the impact of this on employment.

Grandparents who work are slightly more likely to provide at least some care than those who are retired (Wellard, 2011: 15). However, this includes grandparents providing small amounts of care and does not take into account the fact that working grandparents are likely to be younger. When one looks at the employment status of grandparents providing care, we see that retirees are the largest group (Wellard, 2011: 16). Qualitative research suggests that some women may be retiring to help look after grandchildren (Loretto and Vickerstaff, 2013). There is, however, a need for much more research on this, particularly in relation to grandparents aged over 65. In relation to England, ELSA contains relatively little data on grandparenting to be analysed. In relation to the US, Lee and Tang's (2015) results from the HRS relate to people aged 50–61; the influence of grandparenting on employment may change after age 62, when Social Security becomes available. Teasing out the conditions under which grandparent care influences employment beyond age 65 is likely to be complex, however.

Finally, we should also consider the consequences for older individuals who combine care with work in older age. Harrington Meyer (2014) conducted qualitative interviews with grandmothers in the US who combined employment with looking after their grandchildren. She found that many felt pressurised by the intensive nature of having to combine work, typically full-time, with caring. We need to consider factors such as this when identifying policies to arrive at more equitable outcomes for older people in Chapter Seven.

Conclusions and discussion

This chapter has examined the influence of work capability on employment at age 65+. The analysis suggests that education has an important influence on whether or not somebody works. In both countries, individuals with higher education were twice as likely to work as individuals with below high school qualifications. This higher likelihood of working among the educated remained statistically significant in both countries after controlling for other factors such as health (albeit with reduced differences between the groups). In both countries, high qualifications were associated with remaining in a long-held job past age 65 ('Stayers'), and of moving jobs or returning to work following an absence. Education therefore appears to help provide stable careers that enable continued employment (Blekesuane et al, 2008), while making it possible to compete more easily with younger people for jobs (Wang et al, 2008). In both countries, low qualifications were associated with being out of employment for the decade leading up to being 65–74 in 2012.

While the effect of education on employment appears to have been broadly similar in both countries, the chapter indicates that Americans were far more highly educated than their English counterparts. This can be traced back to US 'life-course policies' that have sought to promote self-reliance (see Chapter One). There are good reasons to assume that the higher educational levels of Americans help explain why employment at 65+ is so much higher than in the UK. Previous US researchers have made the link between educational levels and employment levels. For example, analysis by Burtless (2013: 4) suggests that between 1985 and 2010, 'over half of the increase in older men's participation is traceable to gains in educational attainment'. The low educational attainment of many older people in the UK may present a particularly big problem for those seeking work. Kanabar (2012: 30) suggests that one of the probable reasons why he found less 'unretirement' in England, compared with the US studies, is that Americans are much more highly educated. In the UK, there are big educational disparities between older and younger cohorts; these disparities will decline over time, but a generational education gap will remain in the coming decades (see Chapter Seven). Given this, it is questionable whether we will see the level of movement into new jobs past 65 found in the US; Chapter Four certainly did not indicate that this was the case. This leads us to question whether we will see US levels of employment at age 65 in England/the UK.

More broadly, this chapter found that health conditions were widely reported among the 65+ age group, and that these were associated with a lower likelihood of being in employment. In this context, it is interesting to note that, after controlling for other factors, individuals with health conditions were more likely to work if they had higher levels of education. Presumably, this is because qualifications enabled people to have the kinds of jobs that could be performed with health limitations. The question, therefore, is not just *whether* people have health constraints, but if they are able to overcome them and remain in work. Once again, the low-skilled are at a disadvantage in this regard.

Finally, health and caring responsibilities may influence an individual's propensity to work at 65+. In both countries, many older people were engaged in caring for others. US evidence covering people prior to age 65 suggested that caring responsibilities increased the likelihood of women leaving work. Once out of work, it is fair to hypothesise that many probably did not return. The chapter also found that the health of a partner is likely to influence employment, although the impact of this may pull in opposite directions. If a partner has poor health, an individual may have to leave work to care for them, or they may have to continue working in order to make up for the lost income.

Taking all these findings together, it is clear that work–capability issues mean that employment past age 65 is likely to be far from universal in the context of state pension age rises. Given that employment is most common among the educated and healthy, this raises the question of whether or not people working at 65+ are doing so because of 'choice' rather than financial constraint. This is something we examine next in the final empirical chapter.

SIX

The choice to work at age 65+?

Introduction

As we saw in Part One of the book, state pension ages in the US and the UK are to rise significantly in the coming years. Prior to this, however, policy has sought to promote continued employment beyond age 65, particularly in the case of those with inadequate retirement incomes. While finances are therefore a key rationale for extended working lives, analysis in Chapter Five suggests that employment at 65+ was actually most common among the highly educated and healthy. This raises the question of whether employment at this age is simply a 'free choice', rather than the result of financial constraints. In this final empirical chapter, we investigate whether this is the case through an analysis of the English Longitudinal Study of Ageing (ELSA) and the US Health and Retirement Study (HRS). The chapter examines the influence of shared leisure within couples, alongside the stated motivations for working given by people. It also analyses the relationship between financial resources and employment. It finds that the richest appear most likely to work, and the poorest least. However, between these two extremes, there are significant numbers of Americans working for financial reasons. The 'choice' to work is therefore subject to considerable constraint. In England, there is less evidence of financially motivated employment, although it is predicted that this will change following the abolition of mandatory retirement. Although the analysis here is based on England, we can reasonably draw this conclusion for the UK as a whole (see statistical appendix).

The choice to work?

Couples and shared leisure?

In terms of examining potential motives to work, it is useful to start not with the individual, but with the household. It is important to remember that people make decisions about work and retirement in a household context (Loretto and Vickerstaff, 2013). US research finds considerable evidence for joint retirement, namely, people choosing to retire at the same time as their partner or within 18 months (Blau, 1998; Gustman and Steinmeier, 2002; Ho and Raymo, 2009). Ho and Raymo's (2009) analysis of the HRS (covering 1992 to 2004) finds that around a quarter of couples in the US synchronised their retirement timing. US research suggests that joint retirement represents planned behaviour to a considerable degree, and that it cannot be explained with reference to financial incentives. Instead, Blau (1998) argues that it relates to 'preferences for sharing leisure' (Blau, 1998: 622). Blau's (1998) analysis relates to the 1960s and 1970s, but recent research provides some support for the importance of leisure preferences (see Ho and Raymo, 2009: 156). Gustman and Steinmeier (2002: 28), for example, find that 'a measure of how much each spouse values being able to spend time in retirement with the other accounts for a good portion of the apparent interdependence in retirement timing'. Although there is less UK-based research on this topic, Banks and Tetlow's (2008: 11) analysis of ELSA found what they referred to as 'complementarities in leisure amongst [older] couples'. Individuals with working partners were consequently less likely to leave full-time work than those with non-working partners, and more likely to return to employment or work past state pension age (see also Smeaton and McKay, 2003).

While recognising that joint retirement affects significant numbers, some researchers have questioned whether notions of shared leisure are too simplistic. Qualitative research by Loretto and Vickerstaff (2013) found that half of their sample retired, or expected to retire, jointly. However, such individuals were slightly more likely to say that they were retiring to do activities on an individual basis, rather than as part of a couple. Men expressed the meaning of retirement as freedom to pursue hobbies; women, on the other hand, identified freedom from having to juggle paid work and domestic commitments. The research suggested that it was more common for the man to leave work first, and the woman to follow thereafter, described as the 'domination of the male breadwinner's circumstances and decisions' (Loretto and Vickerstaff, 2013: 76). Female employment was therefore influenced more strongly by that of the partner than was the case with men. This is consistent with US research (see Ho and Raymo, 2009: 158), which also suggests that women have been more likely than men to retire in response to pressure from a partner (Szinovacz and DeViney, 2000). Loretto and Vickerstaff's (2013) research, which focused primarily on low- and middle-income couples, found that following a husband into retirement was often seen as an opportunity to leave a boring job.

We might expect joint retirement to have a number of implications for employment beyond age 65. We would expect the presence of a partner in work to increase the likelihood of employment, and the presence of a non-working partner to reduce it. If a partner is still in employment, they may be inclined to remain in work. As men tend to be the older person within a partnership, we would expect this to contribute to the higher likelihood of men working past age 65. Finally, we expect an increased likelihood of working when there is an employed partner to not be explained by financial or other factors.

In order to explore this, Table 6.1 presents the percentage probability of working at age 65–74 in 2010, broken down by partnership status. Partnered individuals are married or part of a cohabiting couple; percentage probabilities of employment are given separately for those with and without working partners. For a small third category, we do not know the employment status of their partner. We also include 'single' individuals, those without a partner due to divorce, separation, widowhood or never having married. It is recognised that single people are a diverse group, but sample size issues make it difficult to disaggregate them further for men and women in both countries. Previous research suggests that older divorced women have comparatively high rates of employment, in the form of those returning to employment following retirement in the US (Pleau, 2010) or working beyond state pension age in the UK (Smeaton and McKay, 2003). This may be due to low retirement incomes as a result of divorce, alongside the positive social aspect of working.

The results in Table 6.1 are presented as 'unadjusted' and 'adjusted' percentage probabilities of working, as was the case in some of the analysis in Chapter Five. Unadjusted percentage probabilities represent the percentages working in each partnership group. They are derived from logistic regression analyses examining whether an individual is in employment or not using partnership status as the sole independent variable. The coefficients from these analyses were converted into Average Adjusted Predictions (AAPs), as per the suggestion of Williams (2012), and then converted into percentage probabilities by multiplying them by 100. Adjusted percentage probabilities are also presented because we are interested in whether the predicted likelihood of working varies between groups *after we take into account the potential impact of other influences*. For example, it might be the case that employment is high among people with a working partner because these individuals tend to be more highly educated or healthier. We therefore want to 'control' for the potential influence of other factors. The factors controlled for in the adjusted results are wealth, private

Table 6.1: Percentage probabilities of working at 65–74 by partnership status, 2010

	All		Men		Women	
	% probability of working		% probability of working		% probability of working	
	Unadjusted	Adjusted (controls for other factors)	Unadjusted	Adjusted (controls for other factors)	Unadjusted	Adjusted (controls for other factors)
USA						
Partnered, partner not working (ref)	24.5	24.0	30.3	30.5	17.5	18.0
Partnered, partner working	43.1***	38.2***	49.5***	47.3***	35.5***	30.0***
Partnered, partner's work status unknown	34.9	30.1	41.4	35.8	23.4	25.0
Single	26.7	30.8**	26.6	29.0	26.8***	28.6***
All	29.5	N/A	34.7	33.0	24.8	26.1
England						
Partnered, partner not working (ref)	9.6	9.7	13.3	13.9	5.8	5.8
Partnered, partner working	38.5***	29.6***	44.2***	36.8***	30.4***	23.5***
Partnered, partner's work status unknown	17.2	15.4	18.3	15.7	16.2	13.3
Single	12.6*	15.1**	14.8	16.5	11.2**	13.2***
All	14.2	N/A	18.5	17.0	10.3	11.4
Base n USA	5399		2329		3070	
Base n England	2774		1281		1493	

Notes: Percentage probabilities are derived from Average Adjusted Probabilities (AAPs) from logistic regression analysis. 'Adjusted' probabilities control for the age, health, education, pension status, home ownership status, gender and wealth (see the statistical appendix). Difference from the reference category is statistically significant at the following levels: *** = $p < 0.001$; ** = $p < 0.01$; * = $p < 0.05$; ° = $p < 0.10$.
Source: Author's analysis of ELSA 2010 wave and HRS 2010 wave.

pension coverage, housing status; self-rated health, the number of health limitations, qualifications held and age (for more on the method used and the variables constructed, see Chapter Five and the statistical appendix).

What is most notable from Table 6.1 is the extent to which having a working partner increases the likelihood of working at age 65–74.

This household effect was particularly important in the case of England. The likelihood of working if an individual had an employed partner was similarly high in both countries: 43.1% in the US and 38.5% in England. However, in cases were a partner was not working, employment rates in the US were much higher than in England (24.5% compared with 9.6%). Women in both countries were less likely to work than men if they had a non-working partner, which is consistent with female employment being more influenced by that of a partner. It is interesting, however, that employment among women in England appears to be particularly influenced by a partner's employment status. The likelihood of employment for an Englishwoman with a non-working partner was only 5.8%; for women with a working partner, the likelihood of being employed was five times that level (30.4%).

One interpretation of the big disparity in employment between those with working and non-working partners in England is the greater effort required to remain in employment. Employers could automatically retire off people at 65 in 2010, and it was down to the employee to make a convincing case for staying on. In such instances, where a partner was already retired, it may have been difficult within the household to justify continuing to work given the expectation that you would leave. In the case of women, as many in the UK have had relatively marginal part-time careers, there may have been a stronger desire to follow their husbands into retirement (Loretto and Vickerstaff, 2015). In the US, where women are likely to have had full-time careers, their propensity to work if they have a non-working partner may be stronger (see Chapter One). Nevertheless, in both countries, spousal employment is an important influence on whether somebody remains in work. All the employment differences between those with working and non-working partners were statistically significant, and remained so when other factors such as wealth were taken into account in the adjusted results. This suggests that leisure preferences probably did play an important part, although we also need to recognise that some individuals will be inactive for other household reasons, such as the ill-health of a partner (see Chapter Five). It is therefore important to look at the motivations that people explicitly say that they have for working beyond 65.

Motivations to work

One of the common justifications for extended working lives is the argument that people want to stay on in employment. The UK Pensions Minister, Ross Altmann, for example, stated in her report *A new vision for older workers* that 'Older people's attitudes are changing – they want to work longer' (Altmann, 2015: 15). Altmann points out that around half of the over 50s surveyed 'want' to work at age 65–69. Survey evidence reported by Rix (2008: 78) likewise reveals that around 80% of surveyed individuals in the US expected to work in retirement, and many baby-boomers contend that they never expect to retire. While these projections may be credible, they tell us less about *why* people have a preference for working beyond their mid-60s instead of retiring.

Research appears to suggest that older people's motivations to work change as they age, so the likelihood of working beyond age 65 may be influenced by this. Inceoglu et al (2011: 300), for example, compares attitudes across age groups and argue that a 'shift in people's motives rather than a general decline in motivation [occurs] with age: older employees were less motivated by extrinsically but more by intrinsically rewarding job features'. Consistent with this, Scherger et al's (2012: 59) analysis of ELSA and the German Ageing Survey found that in both countries, two thirds of people working past pension age were doing so for non-financial reasons. It is plausible that attitudes to employment do change as people age, and we should recognise the need to consider how rewarding work is. However, we should be cautious about drawing the conclusion that an intrinsic desire to work is evident in most people over the age of 65. This analysis reflects a 'survivor effect' – those people with less intrinsic interest in work may already be out of employment, leaving a disproportionately high number of people who really want to be there. McNair's (2006) analysis of older people in the UK revealed that positive attitudes to work declined among those in their early 50s, and rose again among people in their 60s. The explanation given is one of 'a "shaking out" of the labour market in the mid fifties, when many disaffected or demotivated people leave, creating a distinct later life labour market of people who are much more highly motivated' (McNair, 2006: 491). Similarly, Smeaton et al's (2009: 37) survey of older workers found that financial considerations were the biggest reason for working between 50 and 64. At age 65–74, however, enjoyment of work becomes the biggest motivator, experienced by a quarter of respondents. We may expect more people to stay on for financial reasons in the UK as it becomes easier to remain in work following the abolition of mandatory retirement. An early indication of this may be the fact that half of older people in 2008 planning to work after state pension age said that this was because they could not afford to retire (Smeaton et al, 2009). In the past, individuals in this position were likely to have moved into retirement at normal pension age, with little expectation that there was any alternative (Vickerstaff, 2006).

Given the financial rationale for abolishing mandatory retirement in the US in 1986, this raises the question of whether those opting to work beyond 65 conceptualise this as being financially motivated. As we saw in Chapter Two, retirement incomes in the UK have been lower than those in the US, and US experience may provide some indication of the extent to which financially motivated employment will increase. Current research on this is limited, so we present analysis from a one-off self-completion questionnaire given to half of the US HRS sample in 2008. Employed respondents were asked whether they would like to leave work now but will stay because they need the money. If we categorise individuals answering 'yes' as being financially motivated, we can see that two thirds of individuals (65%) aged 65–74 were in this category (see Table 6.2). This is a relatively high percentage when one considers that the measure being used involves people not being able to leave work for perceived financial reasons. For England, the extent to which employment is financially motivated is gauged with a question asked in ELSA in 2008 about why people over state pension age were still in employment. Two responses to this question are categorised as indicating financial motivations for working in Table 6.2: not being able to afford to retire, which is closest to the US measure; and working to improve finances. In England, only a third of workers aged 65–74 were in this broad financially motivated group, split between those feeling financially unable to retire and those seeking to improve their financial position. Of the remaining individuals, the biggest reasons given for working were that they enjoyed their job/ working (42.8%) or to keep fit and active (16.6%). This is consistent with Scherger et al's (2012) analysis, which suggested that workers over state pension age in England were commonly intrinsically motivated; this may change, however, now that people have the option to continue working beyond age 65.

In order to better understand work motivations, it is useful to look at the factors influencing whether somebody was working for perceived financial reasons. We should not automatically assume that individuals with low financial resources are necessarily in employment because they lack the means to retire. At the same time, we should not assume that financially better-off individuals are *not* working for financial reasons. What constitutes having enough money to retire may vary considerably between individuals, depending upon their lifestyle expectations. In a UK context, where retirement at age 65 is seen as inevitable, individuals may be relatively accepting, or at least

Table 6.2: Stated motives for working at age 65–74 in 2008

	Motive for working	% of workers	95% confidence interval
USA			
Financial motives	Would like to stop work but needs the money	65.5	(61.4–69.5)
Non-financial motives	Not prevented from leaving due to money	34.5	(30.5–38.6)
Total		100%	
Base		700	
England			
Financial motives	Not afford to retire/improve financial position	32.3	
	– Could not afford to retire	17.4	(13.8–21.8)
	– To improve pension/financial position	14.9	(11.5–19.1)
Non-financial motives	Did not know what to do after stopped working	4.4	(2.7–7.2)
	enjoyed job/working	42.8	(37.7–48.0)
	to keep fit and active	16.6	(13.2–20.8)
	to retire at the same time as partner	0.9	(0.3–2.9)
	persuaded by employer to stay on	2.9	(1.6–5.3)
Total		100%	
Base		381	

Source: Author's analysis of ELSA 2008 wave and HRS 2008 wave.

stoical, about the fact that incomes will decline in retirement (see, eg, Vickerstaff et al, 2008). When people have the right to continue in their jobs beyond age 65, as in the US, and can exert greater control over their retirement timing, their expectations may change. Retirement may therefore become more of a financial decision in contexts where mandatory retirement does not exist (Shultz et al, 1998), and individuals may feel a greater perceived need to delay retirement or not retire at all. Evidence of shifting US attitudes is identified by Shultz et al (1998: 47): 'Research before 1980 indicates that as long as income and health are satisfactory, individuals find retirement to be satisfactory.… After 1980, more retired individuals would have preferred to remain in the workforce for increased income'. In other words, expectations about what constitutes a decent retirement income shifted after individuals were given the opportunity to work past age 65.

Table 6.3 gives the percentage probabilities of being a financially motivated worker, rather than a non-financially motivated worker, in the US. These probabilities are given for men and women in different financial, qualification, health and partnership categories. Financial categories include: household wealth quartiles (excluding housing and pensions) equivalised to the individual level; whether an individual has a private pension; and housing status. These variables are described in more depth in the statistical appendix. Adjusted percentage probabilities represent the likelihood of being financially motivated if individuals in a particular category, for example, 'women', had average scores on all the other variables included in the regression.

Looking at the column for men and women combined, those most likely to be working for financial reasons are fairly predictable: those in the lower wealth quartiles; those with no private pension; and those either buying or renting their own home. While these results are perhaps not surprising, the extent of financial motivation among the poorest groups is striking, especially when you consider that this means they would rather not be in employment at all: 82.4% of those in the lowest wealth quintile were financially motivated workers, as were 75.4% of those without a private pension and over 70% of home buyers/renters. In all these instances, the probability of being financially motivated was significantly higher, in terms of statistical significance, than those in the most advantageous financial positions. Likewise, the vast majority of those working with below secondary qualifications were financially motivated (83.1%), as were those working in poor/fair health (78.8%). The adjusted results show that the higher likelihood of people working in these categories disappears once we control for other factors such as wealth. Clearly, workers in the poorest groups were in jobs that they would rather not be doing, so the extent to which working past 65 is a choice, as some assert, depends upon an individual's financial position. Nevertheless, we need to bear in mind that the poorest groups were least likely to be working in the first place, as we will see.

Although financial motivations were most frequent among the poorest workers, they were not uncommon among those in seemingly more advantaged positions. For example, 39.3% of those in the top wealth quintile were financially motivated, as were 59.3% of those with private pensions and 54.5% of homeowners. Financially motivated employment is clearly widespread in the US context, which may,

Table 6.3: Percentage probabilities of workers aged 65–74 being financially motivated, US

	All		Men		Women	
	% probability of being financially motivated		% probability of being financially motivated		% probability of being financially motivated	
	Unadjusted	Adjusted (controls for other factors)	Unadjusted	Adjusted (controls for other factors)	Unadjusted	Adjusted (controls for other factors)
1. Male (ref)	64.1	66.1				
2. Female	67.3	64.7				
1st wealth quartile (ref)	39.3	45.6	42.6	51.3	33.8	36.8
2nd wealth quartile	63.3***	63.9**	59.9*	60.4	69.3***	68.3**
3rd wealth quartile	79.1***	76.7***	78.1***	73.5**	80.1***	78.8***
4th wealth quartile	82.4***	79.4***	85.0***	80.1***	80.1***	80.1***
No private pension (ref)	75.4	70.9	79.2	74.0	71.7	68.0
Has got private pension	59.3***	62.4*	56.2***	59.6*	63.8	66.8
Own home (ref)	54.5	59.0	50.9	53.8	58.7	63.9
Buying home	77.0***	75.6***	76.7***	75.6***	77.5**	74.4
Renting home	70.1*	57.8	66.9°	54.7	72.0°	64.1
College+ (ref)	55.1	63.3	52.3	61.1	60.9	66.9
Some college	64.5	63.3	60.3	58.2	68.2	68.6
High school	65.3°	64.0	67.0°	67.1	63.1	63.4
Below high school	83.1***	65.6 / 72.1	87.9***	74.2	78.8°	72.8
Fair/poor health (ref)	78.8		83.1	77.9	74.7	67.0
Good health	62.1***	71.4 / 64.2	59.9***	61.5**	65.0	67.4
Partnered, no working partner (ref)	63.6		61.6	61.5	68.0	68.2

	All		Men		Women	
	% probability of being financially motivated		% probability of being financially motivated		% probability of being financially motivated	
	Unadjusted	Adjusted (controls for other factors)	Unadjusted	Adjusted (controls for other factors)	Unadjusted	Adjusted (controls for other factors)
Partnered, working partner	64.1	63.7	66.5	64.6	59.5	67.5
Partnered, unknown if partners work	45.4	65.2	54.4	66.1	22.3**	26.3*
Single	70.6	56.0	67.9	69.0	71.6	67.9
Base n	700	700	348	348	352	352

Notes: Percentage probabilities are derived from AAPs from logistic regression analysis. 'Adjusted' probabilities control for age, health and the other variables listed in the table. For the definition of financially motivated employment, see Table 6.2 and the text. Difference from the reference category is statistically significant at the following levels: *** = $p < 0.001$; ** = $p < 0.01$; * = $p < 0.05$; ° = $p < 0.10$. Source: Author's analysis of HRS 2008 wave.

in part, relate to increased expectations about necessary retirement incomes compared with the past.

Table 6.3 shows that there is no significant difference between male and female workers in their propensity to be financially motivated. The separate results for men and women show that the extent to which employment is financially motivated is heavily influenced by household resources. For example, financially motivated employment was higher for men and women in the lowest wealth quartiles and among those buying their home. Men were also more likely to be financially motivated if they had no pension, whereas for women, there was no significant difference between those with and without pensions. This suggests that financially motivated female employment may result more from household- than individual-level resources. It should also be noted that financially motivated employment did not differ significantly between different partnership groups, with the exception of women with a partner whose employment status was unknown. Why this exception should be the case is unclear.

Table 6.4 presents the equivalent results for England. Across the table as a whole, we see that financial motivations were less common than in the US. Financial motivations, as we might predict, were highest among those in the poorest wealth quartile (47.3%), those with no pension (43.3%) and those buying or renting their home (50.9% and

Table 6.4: Percentage probabilities of workers aged 65–74 being financially motivated, England

	All		Men		Women	
	% probability of being financially motivated		% probability of being financially motivated		% probability of being financially motivated	
	Unadjusted	Adjusted (controls for other factors)	Unadjusted	Adjusted (controls for other factors)	Unadjusted	Adjusted (controls for other factors)
1. Male (ref)	30.2	31.4				
2. Female	35.5	33.7				
1st wealth quartile (ref)	24.0	26.5	20.9	24.5	29.1	28.8
2nd wealth quartile	29.8	30.5	26.2	27.6	34.0	35.0
3rd wealth quartile	36.6°	36.8	32.0	31.7	45.1	44.6
4th wealth quartile	47.3**	39.7	53.6**	42.7	38.7	37.6
No private pension (ref)	43.0	38.9	55.1	47.2	36.3	36.1
Has got private pension	28.9*	30.0	25.9**	27.1**	35.0	35.1
Own home (ref)	26.9	28.3	23.8	27.1	31.3	30.9
Buying home	50.9**	50.6**	46.4*	47.3*	56.9*	55.9*
Renting home	43.3*	35.6	46.3*	29.9	36.9	40.3
College+ (ref)	21.5	26.7	19.5	24.3	27.3	31.0
Some college	30.9	30.3	27.7	28.7	34.9	33.4
High school	36.0*	37.4	35.5°	34.2	37.1	38.0
Below high school	37.1*	33.4	36.6*	32.4	37.6	36.9
Fair/poor health (ref)	40.9	38.5	48.4	43.1	27.3	27.8
Good health	31.2	31.5	27.6	28.3	36.5	36.4

	All		Men		Women	
	% probability of being financially motivated		% probability of being financially motivated		% probability of being financially motivated	
	Unadjusted	Adjusted (controls for other factors)	Unadjusted	Adjusted (controls for other factors)	Unadjusted	Adjusted (controls for other factors)
Partnered, no working partner (ref)	28.0	28.6	28.5	28.6	26.8	28.2
Partnered, working partner	33.4	33.9	31.2	32.5	37.6	36.5
Partnered, unknown if partners work	53.5°	55.7*	39.5	39.9	67.6*	69.5*
Single	33.7	31.5	30.1	26.7	36.0	35.3
Base *n*	381	381	223	223	158	158

Notes: Percentage probabilities are derived from AAPs from logistic regression analysis. 'Adjusted' probabilities control for age, health and the other variables listed in the table. For the definition of financially motivated employment, see Table 6.2 and the text. Difference from the reference category is statistically significant at the following levels: *** = $p < 0.001$; ** = $p < 0.01$; * = $p < 0.05$; ° = $p < 0.10$. Source: Author's analysis of ELSA 2008 wave.

43.3%, respectively). This, of course, nevertheless means that around half of individuals in these 'low-income' groups were working for non-financial reasons. This may reflect the fact that it was harder for individuals to remain in work beyond age 65 in England at this time; therefore, as with other income groups, employment was concentrated among those with strong intrinsic work motivations. Among the poorest, some will be little better off financially from working due to losing benefits (see Lain, 2011). In this instance, intrinsic motivations may be important for these individuals to be in work. As we will see in the next section, employment among those with low wealth was particularly low in England around this time, and these individuals may consequently be fairly atypical. As with the US, we see that working men without a pension were significantly more likely to be working for financial reasons, which was not the case for women. Female workers (and men) had a high likelihood of being in financially motivated employment if they were buying their house, however. This, once again, is consistent with women being more likely to work due to household- rather than individual-level finances. Consistent with this, previous research suggests that female employment is more responsive to incentives in a partner's pension than their own (Lain, 2015); this is perhaps unsurprising given that women have historically accumulated smaller retirement incomes than men (Ginn, 2003).

In sum, Americans exhibited a much higher likelihood of being in work for financial reasons than their English counterparts. The higher US employment rates at all wealth levels suggest that in the UK, financially motivated employment is likely to rise following the abolition of mandatory retirement in 2011.

The influence of financial resources on employment

Wealth, home ownership and pensions

While workers with low retirement resources are more likely to be working for financial reasons, it is important to ascertain how common working is among this group. There are a number of reasons for expecting poorer individuals to have a *reduced* likelihood of working overall. We know that poorer people are more likely to have low levels of health and education, for example, and these factors are known to reduce the likelihood of employment (see Chapter Five). Examining the financial position of people working beyond 65 is not straightforward, however, and the picture presented may depend upon the measures of financial resources used (see Lain, 2015). In their examination of people working past state pension age, Smeaton and Mckay (2003: 229) conclude that:

> Working [past state pension age] is associated with financial hardship such as: the absence of an occupational pension, income below £100 for men, still paying a mortgage and, for women, being separated or divorced.... [However,] Those in most extreme need with very low savings have often experienced a lifetime of disadvantage with attenuated employment opportunities leading to reliance upon state benefits, which in turn can function as an employment disincentive.

According to this assessment, working past pension age may be most commonly associated with financial disadvantage, except for those in most extreme need. However, this may underestimate the extent to which wealthier individuals were working. For example, 'absence of an occupational pension' appears to refer to pensions *received*, and a number of these individuals were likely to have merely deferred their pension until they retired. Indeed, in the early 2000s, there were legal constraints on drawing a pension from an employer you were working for (Meadows, 2003: 31). Likewise, the 'income' referred to in the previous quote relates to *non-earnings income*, which is likely to be low for workers deferring their occupational, personal or state pensions (Lain, 2011: 499). Similar conclusions might also be drawn from US research by Parries and Sommers (1994). This research found that working in older age was associated with low levels of non-wage income in the US. Once again, this may reflect the fact that individuals have pensions that they have deferred until retirement, and hence have a low non-wage income.

Research that looks at wealth instead of income, thereby avoiding issues around pension deferral, presents a different picture. For example, from such an approach, Haider and Loughran (2001) conclude that 'labour supply [in the US] is concentrated among the most educated, wealthiest and healthiest elderly'. Closer inspection of these results suggests that employment was most common among the wealthiest, but was by no means confined to this group; the poorest segment nevertheless had the least likelihood of working. Analysis of ELSA suggests that after age 65, there is linear relationship between work and wealth, with increasing employment as you move up the wealth quintiles (Crawford and Tetlow, 2010: 21). The analysis also suggests that those in the lowest wealth quintile had a reduced likelihood of working from age 50 upwards. Lain (2011) compares employment by non-pension wealth in the US and England past age 65 in 2002; he finds that in both countries, the wealthiest quintiles are most likely to work and the poorest quintiles are least likely to be in employment. He also finds that once you control for health and education, differences in the propensity to work across wealth quartiles disappeared in the US, but not entirely in England. He concludes that health and education are likely to be significant factors in preventing those with low wealth from working. At the same time, in the case of England, he suggests that means-tested benefits lost as a result of working may have discouraged employment among some in the poorest segment.

Table 6.5 presents percentage probabilities of working in 2010 at different wealth quartiles in both countries. The measure of wealth used is non-housing, non-pension household wealth. In this instance, therefore, wealth includes savings, investments, businesses and 'other' property/real estate, but excludes pension assets and the value of the main residence. Private pensions and housing ownership status are instead included as separate variables in Table 6.5. Wealth is derived from the 'household' level, which, in this instance, may be an individual or a couple. In the case of people living in couples, we have equivalised household wealth to the individual level using the Organisation for

145

Economic Co-operation and Development (OECD)–modified scale (OECD, no date). This assumes that a couple needs 1.5 times the income or wealth of a single person to have an equivalent standard of

Table 6.5: Percentage probabilities of working at age 65–74, by finances, 2010

	All		Men		Women	
	% probability of working		% probability of working		% probability of working	
	Unadjusted	Adjusted (controls for other factors)	Unadjusted	Adjusted (controls for other factors)	Unadjusted	Adjusted (controls for other factors)
USA						
1st wealth quartile (ref)	34.9	29.8	41.6	37.4	28.5	23.5
2nd wealth quartile	31.2°	28.3	36.7	33.9	25.6	23.3
3rd wealth quartile	28.7**	29.7	34.0*	34.9	24.2°	24.7
4th wealth quartile	23.1***	30.3	25.3***	31.8°	21.4**	28.6*
No private pension (ref)	24.4	27.9	32.2	36.7	18.7	21.0
Has got private pension	32.9***	30.3	36.1*	33.7	29.7***	27.4°
Own home (ref)	27.6	27.9	33.6	33.7	22.6	22.7
Buying home	36.8***	32.8**	40.8***	37.6°	32.4***	28.5**
Renting home	21.9*	28.0	23.9*	30.8	20.6	25.9
England						
1st wealth quartile (ref)	19.3	15.2	23.7	19.5	14.5	11.7
2nd wealth quartile	13.9**	13.2	17.9°	17.8	10.3°	9.6
3rd wealth quartile	13.8**	15.3	18.8	20.2	9.6°	10.6
4th wealth quartile	9.8**	12.8	12.9**	15.9	7.5**	9.2
No private pension (ref)	10.9	15.3	17.5	23.1	8.8	10.7
Has got private pension	15.5**	13.9	18.7	18.0	11.4	10.2
Own home (ref)	13.5	13.2	17.4	16.5	10.1	10.1

	All		Men		Women	
	% probability of working		% probability of working		% probability of working	
	Unadjusted	Adjusted (controls for other factors)	Unadjusted	Adjusted (controls for other factors)	Unadjusted	Adjusted (controls for other factors)
Buying home	28.6***	21.0**	38.0***	29.6**	18.9*	13.2
Renting home	10.8	15.5	13.9	22.3	7.8	9.8
Base n USA	5399		2329		3070	
Base n England	2774		1281		1493	

Notes: Percentage probabilities are derived from AAPs from logistic regression analysis. 'Adjusted' probabilities control for age, education, the number of activities of daily living (ADL) health limits, partnership status and the other variables included in the table. Difference from the reference category is statistically significant at the following levels: *** = $p < 0.001$; ** = $p < 0.01$; * = $p < 0.05$; ° = $p < 0.10$. Source: Author's analysis of ELSA 2010 wave and HRS 2010 wave.

living. Using this equivalised wealth, we then allocated individuals to four equally sized wealth quintiles.

The results in Table 6.5 are consistent with previous research in showing that the wealthiest quartile were significantly more likely to work than those below them in both countries. Just over a third of those in the richest US quartile were working (34.9%), compared with a quarter in the poorest group (23.1); this means that the richest were 1.5 times more likely to be employed. In England, those in the richest quartile were twice as likely to be employed as those the poorest quartile, with a fifth working compared with a tenth. In the US and England, those in the middle quartiles had employment rates between these two extremes. In both countries, however, these differential likelihoods of working across wealth groups disappeared once we account for differences in health, education, age and other factors (see the adjusted results). In other words, the other disadvantaged characteristics of the poorest appear to account for their lower propensity to work – when the poorest have equivalent levels of health, education and so on they are likely to work in similar numbers to the richest. Despite the financial rationale for encouraging employment beyond age 65, it therefore appears to be the case that the richest have been best able to avail themselves of these opportunities. It should be noted, however, that US employment was higher at all wealth levels than was the case in England; as a result, the richest in England were less likely to work than the poorest in the US.

The fact that there were no significant differences in the likelihood of working across the English wealth quartiles after adjusting the results for health, education and so on is a different result from Lain's (2011) analysis covering 2002. This may reflect the different measure of wealth used here (which excludes housing), and the larger number of factors controlled for in this data analysis. It may also reflect a modest increase in the propensity of the poorest to work in England relative to the richest; however, Table 6.5 nevertheless shows that employment remained low for all quartiles in England.

Breaking down the analysis by gender, Table 6.5 shows that in both countries, men and women in the bottom wealth quartiles were significantly less likely to be in work than their counterparts in the richest quartiles. In England, it was also true for both men and women that those in the top quartile were twice as likely to be employed as those in the bottom quartiles. In the case of the US, there was a bigger disparity in employment between the top and bottom quartiles for men than women. This difference could be accounted for by the particularly high level of employment among men in the richest quartile, 41.6% of whom were in employment. Clearly, this wealthy segment of men have been key beneficiaries in terms of exercising their right to work past age 65.

In addition to wealth quartiles, Table 6.5 shows the percentage probabilities of working by whether an individual has a private pension. This includes pensions identified as being received by the individual, or pensions that they are entitled to receive in future. Pensions may be from a current or former employer, or those held by an individual; pensions from current employers may have been 'earned' in the past. In the US, we include Individual Retirement Accounts because these are significant pension vehicles for the self-employed. As Table 6.5 shows, in the US and England, people with a private pension were significantly more likely in statistical terms to be in employment than those without such provision. Overall, 32.9% of those with a private pension worked in the US, compared with 24.4% of those without; in England, the corresponding figures were 15.5% versus 10.9%. This differential likelihood of working was no longer significant in either country in the adjusted results. This is consistent with the preceding analysis, which suggests that the higher rates of employment among those with some level of financial advantage are explained by wider advantages in health, education and so on.

The final financial area examined in Table 6.5 relates to housing status – whether an individual owns their own home outright, is still buying their home or is a renter. Previous research has suggested that having an outstanding mortgage increases the likelihood of working in older age, both in the US (Mann, 2011; Butrica and Karamcheva, 2013) and in the UK (Smeaton and McKay, 2003). It should be noted that it is not the level of housing wealth per se that necessarily influences employment. Bender et al (2014), for example, found that having high levels of housing wealth had no significant effect on retirement timing, presumably because people do not aim to draw on this housing equity in retirement. However, having outstanding mortgages does appear to encourage people to remain in work. There is less evidence to suggest that being in rented accommodation increases the likelihood of working in the same way, which might relate to wider disadvantages experienced by renters. Consistent with this research, Table 6.5 shows that an unpaid mortgage was an important influence on being in employment in both countries. In the US, 36.8% of individuals still paying a mortgage were in employment, which is significantly higher than the 27.6% of outright homeowners. The difference in employment rates between 'buyers' and 'owners' was particularly big in the UK: 28.6% of buyers worked, compared with only 13.5% of owners. There was noticeably high employment among men still paying off a mortgage in England, at 38%; this was close to the employment rate of their male counterparts in the US (40.8%). In neither country was the percentage probability of working high among renters. Indeed, renters in the US were significantly less likely to work than buyers, a difference that disappeared once the wider disadvantage of renters was controlled for.

In order to put these findings into context, Table 6.6 shows how common it was in both countries for people aged 65–74 to have an

Table 6.6: Private pension ownership and housing status at age 65–74, 2010

	USA			England		
	All	Men	Women	All	Men	Women
No private pension	40.5	36.5	44.0	30.2	17.1	42.2
Has got private pension	59.5	63.5	56.0	69.8	82.9	57.8
Total %	100%	100%	100%	100%	100%	100%
Own home	55.1	53.9	56.1	75.0	73.4	76.5
Buying home	29.6	33.0	26.6	7.9	8.5	7.4
Renting home	15.3	13.1	17.3	17.0	18.1	16.1
Total %	100%	100%	100%	100%	100%	100%
Base n	5445	2346	3099	2897	1354	1543

Source: Author's analysis of ELSA 2010 wave and HRS 2010 wave.

outstanding mortgage or no private pension. In the US, around 40% of individuals had no private pension, compared with 30% in the UK. The higher rate of UK private pension coverage reflects the ability of individuals to opt out of the State Earnings Related Pension (SERPs) into a private scheme. Individuals could opt in and out of SERPs over time, so a significant number of these individuals will only have had modest pension entitlements from earlier periods of employment. The disparity in pension coverage between men and women was particularly high in England: 42.2% of women had no private pension, compared with around 17.1% of men.

The differences between the countries in relation to home ownership were large. Around 30% of people in this age group were still paying off a mortgage in the US, compared with only 8% England. The US position reflects an increase in the portion of people aged over 62 with outstanding mortgage debt (Butrica and Karamcheva, 2013).

To summarise these results, the wealthiest groups in both countries appear be most likely to work. These individuals are least likely to attribute their employment to financial reasons, although a sizeable minority nevertheless do this. At the other end of the spectrum, the poorest in both countries have the lowest likelihood of working, something that largely disappears once we control for the wider disadvantages experienced by these individuals. In between these two extremes, however, we see significant numbers in the US working for financial reasons. Further pressures on these individuals to work may relate to the types of pension that these individuals hold and medical insurance. We attend to these topics next.

Pensions and medical insurance

As discussed in Chapter Two, one of the major changes to pensions in both the UK and the US is the shift away from employers providing Defined Benefit (DB) occupational pensions. The shift began in the 1980s in the US, with employers typically replacing DB pensions with Defined Contribution (DC) schemes (Friedberg and Webb, 2005). DB pensions provided a regular source of income to retirees, typically based on previous earnings, and were a key element enabling individuals to retire early or at the pension's 'normal' retirement age (Laczko and Phillipson, 1991; Hacker, 2006). Indeed, DB pensions incentivise retirement around a particular age set by the plan, after which it becomes less attractive to delay receipt and people may leave work as a result. In DC schemes, contributions are paid in, which are invested, and the pension is the lump sum accrued paid upon retirement. In these schemes, there is more incentive to continue working because another year of work represents another year of contributions to the pension lump sum. Employees take the risk that their pension investments result in a sufficient pension pot as they are not guaranteed a stream of income based on previous earnings for life. Additionally, it is known that employers in the US and the UK typically make smaller contributions into DC pensions than their DB counterparts (Hacker, 2006; ONS, 2013b). US research shows that those with DC pensions tend to retire later than those with DB pensions (Munnell et al, 2004; Freidberg and Webb, 2005). Indeed, Freidberg and Webb (2005) point to the changing pension structure as an important reason for the increase in employment among older people in the US.

As we saw in Chapter Five, in the UK, the shift away from employers providing DB pensions occurred later than in the US (Pensions Commission, 2004). At the same time, employers have been slower to introduce DC schemes, which is partly why there is a move towards auto-enrolment (see Chapter Three). However, research by Arkani and Gough (2007) suggested that those with DC pensions in 2002 expected to retire later than those with DB pensions. In both England and the US, we might therefore expect people with DC pensions to be more likely to work beyond 65. In order to investigate this, Table 6.7 presents the likelihood of working at age 65–74 in 2012, broken down by type of pension contributed to in 2002. Note that this excludes pensions from previous periods of employment, unlike Table 6.6. Table 6.7 combines DC pensions with 'hydrid' schemes for the US, which were reported by a relatively small proportion of respondents. Hybrid schemes are similar to DC pensions in that employers make contributions and a lump sum is paid in retirement. A key difference is that hybrids provide a greater degree of predictability because employers guarantee the interest rate. Nevertheless, these schemes provide similar incentives to continue working as DC schemes (Johnson and Steuerle, 2004). Note that only people working as employees in 2002 are include in Table 6.7; this therefore excludes some of the most disadvantaged individuals, who are likely to have been out of work before 2002. It also means that the employment rates of these individuals are higher than when we include people inactive in 2002.

For the US, we see that those with DB pensions in 2002 were much more likely to be out of work in 2012 at age 65–74; 33.3% of those with DB pensions worked compared with 43.3% of those with DC pensions. This pattern of lower employment for those with DB pensions was true for both men and women (although the difference was not statistically significant in the case of men). The bottom portion gives a breakdown of the percentages contributing to different types of pensions in 2002, for the purposes of context. As Table 6.7 shows, the coverage of DC pensions appears to have overtaken the coverage of DB pensions for this cohort in 2002, although the proportions with each type of scheme are similar. If we were to look at private sector workers, we would see a bigger concentration of individuals with DC schemes because DB schemes remain dominant in the public sector to a much greater degree (Johnson et al, 2010).

Table 6.7: Percentages working at age 65–74, 2012, by private pension type held by employee in 2002

	USA			England		
	All	Men	Women	All	Men	Women
Percentages working in 2012 by pension in 2002						
DB (ref)	33.3	37.0	29.0	20.4	22.4	18.4
DC/hybrid	43.3**	44.4	42.3***	21.6	22.1	20.3
Don't know	49.5°	53.3	45.1	22.7	27.3	19.3
No pension contribution	36.5	39.9	34.1	23.2	25.9	20.8
% working – all	38.1	40.7	35.7	22.0	24.0	19.8
Type of pension contributed to in 2002						
DB	31.3	35.2	27.8	33.0	32.8	33.2
DC/hybrid	33.6	33.8	33.4	15.5	21.1	9.7
Don't know	2.2	2.4	1.9	5.0	4.1	5.9
No pension contribution	32.9	28.5	36.8	46.5	42.0	51.3
Total %	100%	100%	100%	100%	100%	100%
Base	2167	941	1226	1097	539	558

Note: Excludes those not working as an employee in 2002. Difference from the reference category is statistically significant at the following levels: *** = $p < 0.001$; ** = $p < 0.01$; * = $p < 0.05$; ° = $p < 0.10$.
Source: Author's analysis of ELSA 2002 and 2012 waves and HRS 2002 and 2012 waves.

For England, we see no significant difference in employment between those with DB, DC or no pension at all in 2002. This may perhaps seem strange given Arkani and Gough's (2007) research suggesting that DC pensioners would retire later. However, one needs to bear in mind the policy legacy in England that made it more difficult for people to work past age 65, with a greater tendency for people with intrinsic work orientations to remain in work (see the earlier section 'Motivations to work'). Analysis by Banks et al (2007) examined the extent to which people respond to financial incentives in DC and DB pensions by working or retiring. They found that pension accrual and pension wealth were important influences on the employment of men aged 50–59, but had a weaker influence on men aged 60–64 and women of all ages (Banks et al, 2007: 38). The type of pension held is therefore likely to have influenced retirement timing to a degree in UK, but not after age 65, when only a small minority continue in employment. One might argue that people have a poor understanding of pensions in the UK (Weyman et al, 2012), so their ability to respond to financial incentives to work or retire is poor. That said, Arkani and Gough (2007) did find different expectations about retirement on the basis of pension type. As Shultz et al (1998) point out, the ability to respond to financial incentives to work depends to a degree on whether people are allowed to work. Given the abolition of mandatory retirement in 2011, we might expect more people with DC pensions to work longer. In the early 2000s, the proportion of older workers with DC pensions was relatively low in England (see lower segment of Table 6.7), reflecting the fact that private sector employers failed to sufficiently replace closing DB schemes with DC pensions (Pensions Commission, 2004: 118). The percentage with DC pensions is also set to grow, however, with the introduction of auto-enrolment (see Chapter Two); this may increase the importance of people working to enhance their pensions.

The final financial aspect we examine here is employer medical insurance, which is a known fact facilitating early retirement before age 65 in the US. Unlike the UK, which has a universal health service free at the point of delivery, there have been very limited opportunities to acquire public health insurance in the US before age 65. Publicly provided 'Medicaid' before age 65 is only available to the blind, disabled and those in very low-income groups (Kapur and Rogowski, 2011: 51). Most health insurance coverage before age 65 has consequently been provided by employers (Blau and Gilleskie, 2006). As a result, there is considerable research indicating that being covered by *retiree* health insurance provided by an employer significantly increases the likelihood of leaving work before 65 (see Kapur and Rogowski, 2011: 51). It is important to note that this coverage may be an through individual's employment or via a spouse. Health insurance has a number of other consequences, including tying people to full-time employment during 'working years' because part-timers tend to be excluded from coverage (Green, C.A., 2006: 367; Lyonette et al, 2011). Individuals with employer-provided health-care insurance that does not cover retirees may also be less inclined to leave work before age 65. After age 65, individuals become eligible for publicly funded Medicare; consequently, health insurance becomes less of a concern for remaining in employment (Kapur and Rogowski, 2011: 51). This does not, however, mean that medical insurance has had no effect on employment beyond age 65. Analysis by Green, C.A. (2006) based on 1993/94 data showed that people in poor health working beyond age 65 worked significantly more hours than their healthy counterparts. The explanation given was that these individuals were working full-time in order to get medical insurance covering drug costs not included under Medicare. Since 2006, however, Medicare Part D enables individuals to claim for at least some drug costs, potentially reducing the influence of this on employment.

In order to investigate this further, Table 6.8 gives the percentage probability of working at age 65–74 in 2010, broken down by whether an individual is covered by medical insurance from a current/previous employer. This shows that 43.2% of those with employer-provided medical insurance were in employment, a larger share than the 25.4% with no medical insurance in employment. A number of individuals may have particularly valued the additional cover provided by the insurance, particularly those with health problems. At the same time, however, medical insurance is clearly not the defining factor influencing employment beyond age 65 for most people. Two thirds of those in employment at this age were *not* covered by medical insurance. Likewise, 81.7% of individuals out of work were not covered. This

Table 6.8: Employment at age 65–74, broken down by medical insurance coverage, US, 2010

	% probability of working	% breakdown of coverage: employed	% breakdown of coverage: non-employed
Has employer medical insurance from current/previous employer	43.2	33.3	18.3
No employer medical insurance	25.4	66.7	81.7
Total	29.7%	100%	100%
Base *n*	5396	1428	3968

Source: Author's analysis of HRS 2010 wave.

is consistent with the assertion that medical insurance has less of an influence on employment beyond age 65, as per the arguments of Blau and Gilleskie (2006) and Kapur and Rogowski (2011).

Conclusions

The influence of finances on employment beyond age 65 is likely to be related to whether or not mandatory retirement has been disallowed, thereby enabling individuals to remain in employment (Shultz et al, 1998). This was a key motivation for abolishing mandatory retirement in the US in 1986, and analysis in this chapter indicates that financial motivations for employment were strong in the US. The groups most likely to work appear to be the wealthiest, presumably because they have interesting jobs that they enjoy. The majority of these individuals say that they would work even if they did not need the money. The groups least likely to work appear to be the poorest – those with low wealth and no pension; the lower rates of employment of this group are explained by lower levels of health, education and other factors controlled for in this analysis. The adjusted results suggested that when the poorest segments have comparable levels of health and education, they work in similar numbers to the richest; the fact is, however, that the factors influencing whether or not they are able to work are not evenly distributed across the populations. When these individuals in poorer groups work, they overwhelmingly say that they would leave work if they could afford to, but the proportions working past 65 are *comparatively* low.

In the US, between the extremes of the rich and poor are significant numbers who are in work financial reasons. These individuals are not typically renters, but are often home-buyers. They are perhaps the group most likely to have DC pensions, rather than belonging to DB pension schemes. Outstanding mortgages were common among this group, which is an important influence on employment beyond age 65. Nevertheless, considerable numbers across the different wealth groups said that they were working for financial reasons, some of which may be due to increased expectations about the lifestyle that they feel they need relative to past cohorts. We see that the employment of women as well as men was in response to financial factors. This was evident in the proportion of women working when there was an outstanding mortgage, and when they had a DC rather than DB pension. Spousal employment appeared to exert a strong influence on whether an individual was working, but this was true of both men and women.

The UK context has clearly been different from that of the US in that it has been less straightforward to remain in employment beyond age 65. Consequently, this has arguably contributed to lower rates of employment, and a greater concentration of individuals working because they value their job for non-financial reasons. Only a third of people working at 65–74 in 2008 said that they were working for financial reasons. Not all of these individuals were wealthy, as the analysis shows, but factors such as pensions appeared to have less influence over whether somebody worked beyond age 65. As in the US, the wealthiest segments of the population appear to be most likely, and the poorest least likely, to work. Once again, low levels of employment among the poor were accounted for once we controled for differences in health, education and the other factors included. As the US evidence suggests, abolishing mandatory retirement is likely to have less impact on the poorest segments than the richest.

The one area where financial influences appeared to increase employment in England was in relation to housing. Those individuals in the UK with an outstanding mortgage were significantly more likely to be working than those owning their home outright. However, only around 8% of people aged 65–74 in the UK had an outstanding mortgage, compared with a third in the US. In this sense, and also, to a degree, in relation to health insurance, Americans have a clearer financial need to remain in employment. Nevertheless, given the relative modesty of UK retirement incomes (see Chapter Two), we would expect the abolition of mandatory retirement to increase the numbers working beyond age 65 for financial reasons. At the same time, US experience suggests that many people who expect to work past 65 are not able to do so. We therefore need efficient and equitable life-course policies to support individuals in making choices about working or retiring at 65; we examine these in Chapter Seven.

Part Three
Current paths and
policy alternatives

SEVEN

Current paths and policy alternatives

Introduction: the state and the reconstruction of retirement policy

Governments in the UK and the US have sought to reconstruct retirement. In comparative accounts of retirement, the role of the state in 'liberal' countries such as the UK and the US is assumed to be weak. However, governments in both countries have proactively increased the financial necessity to work beyond age 65 considerably, while dissolving the notion of fixed retirement ages. The changes have been both positive and negative – they increase the theoretical choice that individuals have over retirement timing while reducing the amount of financial security that many individuals have. If we recognise that the state *necessarily* plays a significant role in shaping and reshaping retirement, we are then in a better position to argue for policies that promote greater autonomy *and* security over retirement decisions.

On the positive side, both the UK and the US have abolished mandatory retirement in most circumstances, increasing the theoretical autonomy individuals have over retirement timing. This means that employers can no longer routinely rely on fixed retirement ages, and older people have a much stronger legal claim to continue working past 65. This occurred in 1986 in the US and 2011 in the UK; in both cases, there was resistance from employers for this significant state intervention in the labour market. Likewise, governments have intervened in the area of occupational pensions. In the US and the UK, it is now easier to take a pension with an employer you currently work for, while in the US, employers have to continue contributing to pensions beyond 'normal' retirement age. Furthermore, governments have reformed state pensions in both countries so that people can claim a full pension while continuing to work. Policies such as these blur the divide between work and retirement, and for some individuals, this will be a positive development. In particular, it will allow *some* people to gradually retire, whereby they reduce their hours in the lead-up to 'full' retirement; this is seen as desirable by many individuals (Abraham and Houseman, 2005; Vickerstaff, 2007).

While the aforementioned policies can be considered broadly positive, the more problematic side to this reconstruction of retirement relates to the financial pressures to work past 65. It is important to note that in both countries, the abolition of mandatory retirement was an example of policy 'conversion' (to draw on the concept of Streeck and Thelen, 2005). The roots of this policy were originally aimed at addressing unfair age discrimination in the US and the UK. However, in both countries, a key rationale for extending age discrimination legislation to those above 65 was to promote continued employment, particularly for those with inadequate retirement incomes. This has to be viewed alongside changes to retirement incomes that increase the financial need to work past 65. In the UK, the state pension age is rising rapidly to 66 by 2020 for men and women, and will ultimately rise to 68; it will also be reviewed on a regular basis and is arguably likely to rise still further. By way of context, in the early 2000s, women could claim a state pension at 60 and men at 65; this therefore represents a significant increase over a short period. At the same time, the age at which individuals with low incomes can receive UK Pension Credit is also rising. This was previously available at age 60; it therefore represented a safety net for older people exited from work 'early'. This will now rise in line with the female state pension age, so that by 2020, people have no access to this benefit until age 66. Instead, people will have to rely on much lower working-age benefits if they do not work (see the later section 'Strengthening support for those exited from work before state pension age'). Alternatively, individuals may have to draw on any private pensions early, meaning that this is significantly depleted by state pension age.

In the US, the 'normal' Social Security age has already reached 66, and will reach 67 in 2027. Individuals needing to draw on Social Security income before age 67 will be in a more fortunate position than their UK counterparts as they will still be able to take a reduced pension from age 62. However, the rise in the 'full' retirement age to 67 results in an even bigger reduction for early receipt, increasing pressures to work. At the same time, access to means-tested Supplemental Security Income has become extremely limited as a result of 'policy drift'; the assets allowable under the scheme have not risen in decades, resulting in very restricted eligibility.

Concurrent with these changes, in both countries, there has been a significant decline in Defined Benefit (DB) occupational pensions, which provided predictable, secure retirement incomes for individuals over the course of their retirement in the past. These pensions are being replaced by Defined Contribution (DC) pensions in both countries;

these are typically less well funded and do not provide the financial security of DB schemes (Hacker, 2006; Ginn and MacIntyre, 2013; ONS, 2013b). Taking all these changes together, we can see that increased theoretical opportunities to work beyond age 65 are being provided alongside greater financial pressures to be in employment at this age. However, we cannot take it for granted that employment at 65+ is as unproblematic as policy assumes. In this chapter, we therefore present 'current paths' – future prospects for employment beyond age 65 based on current trends. This draws on our analysis of the English Longitudinal Study of Ageing and the US Health and Retirement Survey in Part Two of the book. The findings from the ELSA analysis should reflect the situation in the UK as a whole, given that the vast majority of the UK population lives in England (ONS, 2012) and rules governing pensions and employment rights are the same across the UK. Following this, we then set out 'policy alternatives'; these are 'life-course' policies to increase security and autonomy in older age. Finally, the chapter examines what has happened to the 'policy logics' of 'paternalism' in the UK and 'self-reliance' in the US that we identified in Chapter One for the early 2000s. Having done this, we are in a better position to consider prospects for adopting more positive policies for older people.

Current paths and future prospects for employment at 65+

The US is likely to yield some insights about employment prospects at 65+ in the UK given that US employment at this age is higher and has been the subject of policy for longer. This book shows that high US employment beyond age 65 is not simply the result of people in career jobs working a few more years. This is perhaps surprising given that the abolition of mandatory retirement in 1986 has probably had more impact on retention than on recruitment (see Chapter Three). Americans aged 65–74 in 2012 were more likely than their English counterparts to still be in the jobs that they were doing in 2002. At the same time, however, Americans were more likely to work as a result of moving jobs in older age, or returning to work following an absence. There are number of reasons why it might be necessary to move jobs in order to work past 65. Individuals may have to move jobs in order to reduce their hours or find a more sustainable job (Abraham and Housman, 2005; Alden, 2012). In both countries, most people working past 65 in 2012 had reduced their working hours. For some, this might be seen as a necessity in terms of staying on in work. In the US and UK, a significant number of jobs held by older workers involved physical exertion, while evidence from the US indicated that job stress was common. Added to this, in both countries, men working at 65–74 in 2012 had been working relatively long hours in 2002; it may be hard for workers to maintain these hours in older age. In addition to issues around working time, individuals may also find themselves out of a job in older age as a result of redundancy, or due to a period of ill-health or caring. Their ability to return to work and move jobs may be vital for their prospects of working up to and beyond age 65.

Given the preceding discussion, a significant increase in employment at age 65 in the UK would require individuals not only to remain in long-term jobs, but also to move into new jobs where necessary. Evidence from Lain and Loretto (forthcoming) suggests that the increase in employment at age 65–69 in the UK since the early 2000s has been due to people in long-term jobs remaining in work longer; there was little evidence of increasing numbers of people working as a result of having moved jobs (see also Chapter Four of this book). There are a number of reasons why this might be the case. One factor is the recession that hit the UK towards the end of the 2000s, which probably reduced the potential recruitment of older people (something that also happened in the US). In addition, however, it is likely that the low qualification levels of older people in the UK harms their potential recruitment prospects. As we saw in Chapter One, high US educational attainment among older people reflects a broader US focus on promoting 'self-reliance' over the life course. In both countries, having high levels of education increased the likelihood of working, irrespective of whether this was due to job continuation, job movement or a return to employment following an absence. Education is likely to influence people's ability to have stable careers that allow continued employment (Blekesaune et al, 2008), although some older people will be lucky in maintaining secure employment with limited qualifications. However, older individuals with low qualifications are likely to find it particularly hard to compete in the labour market if they need a new job (Wang et al, 2008). Employers may be happier to continue employing an experienced older person with low qualifications than they would be to recruit them. Overall, in both countries, somebody with higher education aged 65–74 was twice as likely to work as someone with below secondary qualifications (see Chapter Five). This relationship remained statistically significant after controlling for other factors, such as health. The low qualification levels of people in the UK are therefore likely to be a contributory factor in explaining why they are less likely to move into jobs in older age (Kanabar, 2012). In general terms, employment beyond age 65 in England/the UK may therefore be more confined to those continuing in secure long-term jobs. As the preceding discussion suggests, however, in both countries, the paths that people follow to work or inactivity at 65 are likely to be influenced by their socio-economic position.

The evidence in this book suggests that despite the financial rationale for extended working lives, it is the wealthiest who are most likely to work past 65 in both countries. This appears, in part, to be related to the advantaged position of these people. When we control for their better health and education, there is no significant increased likelihood of these individuals working (see Table 6.5 in Chapter Six). These individuals are likely to have interesting jobs and a fair degree of autonomy in deciding whether to retire early or late. The majority of those in this position said that they are working for non-financial reasons in both countries. However, even among the seemingly well off, a significant minority in the US say that they are working for financial reasons. This may reflect difficulties in assessing the financial needs of individuals. However, it probably also indicates increased expectations about retirement lifestyles. With the abolition of mandatory retirement in the UK, we may expect a significant growth in employment among this group.

At the other end of the spectrum, the poorest have the least likelihood of working at 65+ in both countries, and the lowest potential prospects for doing so in future. This appears to be related, in part, to their disadvantaged positions; in both countries, once we control for education, health and a range of other factors, the lower likelihood of working relative to the richest disappears. When they have equivalent levels of health and education, they appear to work in similar numbers to the richest; the point is, however, that they are not in this position and clearly face significant barriers to working past 65. This is something that needs to be considered much more carefully by policy.

While the poorest are least likely to work in *both* countries, the poorest in the US were more likely to work than the poorest in England. In the US, the vast majority of those in the poorer groups said that they were working for financial reasons. In England, a significant number in this category said that they were working for non-financial reasons. This may partly be because benefits such as Pension Credit are withdrawn as a result of working (Lain, 2011), which may make it more important for poorer people to be intrinsically motivated in order to work. With the abolition of mandatory retirement and an increase in the state pension age, we will probably see an increase in these individuals working past 65. However, US experience suggests that there are constraints on how many people in this category will end up working, even in a context where people have the right to work past 65.

In between these two extremes are people in the middle financially. In the US, significant numbers of these individuals work at 65+, most claiming to do so for financial reasons. These workers are not typically renters, but a significant proportion are still paying off a mortgage. They tend to have a private pension, but it often appears to be a DC pension rather than a DB scheme. In England, the number of workers in this middle position is low, as it is for all wealth groups. However, we might expect this to be a group where we will see a rise in employment following the abolition of mandatory retirement age. They are unlikely to have the extremes of disadvantage that reduce the employment prospects of the poorest. In this context, some have suggested that this group are most susceptible to financial incentives to continue working (Weyman et al, 2012). While this is plausible, we should nevertheless appreciate that many of these individuals face constraints on working past 65. US experience suggests that it may be harder for individuals to work in older age than they anticipate. Many Americans say that they expect to work 'in retirement', often part-time, but fewer of these individuals appear to end up doing this (Abraham and Houseman, 2005; Maestas, 2010; AARP, 2014). From an individual perspective, around a third of people aged 65–74 have a work-limiting health condition in the US (and UK) (see Chapter Five). Health conditions are often unexpected, and they reduce the likelihood of working considerably (Williamson and McNamara, 2003). From a labour market perspective, it is known that the recruitment prospects of displaced older workers are far below that of younger age groups (Johnson and Mommaerts, 2011). Finally, the recruitment prospects of older people in the UK are likely to be even more constrained given their low qualifications (Kanabar, 2012).

Life-course policies to support retirement and work in older age

The preceding discussion suggests that policies to reconstruct retirement have increased the theoretical opportunities to work past 65, alongside financial pressures to be in employment. When we examined 'current paths', it was clear that continued employment at 65 is not as straightforward and unproblematic as policy assumes. We therefore propose a series of 'life-course policies' that would enhance individuals' autonomy over retirement timing, while supporting retirement as a period of financial security. The concept of 'life-course policies', as devised by Leisering (2004), was introduced in Chapter One. This recognises that policy needs to support people across the life course, starting with education, if older people are to arrive at a position of security and autonomy in older age.

Policies to support education

It may seem strange that education is a policy area highlighted in a book about extended working lives. As discussed earlier, however, education strongly increased the likelihood of working past age 65 in both countries, whether this was the result of staying in a long-term job, moving jobs or returning to work following an absence. Low-educated individuals are likely to have precarious careers, and they will find it particularly difficult to maintain a career that will keep them in work into their 60s and beyond. It is therefore vital that a renewed effort is made to ensure that people leave education with qualifications. Older people today face a particular problem in the UK: 45% of the cohort aged 65–74 in 2010 had below secondary-level qualifications in the UK, compared with 17% in the US. Older Americans are also more likely to have college degrees than their English counterparts. The wide educational disparity between older and younger cohorts will decline over the coming decades in the UK (OECD, 2014). However, a significant minority still leave school with below secondary-level qualifications in both countries – about 15% in the UK and 10% in the US (OECD, 2014: 43). Ensuring that individuals receive a sound education early in life will give them greater potential autonomy over their employment choices in later life.

In addition to educating young people, there needs to be a much greater emphasis on lifelong learning if people are to remain in employment longer (Phillipson, 2009). Lifelong learning would help enable people to catch up on skills that they missed out on, to update their skills and to help them change careers. At the current time, only a very small fraction of spending on post-school education in the UK is focused on older people. In 2009, only around 2.5% of spending was on the age group 50–74; 86% was spent on the age group 18–24 (Schuller and Watson, 2009: 7). It is important that young people receive a large share of the funding for post-secondary education in order to provide them with a foundation for their careers. However, there clearly needs to be a much greater emphasis on providing education and training for older people. Schuller and Watson (2009) argue for a rebalancing of spending in the UK so that the percentage of spending on those aged 50–74 rises from 2.5% to 4%. They identify general entitlements that should be available to everyone, that is, free access to learning to acquire basic skills (literacy and numeracy) and a financial entitlement to support in order to acquire secondary-level qualifications. They also identify 'transition entitlements', which help people make difficult transitions (leaving prison, moving area or retiring).

Although this is not an argument made by Schuller and Watson (2009), it would also be advantageous to offer 'transition entitlements' for individuals to acquire skills or to change career. This would need to be organised in order to benefit people across the socio-economic spectrum. The low-skilled are least likely to participate in post-secondary education (OECD, 2014: 391), and they would need a much greater financial contribution towards the costs of training. Individuals would also benefit from gaining the right to careers guidance across the life course, linked with the possibility of receiving training entitlements described earlier. This would increase spending on this area at a time when adult education is undergoing substantial cuts (*The Guardian*, 2015). However, adult education has to be seen as an investment rather than a cost (*The Guardian*, 2015). It should not be seen as a panacea to solve all problems associated with extended working lives. Nevertheless, policies of the sort described earlier could help extend working lives by enabling people to make positive job transitions and changes 'before it was too late'.

In the US, there is a more significant culture of education in later life than in the UK. For example, more than a quarter (25.4%) of undergraduate students enrolled in courses in the US in 2011 were aged over 30, with over a tenth (11.4%) aged 40+.[1] In the UK, on the other hand, only just over one tenth (11.3%) of undergraduate students were aged over 30 in 2013.[2] While US higher education does have problems related to the variability of provision, US experience suggests that there is scope for more study at this level in the UK. In a UK context, this may mean expanding provision in properly funded centres of vocational education. However, the preceding policy suggestions for the UK are likely to have relevance for the US context as well, particularly with regard to ensuring that education and training is provided below degree level for those who most need it. This would mean ensuring that costs for adult education courses do not deter individuals (Tate et al, 2011).

Improving policies to support career/family factors

Improving childcare provision

As with education, it may be unexpected for childcare to be raised as an important policy issue with regard to employment and retirement. However, childcare can be important for a number of reasons. First, the cost of childcare has resulted in many women working part-time in the UK (Gash, 2008); with a weaker attachment to the labour market at earlier ages, this potentially reduces their likelihood of working in older age. Women have often worked part-time around family responsibilities in a 'modified male breadwinner' system (O'Connor et al, 1999). In 2003, 42% of women in employment worked part-time, a figure that has not changed significantly over the last 30 years (ONS, 2013c: 1). Once in part-time work, they often stay working short part-time hours. If this work is unrewarding and contributes a relatively small amount to the household income, it is perhaps unsurprising if they retire early as part of a household decision-making process (Loretto and Vickerstaff, 2015). Childcare subsidies can therefore help women to develop rewarding careers that are not derailed by women moving into marginal part-time work to deal with family responsibilities. Subsidies for childcare have improved considerably over the last decade, but there is still some way to go in terms of arriving at an accessible, universal subsidised childcare system (Family and Childcare Trust, 2014).

There is also an issue related to women being out of the labour market entirely during the years when there is a young family. In the US, Harrington Meyer and Herd (2007: 171) argues that 'for many women, given the high price and relatively inadequate support of quality daycare for their children, it does not make financial sense to work'. It is therefore probable that women in this situation, in both countries, will also have a weaker attachment to the labour market in older age. Tax subsidies for middle-income individuals and subsidised childcare do exist in the US, but they are insufficient to buy quality daycare. Harrington Meyer and Herd (2007) therefore argues for a universal childcare policy, based on daycare centres.

Subsidised childcare would also help ensure that older people do not feel obliged to leave work, or to reduce their hours, in order to look after their grandchildren. Unlike in the UK, female employment in the US is often tied to full-time work (Lyonette et al, 2011). With limited affordable quality childcare, parents in couples often work different shifts in order to cover childcare and rely on the broader family to help out. As we saw in Chapter Five, significant numbers of grandparents in the US help look after their grandchildren while their adult children are working. Lee and Tang (2015) found that women aged 51–60 had a significantly increased likelihood of retiring if they looked after their grandchildren for over 100 hours a year. Investing in childcare for parents could therefore help some grandparents remain in work. It would also reduce the pressure on grandparents who have to combine working with caring for grandchildren. Harrington Meyer (2014) interviewed grandmothers who combined paid employment with providing care for their grandchildren so that their adult children could work. Many of these grandmothers wanted to help out with their grandchildren but found the amount of care that they had to provide alongside working very difficult. Older women, in both countries, should not have to put themselves under strain in order to work and provide care.

Finally, the US should follow the lead of the UK and grant employees the right to take time off in the event of an emergency involving a family member or a dependant. In the UK, this legislation defines dependants broadly, to include children, grandchildren, parents or anyone else dependent upon an individual's care.[3] Employers have to allow this time off for a range of emergencies, including illness or unanticipated problems with childcare provision. For older workers, this is potentially very helpful if, for example, an aged parent is taken ill, has an accident or requires immediate assistance. The ability to the take time off to deal with emergencies may therefore make it easier for older people to remain in employment.

Strengthening support for those exited from work before state pension age

Although it is to be expected that average retirement ages are going to rise, it remains important that systems of financial support are available if individuals are exited from work before state pension age. In the past, Pension Credit in the UK 'caught' people from age 60 if they found themselves without work. It was more generous than unemployment-based Job Seekers Allowance, social-assistance-based Income Support or disability-based Employment and Support Allowance. In 2013, Pension Credit for a single individual was worth £142.70, whereas the other benefits just listed were worth only half that amount, at £71.70. With the age of pension credit eligibility rising from 60 to 68, we therefore see the opening up of an eight-year period when people unable to work for reasons of unemployment or disability will find themselves having to survive on very low benefits. Of course, this raises the problem of low benefit levels for all age groups in the UK.

The alternative to this is to revitalise earnings-related social insurance so that people can earn entitlement to benefits paid at higher levels (Bell and Gaffney, 2012). In this regard, disability insurance would be particularly important. While disability benefits would not be older worker benefits per se, they would disproportionately support older people. In 2013, around 10% of people aged between 50 and state pension age were not working for reasons of ill-health (DWP, 2014b: 24). It is therefore important that these individuals are supported properly in the lead-up to state pension age. In the US, Social Security includes a social-insurance-based disability pension; the UK should follow the lead of the US and introduce their own scheme.

Reforming policies to support retirement and late careers

Retaining the option of a state pension at 65

There is a strong argument to be made for continuing to allow individuals to access state pension income at age 65 in the future in the UK and the US. Although 'normal' state pension ages are rising across a range of countries, it is important to recognise that the UK's reforms are atypical in removing access to a state pension until after age 65. Countries that plan to increase state pension ages above 65 will often allow individuals to take a reduced pension before this. Out of 34 countries listed in the Organisation for Economic Co-operation and Development's (OECD, 2011: 113) *Pensions at a glance 2011*, eight countries had legislated a future 'normal' state pension age of over 65. Seven of these countries had legislated a normal state pension age of 67 (Australia, Denmark, Germany, Iceland, Israel, Norway and the US). The remaining country, the UK, had a state pension age of 68. More recent projections suggest that out of the 27 EU countries, 12 will have a normal state pension above 65 in 2060 (EC, 2014: 11). However, only seven countries will not allow an early (reduced) pension to be taken at or before 65 (Denmark, Greece, Italy, the Netherlands, Slovakia, Ireland and the UK). In the US, people will continue to be able to receive a reduced pension from age 62; in 2027, the state pension will be reduced by 30% if they receive it at 62 instead of 67. If they choose to retire at 65, they will receive a pension reduced by 13.3%. Someone on average earnings throughout their working lives retiring at 65 would receive a state pension worth 38.7% of their previous earnings (rather than 45% at age 67) (see Chapter Two). In the UK, options for providing a reduced pension at 65, instead of 68, are constrained by the fact that the 'full' Single Tier Pension (STP) is already projected to be provided at such a low level. Current projections suggest that it will only be worth 30% of average earnings in future. There is, however, a strong argument for providing the *full* STP pension at age 65.

The first thing to note is that maintaining a state pension age of 65 in the UK is arguably economically feasible, if there was a political will to do this. In 2010, the UK spent 7.7% of gross domestic product (GDP) on pensions (including means-tested Pension Credit), compared with an average across OECD countries of 9.3% (OECD, 2011; EC, 2002). In the UK, the amount spent on pensions is projected first to fall, and then to rise to 8.2% in 2050 and to 9.2% in 2060. In other words, the amount to be spent on pensions in the UK as a proportion of GDP in 2060 is lower than the average amount spent by OECD countries in 2010. In 2060, across 25 OECD countries, the average amount spent on state pensions was 12.3% of GDP. This suggests that there is political room for manoeuvre in maintaining a state pension age of 65 in the UK. There is certainly little evidence of an appetite for state pension age rises, with 77% of those surveyed in the UK thinking that they are 'unfair' (Macnicol, 2015: 203). It should also be remembered that some of the costs of providing a state pension between the ages of 65 and 68 would otherwise be spent on unemployment and disability benefits.

There are a number of reasons for maintaining a state pension age of 65 in the UK, while allowing people to continue working if they want to. As we saw at the very start of the book, Ros Altmann, UK Pensions Minister, has argued that 'rethinking retirement' 'is not about forcing people to work on, but supporting those who want to work' (Altmann, 2015: 9). Withdrawing state pensions until after 65 *is* forcing people to work. A growing body of research suggests that in terms of well-being in older age, what matters is the degree of choice people feel they have over the work decisions they make (see, eg, Matthews and Nazroo, 2015). Obviously, in an ideal world, people would exercise a much higher degree of work/retirement autonomy *before* age 65. However, the idea of a dependable pension at a known age will arguably be of comfort to those struggling on in employment in older age, eager to leave to pursue other activities. The alternative prospect of raising the state pension age to 68 and periodically reviewing it may have the consequence of breeding distrust that the goalposts are being continually moved. Such a consequence may make individuals less likely to save if people feel insecure about their likelihood of retiring. The age of 65 has become synonymous with the receipt of a pension in the minds of individuals; we should maintain this commitment.

While there is a strong case for retaining a state pension at 65, we should not assume that this is incompatible with people working longer. There is a large weight of evidence to suggest that individuals often want to reduce their working hours prior to full retirement (for the UK, see, eg, Vickerstaff, 2007; for the US, see Abraham and Houseman, 2005). Indeed, as we saw in Chapter Four, most people continuing in employment past 65 do so part-time. The ability to take a pension while working may make part-time employment attractive because the pension will offset some, or all, of the lost earnings. New Zealand is a country where there is little incentive to delay receipt of the state pension beyond age 65, and yet there has been a big growth in part-time employment among this group (Lain and Vickerstaff, 2014). State pensions can therefore be very compatible with working longer if people are given the opportunity to do so.

On a final point in relation to state pensions, it is important to recognise that some people have left school early and worked continuously thereafter. In the UK, state pensions will require 30 years of contributions in future, but somebody leaving school at 16 may have paid contributions for 49 years. Many of these individuals will have worked in manual jobs and have below average life expectancy. It is therefore a particular injustice that these people should have to work until 68 to receive a pension.

Restoring financial certainty to supplementary pension income

In the UK and the US, we have seen a mass decline in DB occupational pensions. These were usually based on the individual's former salary, and the employer was responsible for ensuring that there were enough funds to make payments. Such schemes were not without their limitations, most notably, the fact that coverage was only partial in both countries. They nevertheless brought supplementary income to a significant number of households. In the UK, around half of workers had an occupational pension in the early 1990s (Clark, 2006: 149); in the US, a similar proportion of private sector workers had such a pension (Buessing and Soto, 2006). More often than not, these individuals had DB pensions, which potentially provided individuals with dependable, regular pension payments for the rest of their lives (Hacker, 2006).

In the US, employers replaced DB pensions with DC schemes. As Hacker (2006) has pointed out, employers tend to contribute less to DC schemes and the lump sums that they pay out can be highly variable depending upon stock market performance. This reduces the amount of security that many households will have. DB occupational schemes will not be returning, however, and, as Hacker (2006) points out, this makes Social Security an even more important source of financial security for households. It is therefore important that Social Security is protected from attempts to privatise it (see Béland and Waddan, 2012). In the UK, the decline in DB occupational pensions was not met with a sufficient rise in the number of DC pensions (Pensions Commission, 2004). The government therefore introduced 'auto-enrolment'. Under this policy, employers without an adequate occupational scheme will be compelled to contribute to a DC scheme if the employee also contributes. In the UK context, it remains extremely important that individuals have supplementary pension income as the STP is only expected to be worth around 30% of average earnings in the future (Pensions Commission, 2004).

The introduction of compulsion on the part of UK employers to contribute to supplementary pensions is a welcome development. However, there remain questions about whether this is an ideal arrangement for everyone, particularly those on low incomes and many women. The government predicts that a median earner saving from age 30 would receive a wage replacement rate of 15% from auto-enrolment (Ginn and Macintyre, 2013). However, it would be unable to guarantee such a replacement rate given that stock market outcomes can be unpredictable and highly variable. After the stock market crash in 2007, the value of assets in UK DC pensions fell by a third (*The Guardian*, 2008). While the value of these schemes may have returned to pre-crash levels since then, this was bad news for those people needing to draw on this income at the time. One of the benefits of earnings-related schemes is that the risks can be shared between cohorts. In the case of the default auto-enrolment scheme, the National Employment Savings Trust (NEST), it is argued that a cautious investment strategy is being adopted. What kind of pensions will be generated by NEST, or by other schemes, cannot be known in advance, however. An alternative proposed by Ginn and MacIntyre (2013) is a Voluntary Earnings-related State Pension Addition (VESPA). This has the advantage of providing the security of earnings-related provision with the ability to pay credits for time spent caring, benefitting women. Ginn and MacIntyre (2013: 99) argue:

> VESPA ... would be better-adapted to women's needs than NEST-type schemes. Contributions would be as in NEST and carer credits as in state pensions, thus avoiding the penalty for caring years incurred in private pensions. A VESPA would be a fully portable pay-as-you-go scheme, allowing workers to save for their retirement without the investment and annuity risks inherent in defined

contribution schemes. No derived benefits based on marriage would be payable, since these are anachronistic and poorly targeted (Ginn, 2003). Carer credits would require either an intra-VESPA cross-subsidy, as in NI [National Insurance] and in occupational pensions' provision for ill-health and survivor benefits, or a grant from the Exchequer in lieu of tax relief. Tax relief on private pensions is extremely regressive, mainly helping the highest earners; it is also costly, net subsidies to private pension saving being equivalent to 2.2 per cent of GPD (Pensions Policy Institute, 2010). The VESPA fund could be ring-fenced and at arm's length from government, like social insurance funds in other European countries, to minimise political risk.

There should be more attention paid to how we can provide secure, predictable retirement incomes in future; the VESPA proposal is one possible solution.

Strengthening the safety net for older people

In the UK, means-tested social assistance in the form of the Pension Credit is expected to continue to provide a significant number of retirees with supplementary incomes (Foster, 2014). This is because the full STP will be pegged just above Pension Credit level, which means that those with insufficient contributions will still be eligible for Pension Credit. It is therefore important that the level of Pension Credit maintains its real value over time, a commitment that has been made at the current time. In addition, it also needs to be recognised that Housing Benefit receipt will also continue to be needed by a significant minority. Projections in the past have suggested that 15% of pensioner households will still be entitled to Housing Benefit in 2040 (DWP, 2008), and it may be higher if fewer people manage to buy their home in future, as some have suggested. Currently, older households are protected from cuts to Housing Benefit, and it is important that this source of income continues to be available for older people.

In the US, as we saw in Chapter Two, the safety net of means-tested benefits is much weaker than in the UK. Social assistance-based Supplementary Security Income is provided at less generous levels than UK Pension Credit and is harder to receive (Lain, 2011). In particular, the assets allowable for a Supplementary Security Income recipient have not risen since 1989, and have declined dramatically in real terms since 1974 (Elder and Powers, 2006). As a result, inflation means that it becomes harder and harder for those on low incomes to receive this benefit as time goes on; in 2002, only around 3% of the over 65s received this benefit (Lain, 2011: 496). This is despite the fact that the US has a high rate of relative poverty by international standards (see Figure 7.1). It is therefore important that the US does more to help vulnerable retirees on low incomes. Asset requirements for Supplementary Security Income should, as a minimum, be increased as a matter of urgency, making up for its dramatic decline in real terms since 1974. The scheme also needs considerable publicity if it is to attract the poorest to apply. Politically, revitalising Supplementary Security Income will not be easy because the scheme lacks the automatic support afforded to Social Security (see Chapters One and Two). Historically, when debates about the benefit for older people have surfaced in the past, there were concerns that the benefit was being received by older immigrants that had recently moved to the US and had not contributed to the system (Berkowitz and DeWitt, 2013). In reality, only a relatively small number of individuals were in this position. One option would therefore be to introduce a residency requirement, for example, of 10 years. Of course, it would be important to support the small number of low-income individuals entering the US in older age through other means.

In addition to social assistance, as noted in Chapters One and Two, the system of housing benefits in the US is weaker than in the UK. Housing benefits to renters with low incomes, for example, are not provided as a right. Instead, the amount of support available is budgeted, and individuals have to join long queues to receive help; only a fraction of those theoretically entitled to help actually receive it. As we saw in Chapter Six, renters do not have a high likelihood of working in either country, which is likely to be, in part, related to wider disadvantage. It is therefore important that support is readily available, as a right, for these potentially vulnerable individuals.

Strengthening age discrimination laws

On a final point, it is argued here that it would be of benefit to older people, and employers, if age discrimination legislation was strengthened and clarified. The UK reforms still leave open the possibility that an 'Employer Justified Retirement Age' (EJRA) can be established. An EJRA has to be a 'proportionate means' of achieving 'a legitimate end'; this 'legitimate end' must have a social policy objective that is of public interest. Current evidence suggests that mandatory retirement ages have been abolished in the vast majority of cases. A

Figure 7.1: Poverty rates among over-65s, OECD countries, mid-2000s

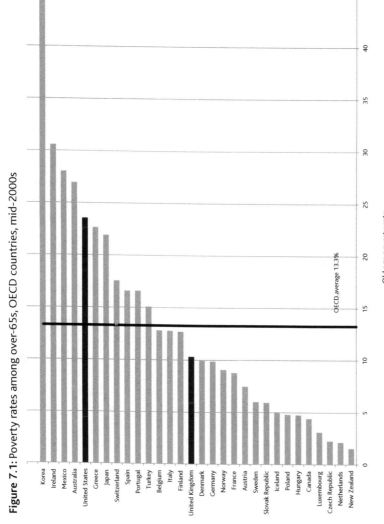

Old-age poverty rate

Percentage of older people with equivalent incomes below half population median

Source: OECD (2009: 64).

survey conducted by the Confederation of British Industry (CBI, 2013) in 2013 found that only around 5% of employers responding had retained a mandatory retirement age. However, a third of employers said that they would like to have a mandatory retirement age but saw this as too risky given uncertainty about the legal basis for justifying these. While it is unlikely that mandatory retirement will return in a large number of cases, the ambiguity is not helpful for older people or employers. It would therefore be advantageous to tighten up the legislation so that it was clear when mandatory retirement is allowable. For example, in the US, mandatory retirement is allowed in a narrow range of circumstances that are clearly specified, for example, in relation to safety issues (Macnicol, 2006). Such an approach would be more suitable for the UK. However, some anomalies in US legislation should also be addressed. For example, there is little reason to exempt age discrimination legislation from firms with less than 20 staff. Our analysis in Chapter Four suggested that small companies were not more likely to get rid of staff at 65. However, people working in small firms should nevertheless be protected from forced retirement at a fixed age.

Paternalism, self-reliance and self-determination

We started this book by considering 'policy logics' regarding work and retirement in the early 2000s. It is therefore appropriate to finish by considering how changes have altered these underpinning policy logics and what the prospects are for adopting a different path. In the early 2000s, a 'self-reliance' policy logic was evident in the US, under which the state encouraged/necessitated employment beyond age 65. The safety net for those with low retirement incomes was weak, but protection from forced retirement on the basis of age was strong. The US has not deviated from its path of self-reliance since the early 2000s, and earlier reforms, such as Social Security age increases, actually came into force after 2000. US self-reliance continues to be based on a model of legal protection from forced retirement and 'earned' entitlements; this is evidenced by the superior long-term prospects of Social Security relative to Supplemental Security Income, which continues to be marginalised. In this 'self-reliance' context, significant numbers of Americans over 65 work for financial reasons. However, as we have seen, fewer people work 'in retirement' than expect to (Maestas, 2010). Furthermore, employment is lowest among the poorest groups, despite the US policy focus of enabling employment for those with inadequate retirement incomes. In this sense, the US self-reliance policy logic fails to deliver what it aims to achieve.

In the UK, a 'paternalistic' policy logic was in operation, under which legal rights to work beyond age 65 were negligible but the safety net for those with low retirement incomes was stronger than in the US. The UK is currently moving closer to a 'self-reliance' policy logic, albeit one that differs from the US. While US self-reliance is based on 'earned' entitlements, UK self-reliance pays more attention to the 'safety net' provided for those on low retirement incomes. For example, most individuals will receive smaller state pension incomes in future than is currently the case (Foster, 2014), but there will be a greater focus on bringing the pension incomes of the poorest segments above means-tested Pension Credit levels. This, it is hoped, will reduce perceived disincentives to save/work (Foster, 2014). The developing UK self-reliance logic is also reflected in the abolition of mandatory retirement, the large state pension age increases and the phasing out of Pension Credit for 'early exiters'.

The former UK policy logic of paternalism was problematic in terms of providing insufficient economic security and limited employment rights; the sociologist Peter Townsend (1981, 1986) described this negatively as the 'structured dependency' of older people. The move towards a self-reliance model increases the theoretical opportunities to work past 65 but leaves many in a more perilous economic position than they would otherwise have been under previous policy arrangements. The evidence in this book suggests that in the late 2000s, around two thirds of those working beyond age 65 in England were doing so for non-financial reasons. This reflected, to a degree, the legacy of a paternalistic policy logic whereby employment at this age was not straightforward and individuals had to go against the norm and actively pursue employment. With the abolition of mandatory retirement in 2011, we expect financially motivated employment past age 65 to increase significantly, in line with the self-reliance policy logic that is developing.

The alternative to 'self-reliance' and 'paternalism' is a policy logic of 'self-determination', representing enhanced autonomy over work and retirement decisions. This would enable greater degrees of financial security alongside legal rights to employment beyond age 65; the policies advocated earlier are suggested in this spirit. Such developments may be seen as unrealistic. However, prospects for delivering such change are greatly enhanced if we acknowledge the potential positive power of gradual, incremental change (drawing on the perspectives of Streeck and Thelen, 2005). It is clear that significant changes have often occurred as a result of incremental changes over the long term. Incremental changes have often detrimentally affected retirees. State pension levels were gradually eroded over time in the UK from the 1980s onwards and access to US Supplemental Security Income became gradually more restricted. However, more recent policy reforms affecting older people will take a number of years to come to full fruition. This provides some potential 'space' to steer UK and US policies towards providing financial security and autonomy for older people. The pension choices we make today, for example, are crucial in deciding the fates of retirees in the future. Likewise, the investments we make today in education and lifelong learning will benefit older individuals, and society more broadly, in the future. What is required is the political will to invest in life-course policies that benefit current and future retirees; without such action, we face very uncertain prospects for retirement.

Notes

[1] Percentage derived from https://nces.ed.gov/datalab/quickstats/createtable.aspx. The source is the US Department of Education, National Center for Education Statistics, 2011–12 National Postsecondary Student Aid Study (NPSAS: 12).

[2] See: https://www.hesa.ac.uk/content/view/3484/#age

[3] Details taken from: https://www.gov.uk/time-off-for-dependants/your-rights

Statistical appendix

Data in Chapter Two: the UK Labour Force Survey and US Current Population Survey

In Chapter Two, we present data on the incomes of people over 65 in the UK and US from an analysis by the author of the UK Labour Force Survey and the US Current Population Survey (see Figures 5.2 and 5.3). The surveys were selected because of their detailed information about the incomes of older people. The surveys analysed were harmonised by the author as part of his earlier PhD research (see Lain, 2009). The author replicated the variables used in the Luxembourg Income Study (LIS) in order to ensure that they were comparable across countries (for more on the LIS, see Atkinson, 2004). These variables were then adapted slightly to ensure that the full range of means-tested benefits were categorised as such (see Lain, 2009).

Data in Part Two: the English Longitudinal Study of Ageing and the US Health and Retirement Study

In Part Two of the book (Chapters Four to Six), the English Longitudinal Study of Ageing (ELSA) and the US Health and Retirement Study (HRS) were analysed. These surveys interview people in their 50s upwards, alongside their partners, on a biannual basis. ELSA was designed in conjunction with those working on HRS, and consequently the surveys have a high degree of comparability in terms of the variables constructed (see Banks et al, 2006). We used comparable data files created by the RAND organisation (for the HRS data) and the Gateway to Global Aging Data (for ELSA) (see Phillips et al, 2014; Chien et al, 2014). Please see the acknowledgements section for more details on the parters involved in creating and funding the data.

The analysis in Part Two focuses primarily on those aged 65–74, although the survey year analysed varies slightly depending upon what is most appropriate. In Chapter Four, we examine the pathways that people take to employment at 65+ and focus on those aged 65–74 in 2012. For that chapter, we also draw on data for these individuals going back to 2002, the year that ELSA started. In Chapters Five and Six, most of the analysis examines those aged 65–74 in 2010; this is because we have a more complete selection of variables related to wealth and financial position in 2010 (Phillips et al, 2014). We also present some analysis of those aged 65–74 in 2008 because questions about the motivation for employment were asked in that wave.

By way of illustration about the sample size, the sample of people aged 65–74 in 2008 was 2,941 for England (including 405 workers) and 5,891 for the US (1,668 workers). Weights provided were used as advised by both surveys to increase the representativeness of the samples; it was particularly important to weight the HRS analysis because of its complex sample structure (Aneshensel, 2013: 167–96). Although the analysis focuses on England, the result should broadly reflect those of the UK as a whole because England represents 84% of the UK population (ONS, 2012).

In Chapters Five and Six, some of the analysis is presented as 'unadjusted' and 'adjusted' *percentage probabilities* of working (or being financially motivated). These results are derived from logistic regression analysis, which is then converted into percentage probabilities; this is explained more fully in the text itself (see also Williams, 2012). The 'adjusted' results, in effect, 'control' for a range of other factors that may influence the propensity for someone to be working (or be financially motivated if in employment). When presenting this analysis, we usually list what the adjusted results are controlled for, without going into detail about each of the variables included. This is to avoid the text becoming overly repetitive. The text directs the reader to this statistical appendix if they want to find out more about the 'control' variables used. For ease of reference, Table A.1 gives an overview of these variables.

Table A.1: Overview of 'control' variables referred to in the text

Description in text	Explanation
'Wealth'	Non-housing, non-pension 'household' wealth, including savings, investments, businesses and other property/real estate (excludes main residence). A household is defined as an individual or a couple. For couples, wealth has been equivalised to the individual level using the Organisation for Economic Co-operation and Development (OECD) modified scale; this assumes that a couple needs 1.5 times the income or wealth of a single person to have an equivalent standard of living. This equivalised wealth was then used to allocate people to four equally sized wealth quartiles.
'Private pension coverage'	This indicates whether a person has a private pension (yes/no). This includes private pensions that we have been able to identify that the individual either receives, or is entitled to receive, in future. Pensions may be from a current or former employer, or those held by an individual. Pensions may be from an earlier period of employment. For the US, we include Individual Retirement Accounts because these are significant pension vehicles for the self-employed.
Home ownership status	Individuals are categorised as being either: (1) outright homeowners, (2) home-buyers (still paying a mortgage); or (3) renters. In the data, a very small number of individuals are in an 'other' category; the numbers involved were too small to be analysed separately. As these individuals do not have the security of home ownership, we have combined them under the category of renters.
Education/ qualifications	Individuals were placed into four categories on the basis of their highest qualification; the categories derive from the HRS variable (see Table 5.1). 'Below high school' indicates below secondary qualifications. 'High school' represents secondary-level education – in the UK, this includes O-levels; in the US, this includes people with a High School Diploma or a General Educational Development (GED) diploma (which is designed to be equivalent). 'College+' indicates having an undergraduate or Master's degree or a PhD 'Some College' represents a qualification between secondary level and 'College+'; in the UK, this includes A Levels.
Self-rated health	Individuals self-defined their health on a five-point Likert scale, ranging from 'excellent' to 'poor' health.
Partnership status	Individuals were categorised depending upon whether or not they were single or 'partnered' (cohabiting or married). The variable includes information about the partner's employment status (see Table 6.1). People could be categorised as being single or partnered with: a working partner; a non-working partner; or a partner with unknown employment status.
Activities of daily living (ADL) limitations	Individuals were asked if they had any difficulties with seven ADLs (see Table 5.4). The number of ADL difficulties were summed for each person, such that individuals could have between none and seven ADL limitations.

References

AARP (2014) *Staying ahead of the curve: The AARP Work and Career Study*, Washington, DC: AARP.

Abraham, K. and Houseman, S. (2005) 'Work and retirement plans among older Americans', in R. Clark and O. Mitchell (eds) *Reinventing the retirement paradigm*, Oxford: Oxford University Press, pp 70–91.

Adams, S.J. (2004) 'Age discrimination legislation and the employment of older workers', *Labour Economics*, 11(2): 219–41.

Adams, S.J. and Heywood, J.S. (2007) 'The age of hiring and deferred compensation: evidence from Australia', *Economic Record*, 83(261): 174–90.

Alden, E. (2012) *Flexible employment: How employment and the use of flexibility policies through the life course can affect later life occupation and financial outcomes*, London: Age Concern.

Alesina, A. and Glaeser, E. (2004) *Fighting poverty in the US and Europe: A world of difference*, Oxford: Oxford University Press.

Altmann, R. (2015) *A new vision for older workers: Retain, retrain, recruit*, London: Department for Work and Pensions.

Altonji, J.G. and Paxson, C.H. (1992) 'Labor supply, hours constraints and job mobility', *Journal of Human Resources*, 27(2): 256–78.

Aneshensel, C. (2013) *Theory-based data analysis for the social sciences*, Thousand Oaks, CA: Sage Publications.

Arkani, S. and Gough, O. (2007) 'The impact of occupational pensions on retirement age', *Journal of Social Policy*, 36: 297–318.

Atkinson, A.B. (2004) 'The Luxembourg Income Study (LIS): past, present and future', *Socio-Economic Review*, 2(2): 165–90.

Atkinson, J., Evans, C., Willison, R., Lain, D. and Van Gent, M. (2003) *New Deal 50plus: Sustainability of employment*, London: Department for Work and Pensions.

Banks, J. and Tetlow, G. (2008) 'Extending working lives', in J. Banks, E. Breeze, C. Lessof and J. Nazroo (eds) *Living in the 21st century: Older people in England*, London: Institute for Fiscal Studies, pp 19–56.

Banks, J., Marmot, M., Oldfield, Z. and Smith, J.P. (2006) 'Disease and disadvantage in the United States and in England', *Jama – Journal of the American Medical Association*, 295(17): 2037–45.

Banks, J., Emmerson, C. and Tetlow, G. (2007) 'Healthy retirement or unhealthy inactivity: How important are financial incentives in explaining retirement', Institute for Fiscal Studies. Available at: http://www.ifs.org.uk/publications/3972 (accessed 27 November 2014).

Banks, J., Blundell, R., Bozio, A. and Emmerson, C. (2008) *Releasing jobs for the young? Early retirement and youth unemployment in the United Kingdom*, London: Institute for Fiscal Studies.

Barnes, H., Parry, J. and Taylor, R. (2004) *Working after state pension age: Qualitative research*, Norwich: Her Majesty's Stationary Office.

Baxter, J. (1998) 'Will the employment conditions of part-timers in Australia and New Zealand worsen?', in J. O'Reilly and C. Fagan (eds) *Part-time prospects: An international comparison of part-time work in Europe, North America and the Pacific Rim*, London: Routledge, pp 265–81.

Béland, D. and Waddan, A. (2012) *The politics of policy change: Welfare, Medicare, and Social Security reform in the United States*, Washington, DC: Georgetown University Press.

Bell, K., Gaffney, D. (2012) *Making a contribution: Social security for the future*, London: Trades Union Congress.

Bender, K.A., Mavromaras, K.G., Theodossiou, I. and Wei, Z. (2014) *The effect of wealth and earned income on the decision to retire: A dynamic probit examination of retirement*, Bonn: IZA.

Berkowitz, E. and DeWitt, L. (2013) *The other welfare: Supplemental security income and US social policy*, New York: Cornell University Press.

Black, C.M. (2008) *Working for a healthier tomorrow: Dame Carol Black's review of the health of Britain's working age population*, London: The Stationery Office.

Blau, D.M. (1998) 'Labor force dynamics of older married couples', *Journal of Labor Economics*, 16(3): 595–629.

Blau, D.M. and Gilleskie, D.B. (2006) 'Health insurance and retirement of married couples', *Journal of Applied Econometrics*, 21(7): 935–53.

Blau, D.M. and Shvydko, T. (2011) 'Labor market rigidities and the employment behavior of older Americans', *Industrial & Labor Relations Review*, 64(3): 464–84.

Blekesaune, M., Bryan, M., Taylor, M. and Britain, G. (2008) *Life-course events and later-life employment*, Norwich: Department for Work and Pensions.

Blossfeld, H.-P., Buchholz, S. and Kurz, K. (eds) (2011) *Aging populations, globalization and the labor market: Comparing late working life and retirement in modern societies*, Cheltenham: Edward Elgar.

Blyth, M. (2002) *Great transformations: Economic ideas and institutional change in the twentieth century*, New York, NY: Cambridge University Press.

Bolin, K., Lindgren, B. and Lundborg, P. (2008) 'Your next of kin or your own career? Caring and working among the 50+ of Europe', *Journal of Health Economics*, 27(3): 718–38.

Bonoli, G. and Shinkawa, T. (2005) *Aging and pension reform around the world*, Cheltenham: Edward Elgar Publishing.

Boushey, G. (2010) *Policy diffusion dynamics in America*, Cambridge: Cambridge University Press.

Boushey, G. (2012) 'Punctuated equilibrium theory and the diffusion of innovations', *Policy Studies Journal*, 40(1): 127–46.

Bozio, A., Crawford, R. and Tetlow, G. (2010) *The history of state pensions in the UK: 1948 to 2010*, London: Institute for Fiscal Studies.

Bridgen, P. and Meyer, T. (2007) 'The British pension system and social inclusion', in T. Meyer, P. Bridgen and B. Riedmuller (eds) *Private pensions versus social inclusion? Non-state provision for citizens at risk in Europe*, Cheltenham: Edward Elgar, pp 47–78.

Bridgen, P. and Meyer, T. (2011) 'Britain: exhausted voluntarism – the evolution of a hybrid pension regime', in B. Ebbinghaus (ed) *The varieties of pension governance: Pension privatization in Europe*, Oxford: Oxford University Press, pp 265–92.

Bridgen, P. and Meyer, T. (2013) 'Fair cuts? The impact of British public service pension reform on workers in the main occupations', *Social Policy and Society*, 12(1): 105–22.

Buchholz, S., Rinklake, A., Schilling, J., Kurz, K., Schmelzer, P. and Blossfeld, H.-P. (2011) 'Aging populations, globalization and the labor market: comparing late working life and retirement in modern societies', in H.-P. Blossfeld and K. Kurz (eds) *Aging populations, globalization and the labor market: Comparing late working life and retirement in modern societies*, Cheltenham: Edward Elgar, pp 3–32.

Buessing, M. and Soto, M. (2006) *The state of private pensions: Current 5500 data*, Chestnut Hill, MA: Centre for Retirement Research at Boston College.

Burchell, B., Ladipo, D. and Wilkinson, F. (eds) (2005) *Job insecurity and work intensification*, London: Routledge.

Burtless, G. (2013) *Can educational attainment explain the rise in labor force participation at older ages?*, Chestnut Hill, MA: Centre for Retirement Research at Boston College.

Butrica, B.A. and Karamcheva, N.S. (2013) *Does household debt influence the labor supply and benefit claiming decisions of older Americans?*, Chestnut Hill, MA: Center for Retirement Research at Boston College.

Cabinet Office (2000) *Winning the generation game: Improving opportunities for people aged 50–65 in work and community activity*, London: The Stationery Office.

Cahill, K.E. and Quinn, J.F. (2014) 'A balanced look at self-employment transitions later in life', *Public Policy & Aging Report*, 24(4): 134–40.

Cahill, K.E., Giandrea, M.D. and Quinn, J.F. (2011) 'Reentering the labor force after retirement', *Monthly Labor Review*, 134(6): 34–42.

Campbell, N. (1999) *The decline of employment among older people in Britain*, Working Paper CASE019, London: London School of Economics.

Cappelli, P. (1999) *The new deal at work: Managing the market-driven workforce*, Boston, MA: Harvard Business Press.

Cates, J.R. (1983) *Insuring inequality: Administrative leadership in Social Security, 1935–54*, Ann Arbor, MI: University of Michigan Press.

CBI (Confederation of British Industry) (2013) *On the up: CBI/ Accenture employment trends survey 2013*, London: Confederation of British Industry.

Cebulla, A., Butt, S. and Lyon, N. (2007) 'Working beyond the state pension age in the United Kingdom: the role of working time flexibility and the effects on the home', *Ageing and Society*, 27(6): 849–68.

Chien, S., Campbell, N., Hayden, O., Hurd, M., Main, R., Mallett, J., Martin, C., Meijer, E., Moldoff, M., Rohwedder, S. and St.Clair, P. (2014) *Rand HRS data documentation: Version N*, Los Angeles, CA: USC Davis Centre for Global Aging Research. Available at: http://hrsonline.isr.umich.edu/modules/meta/rand/randhrsn/randhrsN.pdf (accessed 17 January 2016).

Clark, G.L. (2006) 'The UK occupational pension system in crisis', in H. Pemberton, P. Thane and N. Whiteside (eds) *Britain's pensions crisis: History and policy*, London: Oxford University Press, pp 145–68.

Clark, T. (2013) 'A pension age of 70? That's what is in store for overburdened Generation Y', *The Guardian*. Available at: http://www.theguardian.com/society/2013/dec/05/pension-age-70-in-store-generation-y (accessed 27 September 2015).

Clinton, B. (2000) 'Remarks by the president at bill signing the Senior Citizens Freedom to Work Act of 2000–April 7, 2000', Social Security Administration. Available at: http://www.ssa.gov/history/clintonfreedom.html (accessed 27 September 2015).

Costa, D.L. (1998) *The evolution of retirement: An American economic history, 1880–1990*, Chicago, IL: University of Chicago Press.

Crawford, R. and Tetlow, G. (2010) 'Employment, retirement and pensions', in J. Banks, C. Lessof, J. Nazroo, N. Rogers, M. Stafford and A. Steptoe (eds) *Financial circumstances, health and well-being of the older population in England*, London: Institute for Fiscal Studies, pp 11–75.

Crawford, R., Keynes, S. and Tetlow, G. (2013) *A single-tier pension: What does it really mean?*, London: Institute for Fiscal Studies.

Daniel, K. and Heywood, J.S. (2007) 'The determinants of hiring older workers: UK evidence', *Labour Economics*, 14(1): 35–51.

Davey, J.A. (2007) *Maximising the potential of older workers*, Wellington: New Zealand Institute for Research on Ageing, Victoria University of Wellington.

Disney, R. and Smith, S. (2002) 'The labour supply effect of the abolition of the earnings rule for older workers in the United Kingdom', *The Economic Journal*, 112(478): C136–52.

Disney, R., Grundy, E., Johnson, P. and Britain, G. (1997) *The dynamics of retirement: Analyses of the retirement surveys*, London: The Stationery Office.

DSS (Department for Social Security) (1998) *A new contract for welfare: Partnership in pensions*, London: Department for Social Security.

Dubois, H. and Anderson, R. (2012) *Income from work after retirement in the EU*, Luxembourg: Publications Office of the European Union.

Duncan, C. (2003) 'Assessing anti-ageism routes to older worker re-engagement', *Work Employment and Society*, 17(1): 101–20.

DWP (Department for Work and Pensions) (2007) 'The pensioners' incomes series 2005/6 (revised)', Department for Work and Pensions. Available at: http://campaigns.dwp.gov.uk/asd/asd6/PI_series_0506.pdf (accessed 16 February 2012).

DWP (2008) 'Projections of entitlement to income related benefits to 2050', Department for Work and Pensions. Available at: http://www.irrv.net/forums/alert/documents/RelatedBenefits.pdf (accessed 17 January 2016).

DWP (2013) *State pension age timetables* Department for Work and Pensions, https://www.gov.uk/government/uploads/system/uploads/attachment_data/file/310231/spa-timetable.pdf, date accessed 20/12/15

DWP (2014a) *Automatic enrolment opt out rates: Findings from qualitative research with employers staging in 2014*, London: Department for Work and Pensions.

DWP (2014b) *Working longer: A framework for action background evidence*, London: Department for Work and Pensions.

Ebbinghaus, B. (2006) *Reforming early retirement in Europe, Japan and the USA*, Oxford: Oxford University Press.

EC (2002) *Increasing labour force participation and promoting active ageing*, Com (2002) Final 9, Brussels: European Commission.

EC (2014) *Identifying fiscal sustainability challenges in the areas of pension, health care and long-term care policies*, Brussels: European Commission.

Elder, T.E. and Powers, E.T. (2006) 'The incredible shrinking program', *Research on Aging*, 28(3): 341–58.

Esping-Andersen, G. (1990) *The three worlds of welfare capitalism*, Princeton, NJ: Princeton University Press.

Faggio, G. and Nickell, S. (2003) 'The rise in inactivity among adult men', in R. Dickens, P. Gregg and J. Wadsworth (eds) *The labour market under New Labour: The state of working Britain*, New York, NY: Palgrave Macmillan, pp 40–52.

Family and Childcare Trust (2014) *Where next for child care? Learning from the 2004 Childcare Strategy and 10 years of policy*, London: Family and Childcare Trust.

Fitzpatrick, R. (2008) 'Organising and funding health care', in G. Scambler (ed) *Sociology as applied to medicine*, Edinburgh: Saunders, pp 313–28.

Flynn, M. (2010) 'The United Kingdom government's 'business case' approach to the regulation of retirement', *Ageing & Society*, 30: 421-43.

Foster, L. (2014) 'Towards a fairer pension system for women? Assessing the impact of recent pension changes on women', in K. Farnsworth, Z. Irving and M. Fenger (eds) *Social policy review 26: Analysis and debate in social policy*, Bristol: The Policy Press, pp 29–46.

Friedberg, L. and Webb, A. (2005) 'Retirement and the evolution of pension structure', *Journal of Human Resources*, 40(2): 281–308.

Garfinkel, I., Rainwater, L. and Smeeding, T. (2011) *Wealth and welfare states: Is America a laggard or leader?*, Oxford: Oxford University Press.

Gash, V. (2008) 'Preference or constraint? Part-time workers' transitions in Denmark, France and the United Kingdom', *Work, Employment & Society*, 22(4): 655–74.

Giandrea, M.D., Cahill, K.E. and Quinn, J.F. (2009) 'Bridge jobs a comparison across cohorts', *Research on Aging*, 31(5): 549–76.

Giandrea, M.D., Cahill, K.E. and Quinn, J.F. (2010) *The role of re-entry in the retirement process*, Washington, DC: US Bureau of Labor Statistics.

Ginn, J. (2003) *Gender, pensions and the lifecourse: How pensions need to adapt to changing family forms*, Bristol: The Policy Press.

Ginn, J. and MacIntyre, K. (2013) 'UK pension reforms: is gender still an issue?', *Social Policy and Society*, 12(1): 91–103.

Glaser, K., Montserrat, E.R., Waginger, U., Price, D., Stuchbury, R. and Tinker, A. (2010) *Grandparenting in Europe*, London: Grandparents Plus.

Gobeski, K.T. (2010) 'Occupational mobility after fifty', in J.A. Jaworski (ed) *Advances in sociology research, volume 6*, Hauppauge: Nova Science Publishers, pp 93–112.

Gordon, C. (1994) *New deals: Business, labor, and politics in america, 1920-1935*: Cambridge University Press.

Green, C.A. (2006) 'The unexpected impact of health on the labor supply of the oldest Americans', *Journal of Labor Research*, 27(3): 361–79.

Green, F. (2006) *Demanding work: The paradox of job quality in the affluent economy*, Princeton, NJ: Princeton University Press.

Gruber, J. and Wise, D. (eds) (1999) *Social security and retirement around the world*, Chicago, IL: University of Chicago Press.

Gustman, A.L. and Steinmeier, T.L. (2002) *Social security, pensions and retirement behavior within the family*, Ann Arbour, MI: University of Michigan Research Centre.

Hacker, J.S. (2006) *The great risk shift: The assault on American jobs, families, health care, and retirement and how you can fight back*, New York, NY: Oxford University Press.

Haider, S. and Loughran, D. (2001) *Elderly labor supply: Work or play?*, Boston, MA: Center for Retirement Research at Boston College.

Hall, P.A. and Soskice, D.W. (eds) (2001) *Varieties of capitalism: The institutional foundations of comparative advantage*, Oxford: Oxford University Press.

Hannah, L. (1986) *Inventing retirement: The development of occupational pensions in Britain*, Cambridge: Cambridge University Press.

Hansen, S.W. (1980) 'The Age Discrimination in Employment Act amendments of 1978: A legal and economic analysis', *Pepperdine Law Review*, 7(1): 4.

Harrington Meyer, M. (2014) *Grandmothers at work: Juggling families and jobs*, New York, NY: New York University Press.

Harrington Meyer, M. and Herd, P. (2007) *Market friendly or family friendly? The state and gender inequality in old age*, New York, NY: Russell Sage Foundation.

Hayes, B.C. and Vandenheuvel, A. (1994) 'Attitudes to mandatory retirement – an international comparison', *International Journal of Aging & Human Development*, 39(3): 209–31.

Hedges, A. and Sykes, W. (2009) *Extending working life: Changing the culture. Qualitative research into effective messages*, Norwich: HMSO.

Heywood, J.S. and Siebert, S. (2008) *Understanding the labour market for older workers*, IEA Discussion Paper No 23, London: Institute for Economic Affairs.

Heywood, J.S., Ho, L.S. and Wei, X.D. (1999) 'The determinants of hiring older workers: evidence from Hong Kong', *Industrial & Labor Relations Review*, 52(3): 444–59.

Heywood, J.S., Jirjahn, U. and Tsertsvardze, G. (2010) 'Hiring older workers and employing older workers: German evidence', *Journal of Population Economics*, 23(2): 595–615.

Heywood, J.S., Jirjahn, U. and Tsertsvadze, G. (2011) 'Part-time work and the hiring of older workers', *Applied Economics*, 43(28): 4239–55.

Hicks, P. (2001) *Public support for retirement income reform*, Paris: OECD.

Hirsch, B.T., Macpherson, D.A. and Hardy, M.A. (2000) 'Occupational age structure and access for older workers', *Industrial & Labour Relations Review*, 53: 401.

HM Government (2009) *Building a society for all ages*, London: Stationery Office.

Ho, J.H. and Raymo, J.M. (2009) 'Expectations and realization of joint retirement among dual-worker couples', *Research on Aging*, 31(2): 153–79.

Hofacker, D. (2010) *Older workers in a globalizing world: An international comparison of retirement and late-career patterns in Western industrialized countries*, Cheltenham: Edward Elgar.

Hughes, M.E., Waite, L.J., LaPierre, T.A. and Luo, Y. (2007) 'All in the family: the impact of caring for grandchildren on grandparents' health', *The Journals of Gerontology Series B: Psychological Sciences and Social Sciences*, 62(2): S108–19.

Hutchens, R. (1988) 'Do job opportunities decline with age', *Industrial & Labour Relations Review*, 42: 89.

Hutchens, R. (2010) 'Worker characteristics, job characteristics, and opportunities for phased retirement', *Labour Economics*, 17(6): 1010–21.

Hutchens, R. and Grace-Martin, K. (2006) 'Employer willingness to permit phased retirement: why are some more willing than others?', *Industrial & Labor Relations Review*, 59(4): 525–46.

Inceoglu, I., Segers, J. and Bartram, D. (2011) 'Age-related differences in work motivation', *Journal of Occupational and Organizational Psychology*, 85(2): 300–29.

Issacharoff, S. and Harris, E.W. (1997) 'Is age discrimination really age discrimination? The ADEA's unnatural solution', *New York University Law Review*, 72(4): 780–840.

Jensen, P.H. (2005) 'Reversing the trend from "early" to "late" exit: push, pull and jump revisited in a Danish context', *Geneva Papers on Risk and Insurance – Issues and Practice*, 30(4): 656–73.

Johnson, R. (2011) 'Phased retirement and workplace flexibility for older adults: opportunities and challenges', *Annals of the American Academy of Political and Social Science*, 638: 68–85.

Johnson, R. and Mommaerts, C. (2011) *Age differences in job displacement, job search, and reemployment*, Boston, MA: Boston College Center for Retirement Research.

Johnson, R. and Steuerle, E. (2004) 'Promoting work at older ages: the role of hybrid pension plans in an aging population', *Journal of Pension Economics and Finance*, 3(3): 315–37.

Johnson, R., Butrica, B. and Mommaerts, C. (2010) *Work and retirement patterns for the G.I. generation, silent generation, and early boomers: Thirty years of change*, Washington, DC: Urban Institute.

Johnson, R., Mermin, G.B.T. and Resseger, M. (2011) 'Job demands and work ability at older ages', *Journal of Aging & Social Policy*, 23(2): 101–18.

Jones, A.M., Rice, N. and Roberts, J. (2010) 'Sick of work or too sick to work? Evidence on self-reported health shocks and early retirement from the BHPS', *Economic Modelling*, 27(4): 866–80.

Jones, D.A. and McIntosh, B.R. (2010) 'Organizational and occupational commitment in relation to bridge employment and retirement intentions', *Journal of Vocational Behavior*, 77(2): 290–303.

Kanabar, R. (2012) *Unretirement in England: An empirical perspective*, Discussion Papers in Economics No 12/31, York: University of York.

Kapur, K. and Rogowski, J. (2011) 'How does health insurance affect the retirement behavior of women?', *Inquiry – The Journal of Health Care Organization Provision and Financing*, 48(1): 51–67.

Khawaja, M. and Boddington, B. (2009) 'Too early to retire? Growing participation of older New Zealanders in the labour force', *New Zealand Population Review*, 35: 75–93.

Kidd, M.P., Metcalfe, R. and Sloane, P.J. (2012) 'The determinants of hiring older workers in Britain revisited: An analysis using WERS 2004', *Applied Economics*, 44(4): 527–36.

Kodz, J., Davis, S., Lain, D., Strebler, M., Rick, J., Bates, P., Cummings, J., Meager, N., Anxo, D. and Gineste, S. (2003) *Working long hours: A review of the evidence. Volume 1 – main report*, London: Department for Trade and Industry.

Komp, K., Van Tilburg, T. and Van Groenou, M.B. (2010) 'Paid work between age 60 and 70 years in Europe: A matter of socio-economic status', *International Journal of Ageing and Later Life*, 5(1): 45–75.

Koslowski, A. (2009) 'Grandparents and the care of their grandchildren', in J. Stillwell, E. Coast and D. Kneale (eds) *Fertility, living arrangements, care and mobility*, London: Springer, pp 171–90.

Laczko, F. and Phillipson, C. (1991) 'Great Britain: The contradictions of early exit', in M. kohli, M. Rein, A. Guillemard and H. Van Gunsteren (eds) *Time for retirement: Comparative studies of early exit from the labor force*, Cambridge: Cambridge University Press, pp 222–51.

Lahey, J.N. (2008) 'Age, women, and hiring – an experimental study', *Journal of Human Resources*, 43(1): 30–56.

Lain, D. (2009) *Healthy, wealthy and wise? Working past age 65 in the UK and USA*, Sociology DPhil, Brighton: University of Sussex.

Lain, D. (2011) 'Helping the poorest help themselves? Encouraging employment past 65 in England and the USA', *Journal of Social Policy*, 40: 493–512.

Lain, D. (2012a) 'Working past 65 in the UK and the USA: segregation into "Lopaq" occupations?', *Work, Employment & Society*, 26(1): 78–94.

Lain, D. (2012b) 'Comparing health and employment in England and the United States', in S. Vickerstaff, C. Phillipson and R. Wilkie (eds) *Work, health and well-being: The challenges of managing health at work*, Bristol: The Policy Press, pp 59–78.

Lain, D. (2015) *Domain – financial factors: Understanding employment participation of older workers*, Berlin: Federal Ministry of Labour and Social Affairs (BMAS) and Federal Institute for Occupational Safety and Health (BAuA). Available at: http://www.jp-demographic.eu/wp-content/uploads/2015/07/UK-National-Report.pdf (accessed 17 January 2016).

Lain, D. (forthcoming) 'Employment of workers age over 65: the importance of policy context', in E. Parry and J. McCarthy (eds) *Handbook of age diversity and work*, London: Palgrave.

Lain, D. and Loretto, W. (forthcoming) 'Managing employees beyond age 65: from the margins to the mainstream?', *Employee Relations*.

Lain, D. and Vickerstaff, S. (2014) 'Working beyond retirement age: lessons for policy', in S. Harper and K. Hamblin (eds) *International handbook on ageing and public policy*, Cheltenham: Edward Elgar, pp 242–55.

Lain, D., Vickerstaff, S. and Loretto, W. (2013) 'Reforming state pension provision in "liberal" Anglo-Saxon countries: re-commodification, cost-containment or recalibration?', *Social Policy and Society*, 12(1): 77–90.

Lazear, E.P. (1979) 'Why is there mandatory retirement?', *Journal of Political Economy*, 87(6): 1261–84.

Lee, Y. and Tang, F. (2015) 'More caregiving, less working: caregiving roles and gender difference', *Journal of Applied Gerontology*, 34(4): 465–83.

Leisering, L. (2004) 'Government and the life course', in J. Mortimer and M. Shanahan (eds) *Handbook of the life course*, New York, NY: Kluwer Academic/Plenum, pp 205–25.

Lindert, P.H. (2004) *Growing public: Volume 1, the story: Social spending and economic growth since the eighteenth century*, Cambridge: Cambridge University Press.

Loretto, W. and Vickerstaff, S. (2013) 'The domestic and gendered context for retirement', *Human Relations*, 66(1): 65–86.

Loretto, W. and Vickerstaff, S. (2015) 'Gender, age and flexible working in later life', *Work, Employment & Society*, 29(2): 233–49.

Loretto, W. and White, P. (2006) 'Employers' attitudes, practices and policies towards older workers', *Human Resource Management Journal*, 16(3): 313–30.

Lynes, T. (1996) *Our pensions: A policy for a Labour government*, London: Eunomia Publications.

Lynes, T. (1997) 'The British case', in M. Rein and E. Wadensjo (eds) *Enterprise and the welfare state*, Cheltenham: Edward Elgar, 309–51.

Lyonette, C., Kaufman, G. and Crompton, R. (2011) '"We both need to work": maternal employment, childcare and health care in Britain and the USA', *Work, Employment & Society*, 25(1): 34–50.

Macnicol, J. (2006) *Age discrimination: An historical and contemporary analysis*, Cambridge: Cambridge University Press.

Macnicol, J. (2007) 'The American experience of age discrimination legislation', in W. Loretto, S. Vickerstaff and P. White (eds) *The future for older workers: New perspectives*, Bristol: Policy Press, pp 27–42.

Macnicol, J. (2015) *Neoliberalising old age*, Cambridge: Cambridge University Press.

Maestas, N. (2010) 'Back to work expectations and realizations of work after retirement', *Journal of Human Resources*, 45(3): 718–48.

Mann, A. (2011) 'The effect of late-life debt use on retirement decisions', *Social Science Research*, 40(6): 1623–37.

Marmot, M., Allen, J., Goldblatt, P., Boyce, T., McNeish, D., Grady, M. and Geddes, I. (2010) *Fair society, healthy lives: The Marmot review, strategic review of health inequalities in England post 2010*, London: Department of Health.

Matthews, K. and Nazroo, J. (2015) 'Later-life work, health and wellbeing: Enduring inequalities', in S. Scherger (ed) *Paid work beyond pension age*, London: Palgrave Macmillan, 259–77.

McGeary, K.A. (2009) 'How do health shocks influence retirement decisions?', *Review of Economics of the Household*, 7(3): 307–21.

McNair, S. (2006) 'How different is the older labour market? Attitudes to work and retirement among older people in Britain', *Social Policy and Society*, 5(4): 485–94.

McNamara, T.K. and Williamson, J.B. (2004) 'Race, gender, and the retirement decisions of people ages 60 to 80: prospects for age integration in employment', *International Journal of Aging & Human Development*, 59(3): 255–86.

Meadows, P. (2003) *Retirement ages in the UK: A review of the evidence*, London: Department for Trade and Industry.

Messe, P.J. (2011) 'Taxation of early retirement windows and delaying retirement: the French experience', *Economic Modelling*, 28(5): 2319–41.

Metcalf, H. and Meadows, P. (2006) *Survey of employers' policies, practices and preferences relating to age*, London: Department for Work and Pensions.

Milhoj, P. (1968) 'Work and retirement', in E. Shanas, P. Townsend, D. Wedderburn, H. Friis, P. Milhoj and J. Stehouwer (eds) *Old people in three industrial societies*, London: Routledge and Kegan Paul Limited, pp 288–319.

Minkler, M. and Fuller-Thomson, E. (2000) 'Second time around parenting: factors predictive of grandparents becoming caregivers for their grandchildren', *International Journal of Aging and Human Development*, 50(3): 185–200.

Mohrman-Gillis, M. (1978) 'Age discrimination in Employment Act amendments of 1978: A questionable expansion', *Catholic University Law Review*, 27(summer): 767–84.

Munnell, A.H., Triest, R.K. and Jivan, N.A. (2004) *How do pensions affect expected and actual retirement ages*, Chestnut Hill, MA: Center for Retirement Research at Boston College.

Myles, J. and Pierson, P. (2001) 'The comparative political economy of pension reform', in P. Pierson (ed) *The new politics of the welfare state*, Oxford: Oxford University Press, pp 305–33.

National Pensioners Convention (1998) *Pensions not relief: The National Pensioners Conventions submissions to the government's pension review*, London: National Pensioners Convention.

NEST (2014) *Statement of investment principles: April 2014 to March 2015*, London: National Employment Savings Trust.

Neumark, D. (2003) 'Age discrimination legislation in the United States', *Contemporary Economic Policy*, 21(3): 297–317.

Neumark, D. (2009) 'The Age Discrimination in Employment Act and the challenge of population aging', *Research on Aging*, 31(1): 41–68.

Neumark, D. and Stock, W.A. (1999) 'Age discrimination laws and labor market efficiency', *Journal of Political Economy*, 107(5): 1081–125.

O'Connor, J.S., Orloff, A.S. and Shaver, S. (1999) *States, markets, families: Gender, liberalism and social policy in Australia, Canada, Great Britain and the United States*, Cambridge: Cambridge University Press.

OECD (Organisation for Economic Co-operation and Development) (no date) 'What are equivalence scales?', Organisation for Economic Co-operation and Development. Available at: http://www.oecd. org/eco/growth/OECD-Note-EquivalenceScales.pdf (accessed 27 September 2015).

OECD (2004) *Education at a glance 2004*, Paris: Organisation for Economic Co-operation and Development.

OECD (2005a) *Ageing and employment policies: United States*, Paris: Organisation for Economic Co-operation and Development.

OECD (2005b) *Pensions at a glance 2005*, Paris: Organisation for Economic Co-operation and Development.

OECD (2009) *Pensions at a glance 2009*, Paris: Organisation for Economic Co-operation and Development.

OECD (2011) *Pensions at a glance 2011*, Paris: Organisation for Economic Co-operation and Development.

OECD (2013) 'Protecting jobs, enhancing flexibility: a new look at employment protection legislation', in OECD (ed) *Employment Outlook 2013*, Paris: Organisation for Economic Co-operation and Development, pp 65–126.

OECD (2014) *Education at a glance 2014*, Paris: Organisation for Economic Co-operation and Development.

ONS (Office for National Statistics) (2012) '2011 Census: population estimates for the United Kingdom', 27 March, Office for National Statistics. Available at: http://www.ons.gov.uk/ons/dcp171778_292378.pdf (accessed 28 January 2014).

ONS (2013a) 'Pension trends chapter 5: state pensions, 2013 edition', Office for National Statistics. Available at: http://www.ons.gov.uk/ons/dcp171766_341468.pdf (accessed 27 November 2014).

ONS (2013b) 'Pension trends chapter 8: pension contributions, 2013 edition', Office for National Statistics. Available at: http://www.ons.gov.uk/ons/dcp171766_310458.pdf (accessed 27 November 2014).

ONS (2013c) 'Women in the labour market', Office for National Statistics. Available at: http://www.ons.gov.uk/ons/dcp171776_328352.pdf (accessed 17 January 2016).

Orloff, A.S. (1993) *The politics of pensions: A comparative analysis of Britain, Canada, and the United States, 1880–1940*, Madison, WI: University of Wisconsin Press.

Pampel, F.C. (1998) *Aging, social inequality, and public policy*, Thousand Oaks, CA: Pine Forge Press.

Papworth, J. (2013) 'Annuity rates rise but reprieve may be short-lived', *The Guardian*. Available at: http://www.theguardian.com/money/2013/mar/16/annuity-rates-rise-reprieve-short-lived (accessed 17 January 2016).

Parker, S.C. and Rougier, J.C. (2007) 'The retirement behaviour of the self-employed in Britain', *Applied Economics*, 39(4–6): 697–713.

Parries, H.S. and Sommers, D.G. (1994) 'Shunning retirement: work experience of men in their seventies and early eighties', *Journals of Gerontology*, 49(3): S117–24.

Pensions Commission (2004) *Pensions: Challenges and choices. The first report of the Pensions Commission*, Norwich: The Stationary Office.

Pensions Commission (2005) *A new pension settlement for the twenty-first century. The second report of the Pensions Commission*, Norwich: The Stationery Office.

Pensions Policy Institute (2010) *Pension facts*, London: Pensions Policy Institute.

Phillips, D., Lin, Y.-C., Chien, S., Moldoff, M., Lee, J. and Zamarro, G. (2014) *Harmonized ELSA documentation: Version C: October 2014*, Los Angeles, CA: USC Davis Centre for Global Aging Research. Available at: http://doc.ukdataservice.ac.uk/doc/5050/mrdoc/pdf/5050_Harmonized_ELSA_C.pdf (accessed 17 January 2016).

Phillipson, C. (1982) *Capitalism and the construction of old age*, London: Macmillan.

Phillipson, C. (2009) 'Changing life course transitions: implications for work and lifelong learning', in A. Chiva and J. Manthorpe (eds) *Older workers in Europe*, Berkshire: Open University Press, pp 110–16.

Phillipson, C. (2013) *Ageing*, Cambridge: Polity Press.

Pierson, P. (1994) *Dismantling the welfare state? Reagan, Thatcher, and the politics of retrenchment*, Cambridge: Cambridge University Press.

Pierson, P. (2001) 'Coping with permanent austerity: welfare state restructuring in affluent democracies', in P. Pierson (ed) *The new politics of the welfare state*, Oxford: Oxford University Press, pp 410–56.

Pleau, R.L. (2010) 'Gender differences in postretirement employment', *Research on Aging*, 32(3): 267–303.

Polanyi, K. (2001 [1944]) *The great transformation: The political and economic origins of our time*, Boston, MA: Beacon Press.

Porcellato, L., Carmichael, F., Hulme, C., Ingham, B. and Prashar, A. (2010) 'Giving older workers a voice: constraints on the employment of older people in the north west of England', *Work Employment and Society*, 24(1): 85–103.

Prasad, M. (2012) *The land of too much: American abundance and the paradox of poverty*, Cambridge, MA: Harvard University Press.

Price, D. (2007) 'Closing the gender gap in retirement income: what difference will recent UK pension reforms make?', *Journal of Social Policy*, 36(4): 561–83.

Priemus, H., Kemp, P.A. and Varady, D.P. (2005) 'Housing vouchers in the United States, Great Britain, and the Netherlands: current issues and future perspectives', *Housing Policy Debate*, 16(3/4): 575–609.

Quadagno, J.S. and Hardy, M. (1991) 'Regulating retirement through the Age Discrimination in Employment Act', *Research on Aging*, 13(4): 470–5.

Reskin, B.F. and Roos, P.A. (1990) *Job queues, gender queues: Explaining women's inroads into male occupations*, Philadelphia, PA: Temple University Press.

Rimlinger, G.V. (1971) *Welfare policy and industrialization in Europe, America and Russia*, New York, NY: Wiley.

Rix, S. (2008) 'Will the boomers revolutionize work and retirement?', in R. Hudson (ed) *Boomer bust? Economic and political issues of the graying society*, Westport, CT: Praeger Publishers, pp 77–94.

Rowlingson, K. (2002) 'Private pension planning: the rhetoric of responsibility, the reality of insecurity', *Journal of Social Policy*, 31(4): 623–42.

Ruhm, C.J. (1990) 'Career jobs, bridge employment, and retirement', in P. Doeringer (ed) *Bridges to retirement: Older workers in a changing labor market*, Ithaca, NY: ILR Press, pp 92–107.

Sainsbury, D. (1996) *Gender, equality and welfare states*, Cambridge: Cambridge University Press.

Sargeant, M. (2006) 'The Employment Equality (Age) Regulations 2006: a legitimisation of age discrimination in employment', *Industrial Law Journal*, 35(3): 209–27.

Scherger, S. (ed) (2015) *Paid work beyond pension age*, London: Palgrave Macmillan.

Scherger, S., Hagemann, S., Hokema, A. and Lux, T. (2012) *Between privilege and burden: Work past retirement age in Germany and the UK*, Bremen: Centre for Social Policy Research.

Schor, J. (1992) *The overworked American: The unexpected decline of leisure*, New York, NY: Basic books.

Schuller, T. and Watson, D. (2009) *Learning through life: Inquiry into the future for lifelong learning: Summary*, Leicester: National Institute of Adult Continuing Education. Available at: http://www.learningandwork. org.uk/lifelonglearninginquiry/docs/IFLL-summary-english. pdf?redirectedfrom=niace (accessed 17 January 2016).

Shultz, K.S., Morton, K.R. and Weckerle, J.R. (1998) 'The influence of push and pull factors on voluntary and involuntary early retirees' retirement decision and adjustment', *Journal of Vocational Behavior*, 53(1): 45–57.

Siegel, M.J. (2006) 'Measuring the effect of husband's health on wife's labor supply', *Health Economics*, 15(6): 579–601.

Skocpol, T. (1992) *Protecting soldiers and mothers: The politics of social provision in the United States*, Cambridge, MA: Harvard University Press.

Smeaton, D. and McKay, S. (2003) *Working after state pension age: Quantitative analysis*, Leeds: Department for Work and Pensions.

Smeaton, D. and White, M. (2015) 'The growing discontents of older British employees: extended working life at risk from quality of working life', *Social Policy and Society*: 1–17.

Smeaton, D., Vegeris, S., Sahin-Dikmen, M. and Britain, G. (2009) *Older workers: Employment preferences, barriers and solutions*, London: Equality and Human Rights Commission.

Streeck, W. and Thelen, K. (2005) 'Introduction: Institutional change in advanced capitalist economies', in W. Streeck and K. Thelen (eds) *Beyond continuity. Institutional change in advanced capitalist economies*, Oxford: Oxford University Press, pp 1–39.

Szinovacz, M.E. and DeViney, S. (2000) 'Marital characteristics and retirement decisions', *Research on Aging*, 22(5): 470–98.

Tate, P., Klein-Collins, R. and Steinberg, K. (2011) 'Lifelong learning in the USA: a focus on innovation and efficiency for the 21st century learner', *International Journal of Continuing Education and Lifelong Learning*, 4(1): 1–23.

Taylor, P. and Walker, A. (1997) 'Age discrimination and public policy', *Personnel Review*, 26(4): 307–318.

Thane, P. (2006) 'The "scandal" of women's pensions in Britain: how did it come about?', in H. Pemberton, P. Thane and N. Whiteside (eds) *Britain's pension crisis: History and policy*, Oxford: Oxford University Press, pp 77–90.

The Guardian (2008) 'Pension values decline by third'. Available at: http://www.guardian.co.uk/business/2008/oct/28/recession-pension-decline-money (accessed 17 January 2016).

The Guardian (2015) 'Politicians must start seeing lifelong learning as an investment – not a cost'. Available at: http://www.theguardian.com/education/2015/mar/09/adult-education-funding-cuts-lifelong-learning-investment (accessed 17 January 2016).

Townsend, P. (1981) 'The structured dependency of the elderly: a creation of social policy in the twentieth century', *Ageing and Society*, 1(1): 5–28.

Townsend, P. (1986) 'Ageism and social policy', in C. Phillipson and A. Walker (eds) *Ageing and social policy*, Aldershot: Gower, pp 15–44.

Townsend, P. and Walker, A. (1995) *The future of pensions: Revitalising National Insurance*, Fabian Society London.

United States Congress House Select Committee on Aging (1982) *The end of mandatory retirement: Hearing before the Select Committee on Aging, House of Representatives, ninety-seventh Congress, second session, July 16, 1982*, Washington, DC: US Government Publishing Office.

Vickerstaff, S. (2006) '"I'd rather keep running to the end and then jump off the cliff." Retirement decisions: who decides?', *Journal of Social Policy*, 35: 455–72.

Vickerstaff, S. (2007) 'What do older workers want? Gradual retirement?', *Social & Public Policy Review*, 1(1). Available at: http://www6.plymouth.ac.uk/files/extranet/docs/SSB/Vickerstaff.pdf (accessed 17 January 2016).

Vickerstaff, S. (2015) *Domain – domestic and household factors: Understanding Employment Participation of Older Workers*, Berlin: Federal Ministry of Labour and Social Affairs (BMAS) and Federal Institute for Occupational Safety and Health (BAuA). Available at: http://www.jp-demographic.eu/wp-content/uploads/2015/07/Domain-Domestic-and-household-factors1.pdf (accessed 17 January 2016).

Vickerstaff, S., Baldock, J., Cox, J. and Keen, L. (2004) *Happy retirement? The impact of employers' policies and practice on the process of retirement*, Bristol: The Policy Press.

Vickerstaff, S., Loretto, W., Billings, J., Brown, P., Mitton, L., Parkin, T., White, P. and Britain, G. (2008) *Encouraging labour market activity among 60–64 year olds*, Norwich: Her Majesty's Stationary Office.

Vickerstaff, S., Phillipson, C. and Wilkie, R. (2012) 'Work, health and wellbeing: an introduction', in S. Vickerstaff, C. Phillipson and R. Wilkie (eds) *Work, health and well-being: The challenges of managing health at work*, Bristol: The Policy Press, pp 1–20.

Waine, B. (2009) 'New labour and pensions reform: security in retirement?', *Social Policy & Administration*, 43(7): 754–71.

Wang, M., Zhan, Y.J., Liu, S.Q. and Shultz, K.S. (2008) 'Antecedents of bridge employment: A longitudinal investigation', *Journal of Applied Psychology*, 93(4): 818–30.

Wang, M., Penn, L.T., Bertone, A. and Stefanova, S. (2014) 'Bridge employment in the United States', in C.-M. Alcover, G. Topa, E. Parry, F. Fraccaroli and M. Depolo (eds) *Bridge employment: A research handbook*, Abingdon: Routledge, pp 195–211.

Wang, Y.C., McPherson, K., Marsh, T., Gortmaker, S.L. and Brown, M. (2011) 'Health and economic burden of the projected obesity trends in the USA and the UK', *The Lancet*, 378(9793): 815–25.

Wellard, S. (2011) *Doing it all*, London: Grandparents Plus.

Weyman, A., Wainwright, D., O'Hara, R., Jones, P. and Buckingham, A. (2012) *Extending working life: Behaviour change interventions*, London: Department for Work and Pensions.

Wheelock, J. and Jones, K. (2002) '"Grandparents are the next best thing": informal childcare for working parents in urban Britain', *Journal of Social Policy*, 31(3): 441–63.

Whitehouse, E.R. (2003) *The value of pension entitlements*, Paris: Organisation for Economic Co-operation and Development.

Willets, D. and Yeo, S. (2004) *A fair deal for everyone on pensions*, London: The Conservative Party

Williams, R. (2012) 'Using the margins command to estimate and interpret adjusted predictions and marginal effects', *Stata Journal*, 12(2): 308–31.

Williamson, J.B. and McNamara, T.K. (2003) 'Interrupted trajectories and labor force participation – the effect of unplanned changes in marital and disability status', *Research on Aging*, 25(2): 87–121.

Williamson, J.B. and Pampel, F.C. (1993) *Old-age security in comparative perspective*, Oxford: Oxford University Press.

Wise, D.A. (1993) 'Firm pension policy and early retirement', in A. Atkinson and M. Rein (eds) *Age, work and Social Security*, New York, NY: St. Martins Press, pp 51–88.

Wood, A., Robertson, M. and Wintersgill, D. (2010) *A comparative review of international approaches to mandatory retirement*, Norwich: Her Majesty's Stationery Office.

Index

Note: The following abbreviations have been used – f = figure; n = note; t = table

E